Leslie,

Thanks so much for
your generous enthusiasm and
your scrupulous attention to
details. You made this a
better book.

Nick

Tomorrow Never Knows

Tomorrow

Never

Knows

Rock and
Psychedelics
in the 1960s

Nick Bromell

The University of Chicago Press
Chicago and London

Nick Bromell is associate professor of English and American literature at the University of Massachusetts, Amherst. He is author of *By the Sweat of the Brow: Literature and Labor in Antebellum America* (1993), also published by the University of Chicago Press.

The University of Chicago Press, Chicago 60637
The University of Chicago Press, Ltd., London
© 2000 by Nicholas K. Bromell
All rights reserved. Published 2000
Printed in the United States of America
09 08 07 06 05 04 03 02 01 00   1 2 3 4 5

ISBN: 0-226-07553-2 (cloth)

Portions of this book appeared in somewhat different form in *Tikkun, American Music,* and *Harper's.*

Library of Congress Cataloging-in-Publication Data

Bromell, Nicholas Knowles.
    Tomorrow never knows : rock and psychedelics in the 1960s / Nick Bromell.
        p. cm.
    Includes bibliographical references and index.
    ISBN 0-226-07553-2
    1. United States—Social conditions—1960–1980. 2. Rock music—United States—History and criticism. 3. Rock music—Social aspects—United States. 4. Nineteen sixties. 5. Popular culture—United States—History—20th century. 6. Beatles. I. Title.
HN59.B76   2000
306.4'84—dc21

                                                            00-008794

♾ The paper used in this publication meets the minimum requirements of the American National Standard for Information Sciences—Permanence of Paper for Printed Library Materials, ANSI Z39.48-1992.

This book is for Sam and Leon,
who have shared their music with me.
And for Laurie, my experienced soulmate.

CONTENTS

I want to thank those who first wrote about rock, some of them famous today, others (Deday LaRene, John Cunnick, and John Wolfe) less so: when I read your rock criticism thirty years ago, you confirmed for me that rock was something to think about. I also want to thank those who lived to music with me: my brothers Gavin and Hank, Tom Harris, Ann Blum, Steve Cadwell, Eric Biggs, Linda Rooklin, Bob Danner, Jesse Carr, Kathy Poyntz, Mimi Sprague, Michael Stone, Chris Norris. You are the readers I was always thinking about, and I hope this book falls into your hands wherever you are. Drusilla Walsh provided a charming place to stay in Paris, where this book was begun, and Nikos Phillipakis was a gracious host in Olympos, Karpathos, where my thinking had a chance to mature. Cindy Derwin, Randall Knoper, and Chris Benfey gave encouraging readings of early drafts. Alan Thomas at the University of Chicago Press helped guide me to safe harbor. Finally, with a light in his eyes and a pen in his hands, Eric Saltzman gave tough love and wise advice at key moments along the way. Thanks to all.

"Living to Music"

Remembering Rock and Psychedelics in the '60s

I wake up in the morning and do a Master's Voice thing in front of the speakers for a while; *then* I go outside. Music defines a total environment. . . . Straight musicians understand that kind of involvement, of course; but you can't really communicate to the outside how a hundred thousand children of muzak freaks . . . who in most cases never bother to study or even think about music, are involved in a single art form to the point where they virtually stake their entire sanity on it. Go to a house and someone hands you a joint in front of a record player and it's assumed . . . that you are going to sit for a couple of hours, not talking, hardly moving, *living* to music.

—John Cunnick, Seattle
Helix (1967)

Will we ever know what really happened in the '60s? Or understand what has happened *to* the '60s? Scraped by a muzaked "Help" in the supermarket, stuck in traffic on my way home and ambushed by four bars of "Purple Haze" on the radio, I feel a panic of discontinuity. Did the '60s really take place? How could such intensity fade away, overnight as it seemed, leaving only these spectral songs behind?

But in another moment, another mood, the landscape of the present is the seamless and predictable extension of that past. This day is bound to the '60s by an iron logic that has produced, along with designer jeans and "classic" rock, the middle-class functionary puzzled by his youthful dreams of liberation, pained so gently by a history that has given him so much. Sitting at an outdoor restaurant, savoring a glass of white wine, I wonder why I should be more surprised by Ronald Reagan Airport than by the peace-sign earrings dangling beneath the crewcut of my waitress.

In the flicker of these moods, one looks for a place to stand. One would like to know whether history, one's own history, is in any sense knowable. Knowable not in the sense of getting to the bottom of it or of grasping its meaning or meaninglessness. A plausible fiction would suffice. Or just a metaphor: *America has lived through a decade that tore every page out of the book we call "history," and every page into separate words, and every word into individual letters, and scattered everything to the winds, so that now we have only the memory, untrustworthy, that there ever was such a book.* But that metaphor is no sooner floated than it is sunk. Why not say instead that America *stumbled and regained her balance?* Or that the student revolution *gave birth to a new world order?*

The intuition explored in the following pages is that the '60s fusion of rock music and psychedelics was a way of trying to come to terms with the future we now inhabit, a future in which the footing of the past seems to have dropped out from under us. That whatever else "the '60s" were—and they were far more than this book could ever hope to name—they were also a concentration of cultural energies upon the consequences of growing up in an age when the fatigue of metaphors has become obvious, when the idea of change has collapsed into the idea of continuity, and when narratives about the past, present, and future must find a way to think of these as something other than a sequence. There was something weirdly rigorous and instructive in the act of getting stoned and listening to music as if it mattered. Something to return to and learn from—another frayed metaphor. *Nothing has changed, it's still the same. I've got nothing to say, but it's ok.* Sound familiar?

Lost in a drawer in my mother's desk is a snapshot of the person I was over thirty years ago, in 1968. He's eighteen. He's just started college. He's dressed in jeans and a green t-shirt, and his blond hair is longish but not quite shoulder-length. His face, as I read it now, wears a startled, wary look. He's not going to fight in Vietnam, but that's because he has a college deferment. He marched on Washington, but he's not going to sit on a railroad track and get his legs sliced off by a munitions train. At a Christmas party back home, he'll tell a group of his father's corporate colleagues that he'd rather fight for the Vietcong than for the United States army. But back on campus he argues with the local SDS representative that students who think they're fighting a revolution are just kidding themselves. In the morning, he studies classics and philosophy. In the afternoon, he drifts into someone's dorm room and takes some hits off the joint that's making the rounds and joins the communal immersion in music for several hours. Dylan. Beatles. Hendrix. Stones. Living to music.

That semi-stranger who looks back at me is not, at first glance, so very different from the person he has become. But if I gaze at him long enough and let my memory go back behind his eyes, into what he was thinking and feeling, he becomes formidable—the possessor of an adolescent wisdom I've forgotten, or mislaid. If his expression is startled, it's because he fronts each morning as if it were the roll of cosmic dice, the tumbling dice that come to rest and tell us whether life has any coherence, whether humanity is redeemable or doomed, whether the past will determine the future, whether history itself makes any sense at all. He knows exactly what Dylan means by *Inside the museums infinity goes up on trial.*

What's on trial is the project of collecting and assembling fragments of the past, chunks of bygone years, in the hope of creating a human record that lasts forever and provides a narrative commensurate with all of human time. He gets bitter relief from *Voices echo this is what salvation must be like after a while,* since it seems clear to him that the idea of his soul going on forever in the pallid gloom of heaven is simply another version of this impulse to achieve an immortality of some kind, any kind, however dusty and dead and far from life. And he and his friends laugh at *But Mona Lisa must have had the highway blues, you can tell by the way she smiles,* because here was a line that collapsed the distinctions that history itself seemed to rest on, making fun of the whole enterprise and hinting (there was a hope of some kind here) that the gaze of ancient art upon the present was bemused and sad and tired of the journey. Would his professors, all of whom had devoted their lives to this project of keeping history going on forever, get the joke? (Now that he's become a historian himself, the joke seems richer than ever.)

So if his face wears a startled look, it's because he's a raw adolescent, pimpled and horny yet capable, all at once, of reading Parmenides and Heracleitus. Ideas keep him up all night, unsatisfied. So does lust. His soul cries *I want, I want,* through every minute of the day. What he's suddenly become conscious of is his life, that he's *alive;* yet adults, like ghosts, reach their arms out to enfold him in the company of the dead. That's why his gaze is fierce with scorn as he looks back through the camera's lens into the eyes of his loving mother who seems to have no idea what she's taking a picture of. Thirty years later, that scorn intimidates me when I dare to lock eyes with him and see that I've since grown into a bloated child, naïve and uncommitted, drinking and thinking that I've got it made.

Yet I also answer, as my parents must have, with a worldly sigh. Been there. Done that. Moved on. I know that in just a few weeks, he'll carry his intensity into an all-night acid trip, finding there at last a drama equal to his psychic turbulence. I know that in a few months he's going to stop going to his classes because they're *irrelevant.* I know that when he joins his fellow students in a campus strike in May, he'll be moved as much by the chance to bask in the spring sun as by outrage over the bombing of unknown Cambodians. And I know that if, by smoking marijuana, "I became real to myself for the first time" (Norman Mailer's words), I also became lost in a fog that carried me far away: like I was, you know, blunting whatever mental acuity I had preserved from high school when I said, like, sure, I'll try that. You know what I mean?

❦

Books about the '60s tend to fall into two general categories, neither of which deals with the experience I want to orient myself to—what might have been inwardly felt, in varying ways, by roughly 20 million young people, most of them white and middle class, many of them in college or recently graduated or on their way there: *students,* when that word conferred an identity of some substance, however briefly or misleadingly. Students "living," as John Cunnick wrote in 1967, "to music."

The library's shelves are packed with books about the political movements of the '60s: the struggle for civil rights, the Black Panthers, antiwar organizing, the New Left, SDS, the beginnings of the women's movement and the gay liberation movement. Students took part in all of these. Students were essential to them all. Yet while many of the histories of these movements are informative, even indispensable, they tend to leave out the particular past I want to get at: in exalted terms, the existential and visionary side of the 1960s; more mundanely, the inside of the experience of listening to rock, hearing it as a spontaneous epic poem produced miraculously by your peers for immediate use. Something that could help you make sense of the senselessness of it all by helping you come to your senses, heightening them. Most historians of the political '60s know full well that this living to music was present as a crucial energy that flowed into and powerfully invigorated political ideas and movements. But how to write about it? As Jim Miller confesses in the preface to his brilliant history of the Port Huron Statement, "the gravest omission in my text may well be cultural. Given the political focus of my narrative, it was all but impossible to convey adequately the era's carnivalesque atmosphere of confusion." Or as historian David Farber observes: "To make drug consciousness . . . a major force in the youth movement of the 1960s is not something that comes easily to an academic, but those academicians who have written about the 1960s without any attempt to seriously or analytically relate drug consciousness to the events of the 1960s have done so at the cost of warping and misconstructing much of what went on."

The experience of being what Jimi Hendrix called *experienced*—a compound of music consciousness and drug consciousness—does receive some attention from a second class of books. Their aim, however, is simply to attack it. Outraged, polemical, uninterested in trying to understand what went on in the '60s, they tap into our profound (and warranted) fear of what happened back then, hoping to channel that fear toward conservative political agendas. While several of these critics are smart about the excesses and idiocies of the decade, they tend to oversimplify an endlessly complex and ambiguous moment in American culture. For them, living to music is something to trash, not understand.

In what follows, I try to find some space between these two approaches. This book isn't conventional history or cultural studies or popular culture analysis or musicology or memoir, but a hybrid of all these. It doesn't try to describe objectively what was *happening* but to unearth a vocabulary that might help us connect the '60s more persuasively to our sense of the present. What Michael Herr wrote about making sense of the war in Vietnam seems just as true of the decade as a whole. "The problem was that you didn't always know what you were seeing until later, maybe years later, that a lot of it never made it in at all, it just stayed stored there in your eyes. Time and information, rock and roll, life itself." Now *is* "years later," and knowing what we were seeing and listening to seems long overdue.

According to anthropologist Benedict Anderson, the impulse

to connect past and present is experienced whenever change has seemed abrupt and a culture's consciousness transformed. Out of what he calls "amnesias" and "oblivions" spring narratives that close the gap between what was lived and what can be remembered. But for the '60s that consisted mainly of "living to music," oblivion has not yet yielded such narratives, stories that would weave together political commitment and cultural dreamwork, theory and carnival, student movements and psychedelics and rock 'n' roll. Is this because the change in consciousness was too profound? Or because it was too trivial? If the '60s were any kind of revolution, were they a break from the past or from the future, an inauguration or a culmination? Do those times fail to measure up to narrative, or do the narratives we have fail to take the measure of those times?

Another way of putting these questions is to ask whether we're forgetting this '60s or failing to escape them. These possibilities blur into one another. In 1994, Newt Gingrich celebrated the election of a new Republican majority by being perfectly explicit about his agenda: "There are profound things that went wrong starting with the Great Society and the counterculture and until we address them head-on we're going to have problems." For Gingrich, the Great Society represents the political disasters of affirmative action, feminism, community organizing, environmental activism, and the like. But the deeper object of his fear and loathing is "the counterculture," which represents something everybody knows about and nobody talks about (except by fulminating in vague terms about "right and wrong," "the work ethic," and the like). It's the river that runs steadily and silently through American life these days, the river that welled out of the American psyche thirty years ago, spilling through the fissure blasted by rock 'n' roll and psychedelic drugs. *This* is Gingrich's real enemy: a way of seeing and being in the world that underwrites the possibility, indeed declares the inevitability, of rapid and ceaseless social change.

It's a way that has, superficially at least, taken hold and triumphed. It's the comic-ironic worldliness of *The Simpsons*. It's the self-mocking paranoia of *The X-Files*. It's the trippy feel of Microsoft ads and the total conquest of advertising space by the hyperkinetic vibrations of psychedelicized graphics. It's what historian Thomas Frank has called "hip capitalism," and what this river tells us in every digitalized second of the day and night is to imagine existence as a process of consumption. To live in unrelieved desire for what comes next and to experience the acquisition of the new as a rebellion against the old. In short, to embrace capitalism as the only future, as what the editors of *Fortune* called "the permanent revolution." Yet, as Jimi Hendrix opined when meditating on exactly this subject, *it goes deeper than that*. For this river is also the river that spoke to Heracleitus a thousand years before capitalism was even thinkable, saying *panda rei*—everything moves, everything's flux, nothing remains, foundations are fictions, you're going with the flow whether you like it or not. This is the river conservatives abhor, even when it's the energy that drives the capitalism they cherish.

It's also the river Norman Mailer descried when he walked through Lincoln Park in the summer of 1968 and entered the aural maelstrom of a psychedelicized rock band, hearing "the sound of mountains crashing in this holocaust of the decibels, hearts bursting, literally bursting, as if this were the sound of death by explosion within, the drums of physiological climax when the mind was blown, and forces of the future, powerful, characterless, as insane and scalding as waves of lava, came flushing through the urn of all acquired culture and sent the brain like a foundered carcass smashing down a rapids, revolving through a whirl of demons, pool of uproar, discords vibrating, electrical crescendo screaming as if at the electro-mechanical climax of the age." Not simply big government, universal health coverage, and stronger antipollution laws but this vision of a radically destabilized ontology is what the conservative imagination most fears and despises. "Cultural relativism" is the blandly inadequate name conservatives give their hydra-headed foe, and they fight it, furiously and often futilely, on every front—except, of course, in the corporate boardroom.

At the center of that battle, where cultural self-contradictions become so concentrated as to squeeze forth a realized metaphor, is the War on Drugs. It's a war waged most vigorously and violently, and virtually without public debate or community control, in the neighborhoods of the poor, ostensibly to save them from themselves. The motives behind the war lie, in part, in the psyche of white Americans still failing, as I have, to get to the bottom of their fear of African Americans. But the deeper motive, a fear that operates more publicly and that commands the appropriation of hundreds of millions of dollars of public funds, has its taproot in the suburbs, the lawn-flanked junior high schools, the bleachers, the dens and family rooms of the American middle class. For that's where millions of American kids are still smoking pot and dropping acid, turning on and tuning in. That's where the enemy really lurks.

According to the most authoritative study of national drug use, the Monitoring the Future Study conducted by the University of Michigan Institute for Social Research and funded by the National Institutes of Health, 13.6 percent of all high school seniors graduating in 1997 had tried LSD and 49.6 percent had tried marijuana. Cocaine use was reported by 8.7 percent and heroin by just 2.1 percent. Not only are high school students still choosing pot and acid over all other drugs (except alcohol), they are doing so at the onset of their adolescence. In 1997, 22.6 percent of eighth graders had used marijuana at least once in the past year and 6.7 percent of tenth graders had used LSD in the past year. Rising and dipping only slightly since the study began in 1975, these rates make clear that ever since the 1960s, pot and acid have remained popular drugs—significantly more popular than heroin, cocaine, and crack cocaine. The obvious question to ask, it would seem, is why *these* drugs? What is the synergistic connection between psychedelics and middle-class adolescence? But this seems to be a topic most adults, including the drug war's top analysts, would rather not think about. Apparently no one wants to reflect on the inscape of the experience of getting high or of tripping, to ask *How does it feel?* And so no one wants to go back through amnesia to the obvious starting point of any historical analysis of the subject, back to the moment, now lost in oblivion, when middle-class kids in large numbers first heard about and started using pot and acid: back to the '60s.

What I have tried to write is a book that deals with something that began more than thirty years ago and is still going on, something fundamental and unresolved in American culture. The fusion of rock and psychedelics that John Cunnick called "living to music" lies at the heart of a '60s that was experienced by millions; indeed, it's what many people are pointing to when they say "the '60s." Far more influential than art, film, literature, and other forms of cultural self-expression about which hundreds of studies are written every year, the fusion of rock and psychedelics either inaugurated a way of being in the world, or simply coincided with it, and in either case helped articulate and objectify it. Let us grant right away that when young people listened to rock and smoked pot and dropped acid they were being foolish and hedonistic, and that their attempts to explain why they found these drugs valuable were crude and naïve. But let us admit also that they produced something that mattered very deeply to them—something we are still living with. Living to music is on MTV every day, it's an essential activity of almost every junior and senior high school, and it's an indelible part of the outlook of tens of millions of adult Americans. It's at the very crux of our domestic wars: the "culture wars" and the war on drugs. And it stands at the crossroads where the '60s meet the present.

The reader whose child brings home antidrug leaflets from school will understandably be wondering whether there isn't something perverse about revisiting this particular '60s—the drugs and rock 'n' roll '60s. Even former student activists (and maybe they most of all) will be asking what social good can possibly come out of talking about psychedelics—I mean really talking, not just dismissing them with an ironic laugh or a fulsome jeremiad. Yet while what follows is certainly not a "study" of rock and drugs, I have to trust that it will not be confused either with an intergalactic message sent back to us from Timothy Leary in orbit nor mistaken for the mumbling of that hollow-eyed '60s burnout who's still at his post on a corner of Telegraph Avenue in Berkeley. It's a conversation between two moments. It's a narrative that takes, however absurdly, an oblivion as its subject. It's an attempt to make sense of the paradox that poet W. S. Merwin describes when he writes of the '60s: "We know that age to be utterly beyond reach, irretrievably past, a period whose distance we already feel as though it had stretched into centuries, and yet it appears to be not only recent but present, still with us not as a memory but as a part of our unfinished days, a ground or backdrop before which we live." This book is an effort to walk into the space of those unfinished days and to listen to what we hear there.

CHAPTER 1

"Something That Never Happened Before"

The Early Beatles and the Sense of an Ending

A few days after the first performance on the Sullivan show, I spent the evening with some friends In a café in my hometown. It was, or anyway had been, a folk club. That night one heard only *Meet the Beatles.* The music, snaking through the dark, suddenly spooky room, was instantly recognizable and like nothing we had ever heard. It was joyous, threatening, absurd, arrogant, innocent and tough, and it drew the line of which Dylan was to speak. "This was something that never happened before."

—**Greil Marcus**

● **I WANT TO HOLD YOUR HAND**

(As recorded by The Beatles)
By John Lennon and Paul McCartney
Oh yeh, I'll tell you something
I think you'll understand
Then I'll say that something
I want to hold your hand
I want to hold your hand
I want to hold your hand.

Ol please say to me
And let me be your man
And please say to me
You'll let me hold your hand
Now, let me hold your hand
I want to hold your hand

And when I touch you
I feel happy inside
It's such a feeling that my love I can't hide
I can't hide
I can't hide

Yeh, you g   thing
I think you

When I s   ng
I want to h
I want to ho
I want to hol

And when I t
I feel happ
It's such
can
I can't hi
I can't hid

Yeh, you go
I think you'll
When I feel t
I want to hold
I want t

So let the story begin, absurdly and apocalyptically, at the end. On a dark and stormy night in December 1969, with less than two weeks left in the '60s and with the news in the air that the Beatles were breaking up. The wind was howling around the eaves of my third-floor window when a guy I hardly knew wandered in from another dorm. He sat down on my floor, lit a joint, and we started listening to music together, probably the Beatles' new *Abbey Road* or the Stones' recent *Let It Bleed*. After a while, he began to tell me about a rumor that was connected, through a now unrecoverable logic, to the recent and shocking rumor that Paul was dead. With their piles of money, he said, the Beatles had bought an island somewhere in the world and had scattered clues about the island's location throughout their songs. Any fan who uncovered all the clues and pieced them together would learn the whereabouts of the island and earn the right to go there—and stay there as long as he or she wished.

You began the quest by calling Billie Shears (whose number was plainly listed in the London phone book), and when he answered "Good morning," you had to reply, "Good morning. I've got nothing to say, but it's ok, good morning." Shears would then test your mastery of moments and nuances in *Sgt. Pepper's,* and if you knew all the answers he would give you the first clue—a place to go, a lyric to decode or respond to—and so you were off down a trail that would lead, after many twists and turns, through a glass onion to another place you can be, *listen* to me, to the sanctuary the Beatles had created for us all, a refuge in which the best of the '60s, the very essence of the vision itself, would endure even after they had vanished.

Ah, what a pipe dream. *In the winter of '65, we were hungry, just barely alive,* and though the song was about the end of the Civil War it seemed also to be about the winter of 1969, since we, too, were coming to the end of something. *And in the end* sang the Beatles at the end of what would turn out to be their final album, and their audience wanted desperately to know in the end *what?*

In a week or two, the calendar would display the first day of the next decade, the 1970s. The '60s would be "over." What would that mean, if anything? As the end approached, it seemed fitting to dream the dark dream that Paul was dead and to nourish the intricate hope that the '60s would survive on the Beatles' secret island.

You didn't have to be a stoned adolescent to dwell in this mood and ask these questions. That very month, in December of '69, the *New York Times Magazine* devoted an entire issue to the meaning of the decade, and Richard Rovere voiced the worries of many adults when he wrote that "the decade now drawing to a close . . . has been one in which simple intellectual honesty compelled us to face up to the strong possibility that we humans are just about at the end of our days, that our problems of survival, though most of them yield to abstract analysis and abstract solution, will not be solved because we are simply too human to deal with them."

The strong possibility that we humans are just about at the end of our days. Apocalypse was in the air, fit to print even in the pages of the *Times*. The liberal faith that all problems could be solved—probably by smart, liberal, college-educated white men—had shattered on knowledge gained despite tremendous government and corporate resistance: knowledge about the Vietnam War, about nuclear weapons and nuclear power, about the degradation of the biosphere, about endemic American racism. Smart liberal white men had created many of these problems; smart liberal white men had systematically lied to the American public in order to keep these problems in the dark. It had come to pass that even Richard Rovere, even the *New York Times,* had lost faith in the creed and in themselves. The "abstract analysis" and "abstract solutions" perfected by men like Dean Rusk and Robert McNamara were pitifully inadequate in the face of our own weaknesses. And what are these? What does it mean to say we are "simply too human" if not that we are indelibly stained by original sin, by a predilection for evil? In December 1969, simple intellectual honesty compelled many persons, not just Dylan fans, to admit that we humans were just about at the end of our days, and that the Enlightenment dream of man's infinite perfectibility had become a nightmare or a joke that brought a smile to the lips of Mona Lisa.

As it turned out, the world did not end. (*Ob-la-di, ob-la-da.*) John was the first to die, not Paul. The *Times* and its readers managed to pull themselves out of the muck of their malaise (fatal word, Jimmy Carter). College students got back on track. And the political history of the next thirty years veered away from Armageddon (for a while anyway), becoming instead a struggle to adapt to the collapse of Enlightenment optimism without succumbing to the pull of religious fundamentalism. We stand today at a crossroads, with no choice apparently except the stony path of Cynicism going nowhere or the yellow brick road to the New Age. But back in the '60s, this future was still cloaked. All one could do was experience the present as an indefinable *weight,* the weight of one's consciousness of time, and of time passing, of history, and of the ways awareness itself had debarred one from the simpler, happier life of June and Wally Cleaver. The Beatles sang that we had to carry that weight a long time, so all we could do was keep a kind of vigil there, on the edge of the darkness, with the future approaching in the guise of two riders and the growl of a wildcat. In the Oval Office, Nixon was "ending the war with honor" while nearly tripling the number of American dead (from 16,000 to 57,000) and incalculably worsening the damage done to the Vietnamese and their land. Meanwhile, in dorms and family rooms across America, millions of listeners bent over their stereos and listened for clues. So much of their history had unwound from those speakers that surely their future would too. They listened for clues. They listened to find their way to the Beatles' secret island. They bowed over their speakers and listened. What did they—what did we—hear?

If memory serves me well, we weren't just escaping from reality. Rock was fun, but it was also a vital and spontaneous public philosophizing, a medium through which important questions were raised and rehearsed, and sometimes focused, and sometimes (rarely) answered. At least a part of the audience for '60s rock (what was called the "college market," though it included many who never finished high school) looked to new albums, especially by Dylan and the Beatles, as if a fresh and useful articulation of their own state of mind could be found there. "The fact that we were buying the records," rock critic Jon Landau wrote about early Dylan albums in 1968, "shows where we all were at." The rock audience felt there was a marvelous correspondence between this rapidly changing music and their own rapidly evolving souls. A reviewer of *Abbey Road* in the rock magazine *Creem* began by writing "Another clue from the Beatles . . . a new Beatles album, and all of a sudden there's all this new information to assimilate. . . . Any Beatles album is an artifact in a way that few records can ever be, and since the Beatles are so much a part of who you are, you have to examine it closely." This music *mattered*. But why?

❦

To begin with the Beatles is to begin with the sense of an ending, not just because the breakup of the Beatles signaled the end of the '60s but because the beginning of the Beatles was experienced by many persons as the end of the world, of history, of life as we knew it. "I Want to Hold Your Hand" and "I Saw Her Standing There" were, as New York artist Stan Kaplan has remembered, a kind of apocalypse. "The Beatles' music had just become popular. Maybe a dozen guys started to come to Cornell with 'long' hair, the early Beatle length. The girls liked these guys very much. I remember going to parties and listening to this new music. I would get drunk and listen and think: *The world is going to end. This is the end of the world.* Which was a presage of what, metaphorically, really was going to happen. A world *was* ending." In a piece written in 1969, rock critic Dave Marsh gazed back through the mists of time to 1964 and recalled that "everything before them is sort of blurry; I mean, nothing is quite definite, nothing is important. . . . The next thing I knew there they were and the whole trip was very clear. 'I Want to Hold Your Hand' may not seem significant, but to people my age that is a line of demarcation between history and life as we know it." And Eldridge Cleaver, in his 1968 book *Soul on Ice,* likewise evokes this sense of an ending when he imagines three black men watching from the sidelines as white folks take to the dance floor and get into the rhythms of this new music:

"Man, what done got into them ofays?" one asked.

"They trying to get back," said another.

"Shit," said a young Negro who made his living by shoplift-
ing. "If you ask me, I think it must be the end of the world."

Of course, this end was also felt as a beginning. As the Beatles'
first two hits climbed the charts in December 1963, just two weeks
after the back of John F. Kennedy's head exploded across Jackie's
strawberry-pink suit, a sudden openness to change and possibility
blossomed across America. It was as if the young president's death
had intensified, not cramped, the feeling of optimism in the air, as
if the sacrifice of a young god had been needed to release a tide
of energies long held in check. An immense structure of feelings
was breaking up and giving way before the onslaught of the new,
and not just in the United States but around the world. "Suddenly
you could breathe freely," recalls Vaclav Havel, Czech playwright,
dissident, and Beatles fan; "people could associate freely, fear vanished, taboos were swept away, social conflicts could be named
and described." No one knew what would take the place of the old
order, but the sound that seemed to pave the way for it was the
music of the early Beatles, music that by the end of 1964 was virtually omnipresent, as the Beatles' songs claimed most of the top ten
spots in the hit parade and called imperiously, beguilingly, from
every radio station. "In the beginning," Jim Miller has said of rock
'n' roll, "it was a scandal. . . . After the Beatles, it was important."

Today, this palpable sensation that a world was ending, this
intuition that history had been terminated by a few chords struck
on a guitar, is hard to remember or hear described without a skeptical smile. No matter how hard we stare at the *facts* in this past, at
Richard Rovere musing on "the end of our days," on Dave Marsh
experiencing a line between history and life, we can hardly absorb
them since we know, from our vantage point, that our days did
not end and that history once more overtook and reclaimed life.
Almost inevitably, therefore, we see the '60s through a veil of irony.
We can't help but believe that all those seventeen-year-olds dancing
to the beat of history's demise were actually the duped marionettes
of a history more cunning than they knew. Didn't Lennon himself

conclude "We all dressed up, the same bastards are in control, the same people are runnin' everything. It is exactly the same . . . the dream is over"?

This ironic view of history as an unfolding that delivers its meaning only to the future, so that those who are actually living it can never know what it actually signifies, is hard to resist. It's the very source of the pervasive irony we live in today. But while we tend to believe that this wised-up view of the past is truer than the naïve perspective of those who lived immersed in it, we need to be consistent and acknowledge that our present, too, is wrapped in a history we cannot easily see, that our irony is not natural but the product of particular kinds of experience. And isn't it true that the experience most likely to render us ironists by temperament is disappointment—disappointment that things are not what they seem, disappointment that hopes turn out to be illusions? The conviction that people are the dupes of history is most likely to descend on those who were themselves under the impression that they had gotten out ahead of history, that they were leading history somewhere rather than being pushed along by it, that they were venturing into an unknown that could not be explained or predetermined by what had come before. The ironic gaze upon the past—a gaze that assumes the privileges of a knowing future in relation to that past, and with those privileges a certain complacency about its own knowingness compared to that past—is itself the product of a past. As habitual ironists, therefore, we are not the jaded, canny bystanders we take ourselves to be, but dancers to a tune we've heard so long we've forgotten we're dancing. It was the widely shared sensation that history was ending in the '60s, and with that ending giving rise to new beginnings, that has produced in so many of us the conviction that history has won.

I go to such lengths to disenchant our irony because, at the threshold of the '60s, we encounter this belief in radical change, in endings and beginnings, and we need to grant that belief more authority, more credibility, than most of us are predisposed to do. We have to hear not just the urgency but the truth being spoken when the authors of the Port Huron Statement complain about "the stagnation of those who have closed their minds to the future."

Feeling the press of complexity upon the emptiness of life, people are fearful at the thought that at any moment things might be thrust out of control. They fear change itself, since change might smash whatever invisible framework seems to hold back chaos from them now.

We have to relinquish for a while our belief that we are more knowing and approach this '60s as if we could learn something from it. Even if what we find there is just a million or more screaming adolescents, we have to grant those screams some power, and that power some insight, and that insight some knowledge, and that knowledge some validity, some reach into the future, this "now."

How else can we go back and *hear* the early Beatles, go back and unpack what those tight, jewel-like songs of the first albums meant? While it's undeniable that they meant *something* (how otherwise explain their unprecedented and since then unmatched popularity?), we have to shrug from our shoulders an immense burden of disbelief before we can rediscover a significance in lyrics like

> *Oh yeah I'll*
> *Tell you somethin'*
> *I think you'll understand—*
> *When I*
> *Feel that somethin'*
> *I want to hold your haaaaand*

This is not Billie Holiday singing about strange fruit, or Ella Fitzgerald singing about love for sale, or even Frank Sinatra singing about dancing cheek to cheek. It's simple to the point of crudity. Banal. But this simplicity, infused with an energy that can be recaptured only by *listening* to Beatles songs again, is what explains their appeal and their meaning. Their simplicity said, in effect, that innocence has virtue and validity. Their energy claimed that innocence has power. And while this is true to some degree of all rock 'n' roll, what made the Beatles different was the extraordinary intensity with which they fused innocence and instability—a fusion to be heard in the shift from the downward tilt of "understand" to the unexpected liftoff of "haaaaand," and in the nuanced contrast between "tell" and "feel." Both these pairings seem to balance on the fulcrum of an empty space, a "somethin'," whose mysteriousness is at once denied (you'll understand it) and underscored (I'll *feel* it). Are we talking about an emotion here or an erogenous zone? A hand or . . . what? *Something,* the Beatles sang, they think we'll understand. From the space of that something swiftly rose and spread the possibility of change.

The song on the flip side of this single went even further in making change an imaginable possibility, in legitimating their audience's adolescent belief that change is the natural condition of things. "I Saw Her Standing There" took its teenage listeners to a place that was crucial to their coming of age, to their success or failure as sexually and socially competent youth: the dance. There, the Beatles take up the essential question: *Will something happen?* Will I dare to ask someone to dance? Will someone ask me to dance? What will he say? What will she say?

The Beatles' affirmative answer is delivered directly through the song's fresh and unmistakably joyous sound—its tempo, harmonies, handclaps, the double liftoff of *held her hand in mieee-een.* When their voices rise together in *mieee-een* we hear an energy that can't be held down, that must rise as voiced musical ecstasy to say *Yes. Yes. Yes.* That sudden soaring upward is already the Beatles' distinctive acoustic signature—"I can't *hide,* I can't *hide*" (which Bob Dylan thought was "I get high, I get high"), "she said she *loves you,*" "it's only *love,*" "*Lucy in the sky,*" and so on. We hear this affirmation in another of their little habits, the *yeah, yeah, yeah!* that was so often mocked by adults who obviously couldn't hear what it was really about. We hear it also in McCartney's opening shout—which Greil Marcus fancifully but rightly transcribes as "One, two, three, fuck!"—and we hear it in the peculiar emphasis, not lilting now but textured and serious, with which McCartney sings "just seventeen" and "mean":

> **Well, she was just seventeen**
> **You know what I mean . . .**

Just seventeen is so exactly right: not sweet sixteen, with its blush of virginity lit by sixteen candles, but not eighteen either, the year you grow up and leave home for a job or college (or a place called

Vietnam). Seventeen is perfectly in-between: adolescent energy in its most mature, concentrated, and self-contradictory form. This is where the Beatles' audience was and where it wanted, aesthetically, to dwell. To be *seventeen:* right on that cusp between childhood and adulthood, right on that fault line where the earth's tremors are felt, right there where life is changing and *something* is *happening* every minute.

The song's second line, too, delivered immediacies and intricacies to an audience that absorbed them without noticing. In a 1988 interview with Paul McCartney, Beatles expert Mark Lewisohn discovered that McCartney had written the song's second line as "She was never a beauty queen," and that Lennon, when he first heard the song, instantly improvised "You know what I mean" as the right, the inevitable substitute. When the song was released a few months later, millions of Beatles fans unknowingly heard the first of many "clues" that would accumulate, interweave, and eventually constitute the mythic structure that was the Beatles and their audience together—a structure represented, symbolically, in the myths about the secret island, Paul's death, and the identity of the walrus. "You *know* what I *mean*" announces that the song is not just about *something* happening, but about *knowing* happening and *meaning* happening. The line works because it flows in rhythmic counterpoint to two common sayings in which the accent falls elsewhere than on "know": You know what I mean, and You know what I *mean?* But when the Beatles sing the line, the accent falls on *know*, and so it faintly registers in its audience the possibility that changing, meaning, knowing, and connecting are all intertwined. You just knew that something was happening in these songs that made them special, meaningful. Young Beatles fans claimed these songs as their own, as their language, and we listened to them with a rapture no pop singer since Elvis had provoked. (One young man who listened with such intensity was incarcerated in the federal penitentiary on McNeal Island, Washington; he listened to the Beatles obsessively, as if he heard in them a subtle augury of things to come, feeling an inexplicable bond with them and bragging to a fellow inmate that given the chance he could become even "bigger" than they were. And just five years later, very briefly, Charles Manson would be.)

To hear again after more than thirty years what made "I Saw Her Standing There" so fresh and persuasive, we might compare it to one of its great precursors, Chuck Berry's "Around and Around" (ably covered just months later by the Rolling Stones). The dance evoked within "Around and Around" is a wild affair. The singer tells us that, after standing on the sidelines for a while, he began tapping his feet and clapping his hands until he just had to dance. The dance he joins is entirely communal. No sweetheart or special girl is anywhere in sight. The singer's mind surrenders to his body, his individuality sinks into the group, and he takes his place in the circle, which, like the song itself, is moving around and around. And then reaching into blues roots, memories of juke joints and Saturday night fish fries, Berry's song tells us that this kind of celebration is subversive and threatening to the powers that be. It tells us that the police burst in to restore order. We don't hear the billy clubs swinging, but we sense them in the air.

By comparison, "I Saw Her Standing There" is both more innocent and more assertive. The right to dance at a place consecrated to instability and joy is simply taken for granted, an assumption that reflects the very different social origins of both the song and its audience. But at the same time "I Saw Her Standing There" marks a beginning that might be more unsettling than the dancing in Berry's song. It announces that the world is not just going around and around, repeating itself. It says that change is going to come. It says that something is happening, that we are approaching a line, and that we can, if we wish, just step over it. That *something* would happen in most of the early Beatles songs—it reached *something inside that was always denied,* something that moved people, ripping joy from the hearts of girls, piercing the souls of boys, and making Beatlemania happen.

For Dave Marsh, the affirmation in this song says that we can cross a line that divides history from life, that delivers life as something fresh and anarchic from the grip of the past, habit, convention. According to Eldridge Cleaver, the sound of this music told "Negroes . . . that something fundamental had changed." And both Cleaver and Stan Kaplan heard that change as the end of the world or as the end of one world and the beginning of another. When music makes people feel this way, I think it's fair to call it revolutionary music. For that's what the idea of revolution is all about: revolution is the claim that change can happen cataclysmically, not gradually, and that the fabric of human time is therefore rent with fissures from which emerge new possibilities that are independent of the determinations of the past.

This is the claim that was made by Beatlemania. An extraordinary, indeed in the twentieth-century United States a *singular* phenomenon, it has never been taken seriously by historians of the '60s or of rock 'n' roll. The tendency has always been to be embarrassed by Beatlemania. Documentaries consistently present this moment in the Beatles' career with an awe that is also a sneer. While marveling that the four moptops could exert such orphic force, they pointedly condescend to the young teenagers, almost all of them girls, who pursued and panted, screamed and wept and fainted whenever the Beatles came within reach.

But those who were young at the time will remember that Beatlemania was an essential precondition of the Beatles phenomenon. Beatlemania was a ridiculous spectacle, yet its cultural power—its power to convert others to the Beatles cult—resided squarely in this indifference to ridicule, to what other people thought about you. Those very young girls who, before one's eyes, surrendered absolutely to their passions were the force that demolished so much of the rigid, sexless self-control that prevailed during the fifties. The early Beatles, for better or worse, played a quite secondary role. It was not John Lennon or Mick Jagger, or before them the Beat generation, who succeeded in shattering the surface of conventionality. These men were all, at bottom, poseurs; they acted out leather-jacket fantasies of rebellion for themselves and for a small circle of like-minded male buddies. When they lost self-control, they had to do so by succumbing to the greater force of alcohol or drugs, and they made sure they kept their transgression private. The girls who created Beatlemania—and it's important to acknowledge that Beatlemania was a creation, not a Pavlovian reaction—went much further when they made a public spectacle of their seizures. And I think this is one of the reasons why the Beatles were embarrassed by them. These girls upstaged the "fab four." Their passion swelled into a force that made the lads from Liverpool look suddenly like little figurines of themselves. Acting for adolescents everywhere, they seized and made a world, taking power and space away from the control of adults. In creating Beatlemania, they were demonstrating the force of an impulse—leaders of the New Left would call it "direction action"—that would drive young people just a few years later to seize university buildings and city streets.

To the Beatles' credit (and their manager Brian Epstein's), they handled this energy with grace and generosity. When asked about Beatlemania, they invariably responded with smiles, shrugs, and stammered words that expressed bewilderment, gratitude, excitement, and fear. For the millions of teenagers who were not themselves swept up in Beatlemania and who saw it all secondhand, on news programs or in *A Hard Day's Night,* the Beatles' response to Beatlemania was crucial. Those girls were, we knew deep down, our surrogates. Those girls acted for all Beatles fans. Their passion made them achingly vulnerable, and that vulnerability was, at bottom, everyone's. So when the Beatles demonstrated their respect for that vulnerability, they won the trust of many more fans than chased them through the streets of English towns. (Isn't that a fearless trust that we see glistening in the eyes of those swooning girls?)

Compared with the Beatles, the Rolling Stones, who were also pursued by thousands of screaming teenagers, were *cool.* They were frozen in a pose: indifferent, mean, maybe even dangerous. Instead of responding to their fans' passion with the good humor of the Beatles, they used it as an occasion to demonstrate their cruelty. Rock historian Nik Cohn tells us that when the Stones arrived at a concert, they "stared straight ahead, didn't twitch once, and the girls only gaped. Almost as if the Stones weren't touchable, as if they were protected by some invisible metal ring." And he concludes, "In this way, whatever else, the Stones had style and presence and real control." *Real control* indeed. It was the Stones' insistence on maintaining this control that created much of their charisma; their pose of stony indifference modeled a refusal of sentimentality I and many other fans copied. But it also made them more conservative and less unsettling than the Beatles. The Stones were a great rock band (the band that created the very possibility of being a great rock band), but they were just what you would expect young guys to be: deeply invested in traditional exhibitions of male power.

The Beatles, on the other hand, may have done more than any

other pop celebrities (or perhaps anyone, period) to rewrite what masculinity in America might be. Their appealing mix of authority, vulnerability, and trustworthiness modeled something very new to American culture, including the millions of boys in their audience. The Beatles broke out of the mold of stoic masculine silence and cool irony to celebrate the risks and joys of reciprocal communication. When they sang that all I had to do was call her on the phone, and she'd come running home, they were following a well-worn path. But when they went on to say that the same went for me, whenever she wanted me at all, I'd be there, yes I would, whenever she called, they showed a new way out of tough masculinity.

And girls *loved* this new style. When they encouraged me to grow my hair long, like the Beatles, I realized that it was worth taking the risk of being called a "sissy." ("Maybe a dozen guys started to come to Cornell with 'long' hair, the early Beatle length. The girls liked these guys very much.") The change made possible by the Beatles, the breakthrough they initiated and encouraged, was as much as anything else a change in what it meant to be a "man." As Allen Ginsberg observed in 1984:

> The Beatles changed American consciousness, introduced a new note of complete masculinity allied with complete tenderness and vulnerability. And when that note was accepted in America, it did more than anything or anyone to prepare us for some kind of open-minded, open-hearted relationship with each other and the rest of the world.

The shrill screaming of fans rises above the sound of the Beatles' own voices, hangs in the air of memory, then fades. It was a noise that vocalized so much: desperation, desire, excitement, anger. It was the noise of fans reciprocating, of teenage girls tearing down the walls of Jericho with the power of voiced emotion. And between 1963 and 1972, American culture increasingly allowed itself to be led by these girls and to use them to articulate, as only a scream or an electric guitar can, the profound instability that is felt to underlie life in the late twentieth century.

I suppose that, in other times and places too, young people have gone to bed at night and expected to wake up in a different world. But I suspect that young people in the '60s were the first to have this expectation realized in objective form for them in a popular entertainment they produced and, to a remarkable extent, owned. It may well be that, as some historians have argued and as I have often felt, this expectation was foolishly misguided. Maybe it was all an illusion. Maybe *nothing* was happening. (As David Crosby ruefully remarked: "Somehow *Sgt. Pepper's* did not stop the Vietnam War. . . . Somebody just wasn't listening.") Maybe what looked like a heroic revolt against capitalism, technology, or modernity was in reality just the beginning of capitalism's most recent phase. ("We blew it," says Peter Fonda to Dennis Hopper.) But at the time, dazzled by the spectacle of the youth culture they saw encouraged and reflected in the media, many Americans began to *feel* change as something real. Their willingness to experience rather than deny change, however illusory the change itself might have been, rode on the shoulders of a youth culture and depended on a broad cultural legitimization of what one might call the adolescent perspective. For a short time, just nine years at the most, it became imaginable that one could stay "forever young," and that it was legitimate to do so because youth had a vision, a peculiar insight into modernity, a way of seeing and being in the world that was just as true as the perspective of their parents.

The essence of the youth culture of the '60s was the legitimization of this adolescent vision of life as a river of change—undertaken first through rock 'n' roll and later through psychedelic drugs as well. If belief in youth's wisdom seems to have died out in the age of Reagan, extinguished as well by the din of parents urging their kids to become economic citizens by the eighth grade, youth's attitude has nonetheless been so completely realized and absorbed that, in 1995, a leading philosopher could simply declare that "it becomes necessary to stabilize precisely because stability is not natural; it is because there is instability that stabilization becomes necessary." While as a philosophical position this belief in instability is as old as the pre-Socratics, as an attitude driving popular culture it pushed to the surface for the first time in the early 1960s. Dylan's "The Times They Are A-Changin'" was the song that most explicitly and obviously named it. But the stupendously popular music of the early Beatles—and popular for just this reason—was the force that swept aside the past and uncovered the "founding and irreducible" primacy of change. If that belief looks as if it has disappeared, that may be because it's now everywhere and therefore nowhere.

No one did as much to put this vision into sound and words as the Beatles, who confirmed our sense that the world was radically unstable and open to new possibilities both by producing music that expressed this vision and by changing so continuously themselves. The Beatles were always becoming. Each new album was so different from the last. "What I can say about the Beatles," remarked Warren Zevon in a 1989 interview, "is that . . . everything new they did was supposed to challenge you. The Beatles continued to be new as long as they were the Beatles."

We in the audience could see this mercurial restlessness in the way the Beatles just *looked*. Interviewed again and again, often by aggressive and stupid reporters, they consistently broke through conventions of celebrity decorum to sound fresh and real. (Interviewer: "Where did you get the idea for the haircuts?" John: "Where'd you get the idea for yours?") There was something about the Beatles' insouciant wit that simply sliced through the pall of unreality that usually surrounded pop stars. (Interviewer: "What did you expect to find here in Australia?" John: "Australians, I should suppose.") Even in the silly Edwardian outfits Brian Epstein got them to wear, even with their simpy smiles and oh-so-cute hair shakes, they stood out from the background of a fabricated world as young people who dared to be themselves. (Interviewer: "Do you plan to record any anti-war songs?" John: "All our songs are anti-war." Interviewer: "How has your image changed since 1963?" George: "An image is how *you* see us, so only you can answer that.") Watching the Beatles outwit these adults who condescendingly presumed that rock music had to be banal, and that their power could contain and crush the Beatles, we found our heroes. And so they "sold"—millions upon millions of records. (Interviewer: "Why do you think you're so popular?" John: "It must be the weather I suppose.") For weeks at a time, five or more of the top ten songs would be by the Beatles. Their sound was everywhere. As rock critic Ellen Willis observed: "In 1965, the average person, asked to associate the phrase 'rock 'n' roll,' would probably have said 'Beatles.'" The sales history of their albums, every one of which went to the #1 spot on the charts, is still without peer in the history of popular music.

The Beatles' energy and attitude, the way their music seemed to attack stability at its foundations, was a crucial source of their phenomenal popularity. But we should also take into account something quite different that they brought to their music: their belief, voiced again and again, in the redemptive possibilities of communication. Of love. From "She Loves You" to "All You Need Is Love," their work turned on the pivot of E. M. Forster's moral dictum "Only connect." Of course, rock 'n' roll is rife with songs about letters, phone calls, lovers' misunderstandings, and so on. But the Beatles elaborated on this theme with an insistent creativity that can't be explained by mere convention and that becomes fully self-conscious in their later music. When they sang that half of what they say is meaningless, but they say it just to reach us, or

> *You never give me your pillow*
> *You only give me your situation*
> *And in the middle of negotiations*
> *We break down*

it was obvious that they were thinking not just about the ups and downs of teenage love but about the problems and possibilities of all human encounters. And by 1967, if not much earlier, the Beatles' audience heard songs like these as strengthening a very specific connection: the "you" in question was not just an imagined lover but the Beatles' audience itself. It was as if the Beatles were reaching directly through the speakers of a million stereos in order to make contact with *you*. Were *you* ready? Could *you* hear the word?

Yet this uncanny rapport between pop stars and audience had its indispensable foreground in the innocent enthusiasms of the first two or three albums, where song after song expressed both a need to connect and a confidence in communication. Because so many of these early songs unselfconsciously celebrated the pleasures of getting through, of listening, being heard, telling, and touching, some Beatles fans began to hear intimations of something new, something like subtle messages addressed to themselves as listeners. When the Beatles sang *with love / from me / to you,* they drew out the length of the silences between each phrase in a way that called attention to those gaps and called their listeners' attention into those spaces and seemed therefore to *mean* something. Eventually, such moments of what literary critics call "direct address" became more deliberate. Beatles scholar Ian MacDonald has suggested that "Thank You Girl" (1963) "shows Lennon and McCartney cultivating their audience by encouraging each of their female fans to hear it as gratitude for her part in The Beatles' success." And another song from 1963, "She Loves You," opens up the theme of communication in a different way. What made the song so fresh was its use of the third rather than the first person. By recasting the relationship they are singing about as one between a *she* and a *you* instead of an *I* and a *you* or *her,* the Beatles enormously extended the emotive spatiality of pop. Here was a song that did not lock two lovers into a conventional dialogue, with the teen listener playing the part (necessarily) of an eavesdropper who identifies with one of the two protagonists. Instead, the song is about a triangle, a three-way relationship. The Beatles in effect step back and play the role of a caring friend who mediates between the listener and his or her true love. *They* know what she's thinking of because she's told them what to say. *Their* facility in communicating will get the relationship back on track.

While the Beatles' energy affirmed the possibility of change, their lyrics suggested that such change sluiced through the channels of connection and communication, an idea concretely realized by the Beatles' own success in connecting with their enormous audience. (Early songs in which the difficulties and rewards of communication are directly thematized would include, at a minimum, "From Me to You," "Thank You Girl," "Do You Want to Know a Secret?" "I Saw Her Standing There," "All My Loving," "PS I Love

You," "If I Fell," "Tell Me Why," "Any Time at All," "Things We Said Today," "No Reply," "Words of Love," and "She Loves You." Later songs would include "Drive My Car," "Norwegian Wood," "Michelle," "The Word," "I'm Looking through You," "In My Life," "Here, There and Everywhere," "She Said She Said," "For No One," "I Want to Tell You," "Got to Get You into My Life," "With a Little Help from My Friends," "Within You without You," "A Day in the Life," "Glass Onion," "While My Guitar Gently Weeps," "Julia," "Everybody's Got Something to Hide except Me and My Monkey," "All You Need Is Love," "Come Together," "Something," "You Never Give Me Your Money," "Carry That Weight," "The End," and "I Me Mine.") The intimate click of contact celebrated so innocently in *Well she looked at me, and I, I could see* would later become *Watching her eyes, and hoping I'm always there* and still later, *Somewhere in her smile she knows.* Listening raptly to songs such as these, the Beatles' audience began to invest them with a moral authority I think no pop singers (except possibly Bob Dylan) have had before or since. They were musicians who were also prophets and healers. Their fans started to listen to them as if their music carried answers, pathways, wisdom. By 1967 Gene Youngblood could write without a trace of embarrassment what many Beatles fans were feeling:

> Through the centuries, artists and visionaries have been luring us away on magical mystery tours—inviting us to turn inward upon ourselves. But none have ever commanded the power and audience of the Beatles. The allure, the excitement, the glory of Beatlemusic is the suspicion that the Beatles might just succeed where magicians of the past have failed.

Obviously, though, the Beatles did not succeed, if success means bringing their audience to a state of cosmic enlightenment or permanent joy. And when the Beatles broke up—a disintegration that began just months after Youngblood wrote these words—the entire structure they had built seemed to collapse, and with it so much of the felt presence of an alternative culture within the culture. But if the Beatles did not succeed in this sense, their music certainly did create a framework, invisible to the eyes but audible to the ears, in which something like enlightenment was an imagined possibility. They didn't just represent an attitude that was helpful to their fans. They *enacted* it, they structured it, they *were* it. And maybe the word that brings this into sharpest focus is "ritual."

Jungian psychotherapist Bani Shorter has suggested that "our gods are created by a conscious or unconscious fear of aloneness in the midst of unlimited and overwhelming possibilities," and she understands ritual as a response to this fear: "ritual takes root in a sense of aloneness so bewildering and hazardous that one will sacrifice a previous identity in order to make contact with something more and a strength that resides elsewhere." The Beatles were in this sense a ritual for those teenagers in the early '60s who felt bewildered and alone and wanted desperately "to make contact with something more." The Beatles created a space into which their audience projected as much meaning as they took away. Eventually the Beatles themselves became aware of this dynamic call-and-response between themselves and their audience, a process whereby "meaning" was created by an audience in collaboration with performers. (Think of the fact that it was the audience, acting spontaneously and collectively, that gave *The White Album* the name by which it's known.) "We write songs," said Paul McCartney. "We know what we mean by them. But in a week someone else says something about it, says that it means that as well, and you can't deny it. Things take on millions of meanings. I don't understand it."

> John: If we have any influence on youth at all, we'd like to influence them in a peaceful way.
>
> Yoko: Communicate with them and with each other.

The Beatles came from Liverpool. They did not descend from the heavens with a roll of thunder in a chariot of fire. But they did create an experience that cannot be adequately described if we are afraid to think of the miraculous or the divine. Words like "divine" are just metaphors in any case. They point toward something that can be experienced but not named. They simply indicate that, alongside explanations of the Beatles phenomenon that emphasize the proclivities of capitalism and the ramifications of technology, we have to add one that acknowledges the human thirst for transcendence. Human connection without transcendence (if there has ever been such a thing) does not satisfy. Loneliness is also *cosmic* loneliness. It is not just from ourselves and our culture that we feel alienated, but from Being. This sense of estrangement from everything that might give life meaning is what the writers of the Port Huron Statement were trying to articulate as a political problem when they claimed that people are "infinitely precious and possessed of unfulfilled capacities," and when they opposed "the depersonalization that reduces human beings to the status of things." And for a brief time the Beatles loomed as a gigantic counterforce to this emptying out of life and this reduction of human beings that seem so intrinsic to modern life. This is what Greil Marcus was getting at when he made the claim, so hard for us to take seriously now, that "the Beatles affected not only the feel but the quality of life—they deepened it, sharpened it, brightened it."

John Lennon was intending to outrage when he remarked that the Beatles were "more popular than Jesus." But he was also naming something that was true for me and, I suspect, for many others as well: not just that the Beatles were "popular," but that their popularity had something to do with a sustenance they provided. To me, at least, they offered something I felt I had a *right* to be getting from my culture. It was a feeling of connection, social *and* cosmic. A brightening, a deepening, a sharpening of life. While Elvis too had provided this "strength that resides elsewhere" to his fans, Elvis himself was always blissfully, coolly unreflective. The Beatles went much closer to creating the kind of ritual Shorter has in mind because they seemed to *know* what they were doing. (You *know* what I mean.) For ritual must always be more than spontaneous panic or improvised grasping for transcendence. Ritual is a *form;* it is formalized. Ritual occurs when consciousness creates structures through which we can enact our desire for what consciousness alone cannot reach. Between *she looked at me* and *I could see* came that blank space in which epiphany, contact, could happen. Between *you know my name* and *look up the number* came that moment of decision, of action, the Beatles explicitly asked their audience to take. Between *I saw her yesterday* and *she told me what to say* came the Beatles' insight into existence itself and what gave it meaning.

Between "She Loves You" and "All You Need Is Love," with the latter echoing, parodying, and honoring its own beginnings in the former, came a cultural moment whose status as end or beginning remains undecided, even today.

In 1996, nearly thirty years after Beatlemania, the *Beatles Anthology* was aired on television, drawing an audience estimated at 35 million. It was the highest-grossing year in Beatles history; they took in more than $635 million, selling 7 million new CDs and 13 million rereleases, mainly to teenage buyers. I and the graying friends with whom I watched the program all had tears in our eyes as we watched the black-and-white footage of these boys who embodied and expressed so much of what life once seemed to promise us: "a sense of limitless, unbounded futurity." When Lennon's ghostly voice came through with the simple message that love is the answer to loneliness, that connection is the antidote to unreality, singing *It's real love, Yes it's reeeeal,* I heard again the only truth I have ever believed, the only gospel that has ever broken through my shell of cynicism and my distrust of hope. The Beatles continue to grip me where I live because they came closer than anything I've known since to an experience of hope that is smart because it knows irony and dares to go beyond it.

The vehicle that carried this hip optimism so effectively was at first so simple—those simple yet masterfully crafted songs on their first three albums. As McCartney reflected shortly after the Beatles had completed the complex labyrinth of *Sgt. Pepper's:* "You get to the bit where you think, if we're going to do philosophy it isn't worth it. 'Love Me Do' was our greatest philosophical song: 'Love me do / You know I love you / I'll always be true / So love me do' . . . simple and true . . . it's incredibly simple." But is it futile to try now to unpack this simplicity? Is trying to make sense now of what was partly an effort to *stop making sense* so inherently self-contradictory as to be doomed? The hardest thing in writing these words about the *wonder* of the Beatles is, you know, not sounding too youthfully earnest or, on the other hand, too reliant on the irony-plated armature of academic discourse. The subject demands an adolescent vehemence while calling just as firmly for a distanced gaze, even a sardonic smile, like Mona Lisa's. At bottom, I don't think we can fully explain the Beatles and why they appealed. Everyone then and now has his or her own private sense of what they meant. All we can do now, I think, is rediscover that the reverse weave of this inward experience was always at the same time a public experience, a part of history, the outside of an inside. That fusion was what the Beatles got going and what living to music affirmed. It's what you heard in the screams of their fans.

It's why we stand on the shore of the Beatles' secret island even now.

CHAPTER 2

"Heartbreak Hotel"

At the Crossroads of White Loneliness and the Blues

The inner events of an adolescent demand from what surrounds him life on a grand scale, in a grand style. This is the impulse to apocalypse in the young, as if they were in exile from a nation that does not exist—and yet they can sense it, they know it is there—if only because their belief itself demands its presence.

—Peter Marin (1969)

lonely? Ah yes
but it is the flowers and the mirrors
of flowers that now meet my
loneliness
an' mine shall be a strong loneliness
dissolvin' deep
t' the depths of my freedom
an' that, then, shall
remain my song

—Bob Dylan (1963)

The flick of the light switch, the *thunk* of the refrigerator door, the hiss of air escaping from the newly opened jar of peanut butter. The blue light cast on the living room walls, the minute but deadly chasms of electric sockets, the perpetual hum and whir of motorized life. The smell of brand-new schools without the dust of history, the deadening convenience of time inside the laundromat, the forlorn look of grapes wrapped tight and flat in cellophane. The daylong mysterious absence of the father at his job. The more shadowy absence of the mother whose tactility has been absorbed by her appliances. The advertising oozing from the radio or shouting from the television: omnipresent, yet ignored, like a vast holocaust in a silent dream. One could see, as one gazed out the window, that there was no other place than this. A few trees had been allowed to grow along the street. A yard, much like other yards, adjoined the house. Only the clouds moving swiftly on a March morning, or the pale moon over the rooftops in broad daylight, gave a hint that there was— or once had been—a world of distances and depths, fissures and fragments.

Nothing was wrong with this picture. Everything was. "I experienced my oppression," recalls Osha Neumann of the Mother-fuckers, a New York cultural guerrilla group of the late '60s, "as an inability to grasp anything real beyond my own subjectivity. [I was] in revolt against the experience of unreality." As many of us who grew up then remember, there was indeed something profoundly "unreal" about a middle-class childhood in America in the 1950s. Not just childhood but all of middle-class existence, the massive drive to consolidate a sense of the normal and then submit to it, seemed to promote pervasive unreality at the expense of hard particulars, particulars that might, after all, by virtue of their intrinsic distinctiveness, deviate from that invisible, sacred standard of the norm. Some voices rose in complaint against the bland. The writings of the Beats, movies like *The Wild One* and *Rebel without a Cause,* the cool intensity of bebop—all were responses to the suspicion that in the midst of unprecedented prosperity life had become shallow, false, unreal. In Holden Caulfield's memorable word, "phony." Best-sellers like *A Nation of Sheep* and *The Organization Man* broadcast dire warnings that Americans were mistaking conformity for community, security for strength, vivacity for vigor. Even John Kennedy's campaign against Richard Nixon recognized and played on this national self-doubt, articulating people's fears that prosperity meant flabbiness, that America's amazing success was also making it "soft."

But if you were young and white, no voice dissented as powerfully as Elvis Presley's. For my older brother and me, as for many thousands of white teenagers, the first rock song ever was Presley's cover of Willie Mae "Big Mama" Thornton's "(You Ain't Nothin' but a) Hound Dog." We responded to its *sound* long before we understood the words and years before we had an inkling that we were unhappy in our well-ordered world. Beneath its honeyed flow, Elvis's voice had a buzzsaw back there in the shadows, and if you were young that snarl sounded like a challenge, like defiance, a subtle but unmistakable *Fuck You!* to the world. Its power, I understand now, is immensely strengthened by the claustrophobic, box-like structure of the twelve-bar blues form that contained it. Like the voices of all great blues singers, it beats against the confines of those walls even while its power derives from the intensification of feeling their solidity makes possible. Together, voice and form seemed to understand and attack the vague and pervasive unreality we were unknowingly oppressed by. Without the pause that almost always falls in a twelve-bar blues between the first half of a line and the second, Elvis would not have been able to deliver with such force the words that are really the essence of this song. *They said you was high-class,* pause—

But that was just a lie!

Just a lie. The world was a lie. Adults were liars. Liars of the worst kind because they didn't even know they were lying.

Ten years later, rock music would become much more explicit about the way the world itself was becoming fake. But back in 1956, Elvis unwittingly tapped into the power of the blues and specifically into their power to unmask the lie, to deliver the gift of what W. E. B. Du Bois called "second sight," the canny gaze of one who sees the lies oppressors tell themselves. Elvis fans loved his vulnerability, his croon, his moon-in-June romanticism, but they knew that what singled him out and made him different was the rage they heard in the timbre of his voice and in the musical forms he had chosen for that voice. Their affiliation with his anger is what Stanley Booth witnessed at a July 4 concert that year, when Elvis's "voice became a growl, an act of rebellion. . . . If the police had not been there, forming a blue wall around the stage, the audience might have eaten Elvis's body in a Eucharistic frenzy. They were his and he was theirs, their leader: it was an incandescent moment." His naming of the "lie" became the schism, the fault line that cracked open the veneer of reality and revealed its unreality. It was the beginning of a generation's dream vision, of their Dantesque journey into an underworld that allowed them to see with piercing clarity all that was false and phony about the world above ground.

But on reflection that metaphor doesn't quite work. What made the lie against which these adolescents rebelled so infuriating and so baffling was that it was already *inside* us. For Elvis's audience, the oppressors were not really visible, much less were they nameable. Oppression was something that had been internalized, had become, as Neumann's phrase suggests, a part of one's subjectivity, of one's self. Elvis's fans were as plastic as the world, and we knew it; if we were to undertake a Dantesque journey it would have to be into ourselves, not just out of this world.

We can hear the first musicking of this predicament in Elvis's next big hit, "Heartbreak Hotel." (I apologize for using the grotesque neologism "to musick," which I borrow from musicologist Christopher Small, but it is the only word I know of that conveys music's nature as a *verb*—as movement or activity with purpose.) If Elvis's first hit was a wedge driven into the flank of hypocrisy, his second was more of an exploration, an effort to name what it felt like to live within such a world. Pried out of the context of the whole song, winnowed from the urgent melancholy of Elvis's voice, the song's lyrics look lachrymose and narcissistic. But to the ear attuned to Elvis's gift, these words find *the* word that will be taken up and used again and again by the musicians who created '60s rock. From the depths of an echo that is the aural analog of the hotel itself (Brian Eno remembers it as one of the formative influences on his own musical development), Elvis's voice rings out with startling defiance. He is not just singing. He is announcing a new sound with its new and peculiar suitability to new circumstances. Heard purely as sound, the opening lines

> *Well, since my baby left me*
> *I found a new place to dwell*

carry no hint of the gloom that will follow on their heels. Quite the contrary. The lines are ecstatic. They point toward openness, transcendence, even joy. The ecstasy might derive from Elvis's personal discovery, in the RCA studio, of the inner core of his voice, which we hear now for the first time. But for his audience, it sprang from the discovery of a power to articulate, with passion, the conditions of existence as one felt them. One dwells in one's *place* in history, and for those who came of age between 1955 and 1965 that place certainly felt *new*—completely unlike the world our parents had grown up in. We dwelt there because a loss of some kind had occurred. The departure of something: no words like *love, meaning,* or *familiarity* can rise, as Elvis's voice rises, to the challenge of expressing the fundamental unseen loss that has already occurred, the doom of a new way of being in the world, the departure of this *baby* who is at once one's sweetheart and one's childhood. Elvis's voice rises to announce and, yes, to celebrate this condition, and then the voice abruptly descends,

> *down at the end of some lonely street*

with its soft spiraling, down down down, through the four lines
of the refrain

> *I am so lonely*
> *I am so lonely*
> *I am so lonely*
> *I could die.*

When Elvis's voice hits bottom, we have reached the core of
the song, the dark heart of this old hotel. The word is *lonely*. Elvis
defines the new situation and names it as a new place in which the
generation just coming of age will be forced *to dwell*. The home
becomes a hotel; the private becomes public; surrounded by lonely
others, one is jostled in one's loneliness. This is the place where
the state of being alone is replaced by the state of being *lonely*, a
loneliness we will hear twelve years later as John Lennon, upping
the ante, sings in "Yer Blues": *Well I'm lonely, gonna die!* It is the
loneliness we would seek to overcome through shared music,
through free sex, through the myth of a generation, through the
pharmacology of Dr. Hofmann (inventor of LSD), and through the
cult of love and connection musicked by the Beatles.

But Elvis's voice does not stay stuck in the basement of this
hotel. Right after *I could die*, we are whisked back up to the exalted
heights where the song began. The instruments and Elvis's voice
join in a concerted attack on the condition that the song is bodying
forth: *Well, and though it's always crowded . . .* If *I am so lonely* is
the heart of this song, this abrupt reassertion of the promise announced in the opening lines is its distinctive sound, its magic.
Looking back with the wisdom of elders, we might judge this reassertion to be naïve. But heard with the ear of youth, its anger is
magnificent. It's not "optimistic," it's pissed off. It holds the future
in its hands, refusing to submit or return to the past. It will explore
the inscape of its condition, forcing this hotel to yield its secrets.
What Elvis's fans are looking for is not a way out. This is *our* hotel;
it is *our* dwelling. We must find a way *in* to it, however paradoxical
our quest might be.

I want to take Elvis's word *lonely* as the word that names this condition, not just because it was used so often in the years I'm writing about but because it is a sentimental word, reminding us that the adolescent's response to modernity is a feeling of betrayal, a bruise. In its broadest form, this condition was nothing new. Personal identity has been in a state of some crisis at least since the emergence of capitalism, and Descartes would have recognized with a smile Neumann's "inability to grasp anything real beyond [his] own subjectivity." Yet the 1950s were not just a replay of the 1650s. At about the turn of the twentieth century, many people in Europe and the United States seem to have begun describing their "selves" in a new way. The notion of an isolated self set off against the world began to lose its plausibility as Americans increasingly experienced themselves as an integral part of a vast and complex social network. Lecturing at the University of Chicago in the early 1920s, sociologist George Herbert Mead proposed that, in modern cultures, our sense of who we are derives in large part from our sense of how others perceive us. Mead argued that the self is not so much a thing as a social process. We put together our sense of who we are as we interact with others and infer from their behavior whom they see us to be. Mead was just one of many philosophers and critics—William James, John Dewey, Walter Lippmann, W. E. B. Du Bois, and Lewis Mumford were others—who tried to put into words this new, interdependent subjectivity as it emerged in the first decades of the twentieth century. All recognized that we had started to experience a dialectical dependence *on* others as we constructed a self that was supposed to distinguish us *from* others. This new self they dubbed a "social self."

By 1956, when I entered the first grade and Elvis Presley entered the RCA studios to record "Heartbreak Hotel," the social conditions of capitalist modernity that Mead and his colleagues had observed in their emergent phase had become much more completely established throughout the United States. How did it feel to be a self caught up in such a network of interdependence? asked sociologist David Riesman in *The Lonely Crowd,* published in 1950. Riesman described the "changing American character" as one that achieved "behavioral conformity . . . not through drill in behavior itself . . . but rather through an exceptional sensitivity to the actions and wishes of others." Whereas earlier generations of Americans had regulated their behavior by submitting to tradition or by internalizing social norms, what Riesman called the "other-directed" personality emerging after the Second World War did so by continuously adjusting to the perceived demands and responses of those around him. As a consequence, he wrote, "the other-directed person has no clear core of self . . . no clear line between production and consumption; between adjusting to the group and serving private interests; between work and play." Lacking a "clear core of self," the new (usually white, middle-class, and suburban) American self had few inner resources with which to enjoy and benefit from solitude. He lived, said Riesman, in "the terror of loneliness."

We can hear this terror in "Heartbreak Hotel," I think, but we can also detect another emotion. Loneliness is painful, of course, and we seek to avoid it. We want to be more connected with those around us, especially if we have been taught since infancy to find ourselves in the reciprocating gaze of others. (The child-rearing philosophy of Dr. Spock encouraged mothers to develop precisely this kind of intense, one-on-one relationship with their child.) And yet, as adolescents at least, we also feel just the opposite. We *desire* loneliness because it offers us a chance to conceal ourselves and within that private darkness to hope that we can exist for ourselves before we exist for and from others. We hunger for songs about loneliness not just because they express what we dread but because they offer what we need: a space, a place to go. Who has not, after all, wanted to join Elvis Presley in Heartbreak Hotel?

I, for one, remember feeling that my identity depended so much on the affirmation of others that "I" might not really exist. By the time I turned thirteen in 1963, I'd started to feel that a true authenticity of self—a self as solid and hard as a rock—was simply not achievable anymore, no matter how much my culture paid lip service to the ideal. As I would later read on the liner notes to Dylan's *Highway 61 Revisited:* "I cannot say the word eye anymore . . . when I speak this word eye, it is as if I'm speaking of somebody's eye that I faintly remember . . . there is no eye—there is only a series of mouths."

Because I couldn't find a self that was dense, substantial, and independent of others, the loneliness that was evoked and sustained within countless rock songs became for me a space within which these conflicting and ambiguous feelings could be explored in relative safety—since the songs, like all art, held them at one remove. When in 1966 the Beatles asked where all the lonely people came from, I already knew the answer: they came from the way life *is,* from the way things have been set up. *We* are Eleanor Rigby. And when in 1969 The Band sang Bob Dylan's "I Shall Be Released," I didn't know that "lonely crowd" came from David Riesman's book, but I did know that the phrase named something that I felt, and that the song expressed my bewildered sense of entrapment and loneliness, futility and hope:

> *Standing next to me in this lonely crowd,*
> *Is a man who swears he's not to blame.*
> *All day long I hear him shout so loud,*
> *Crying out that he was framed.*

That "man" was, of course, Dylan. It was also me. And it was everyone my age I knew.

This sense of being doomed to loneliness, of being set up or "framed," was produced in part by our own good fortune. Growing up in the economic boom of the 1950s, middle-class teenagers of the late '50s and '60s suddenly had money. Lots of it. We were a $12 billion consumer market in our own right and spent $13 billion of our parents' money, too. We bought 55 percent of all soft drinks, 53 percent of all movie tickets, 43 percent of all records, and 20 percent of all cosmetics. One out of five high school seniors owned a car. In possession of such power, white youth of the middle and upper classes could lay claim to a measure of social recognition undreamed of by earlier generations. But while many of us had power in the marketplace, everywhere else we were expected to remain kids. We were nagged about clothes, posture, music, food, alcohol, dating, and sex. We were nagged about everything of importance in a teenager's life. Every-where we turned, people were trying to sell us things by telling us who to be.

"The mission of the adult world," opined one writer of the '50s, "is to help teenagers become adults by raising their standards and values, to make adolescence a step toward growing up, not a privi-lege to be exploited." But adolescence *was* exploited, not so much by teenagers themselves as by everyone interested in selling things to them. American adolescents were told again and again to "be yourself" and "think of others." We were the privileged heirs of society, yet we were also outcasts relegated to its margins. We were simultaneously insiders and outsiders. We were powerful and powerless. We were in-between. We were nowhere, looking for a place to dwell that was ours.

But while the vocabulary of economic history tells half the story, there is another half that requires metaphor. For the first eighteen or so years of a prosperous youth, one regards the reality one is given as the only possible reality. For eighteen years, we believe that nothing more exists because we are satisfied that what is is enough. Complications are easily absorbed; the unfamiliar is easily drawn in and focused. The facts about ancient Egypt that we absorb in elementary school are linked invisibly to the patterns in the sidewalk we peruse on our way home. The shadows on our bedroom wall, the names of hurricanes, the theme songs of our favorite TV shows, and the heft of peanut butter sandwiches consti-tute an ordered whole in which we trust. Most of the time anyway. For occasionally and unpredictably, we experience what Virginia Woolf called "moments of being" when we see the world not as we have been taught to, not the familiar and seamless and already bland everydayness that adults take for granted, but existence as such—naked, immediate, present. Woolf remembers a moment when she lay in bed on a summer afternoon and watched the tassel of the cord hanging from the window shade move back and forth in the breeze. I remember finding a blue comb lost beneath the leaves of a shrub in the garden. At such moments, the sheer be-ingness of these things floods us with light we have not yet learned to fear.

Until we reach a certain age, we live fairly comfortably with these sudden incursions of a Being that feels unmediated by parents, culture, upbringing, history. We know, without being particularly upset, that the cities of knowledge are built beside the river of mutability. But at eighteen or thereabouts something happens that we spend the rest of our lives trying either to forget or to understand. We suddenly see a contradiction between the bland complacency of a society and the sharp irruptions of a formless Being. Our moments of naked confrontation with it cut a fissure through the surface of the world we thought we knew—a fissure that opens into another dimension, into other worlds, into the void. Like Persephone, we are swept up and swallowed. This agonizing insight of adolescents was described by Peter Marin in 1969 as "an impulse to apocalypse in the young, as if they were in exile from a nation that does not exist—and yet they can sense it, they know it is there."

We *did* know it was there, and the essence of the '60s I am trying to understand more than thirty years later was this impulse to apocalypse—apocalypse in the double sense of both revelation and cataclysm. This '60s was the cultural legitimization of an experience that is usually private and fugitive. At the edge of the fissure, a counterculture grew like the dense colonies of mysterious organisms that thrive only in the depths of the ocean near life-giving jets of hot gas and molten lava. In *this* '60s, millions of young persons recognized in each other's eyes the look of one who has seen through to the strangeness on the *other side* that reveals the strangeness of this, the nearer side. This was the look of *the girl with the sun in her eyes,* it was Jimi Hendrix's condition of being *experienced,* it was the *something happening here* that Mr. Jones would never understand. It was what Norman Mailer called "the revelatory mystery of the happening where you did not know what was going to happen next." It was what the Beatles meant when they said they would love to turn us on. The decade's elaborate and joyful codes of gesture, glance, and dress all referred to this most ordinary yet subversive perception. Suddenly, the secret was out. From the limbo of our in-betweenness, we saw what most adults have required themselves to forget: that existence is, and therefore might not be. That contingency undergirds being. That cultures are founded on fictions. That rules are a way of forgetting, not just a mode of repression. We needed a form that could represent this vision to ourselves, that could express our second sight and our fear of, and need for, loneliness.

Rock was the form we found, and for good reason.

"If I could find a white man who had the Negro sound and the Negro feel, I could make a billion dollars." These famous words of Sam Phillips, owner of Sun Records, must stand at the top of the first page of any history of rock 'n' roll, testifying to the uneasy confluence of race, gender, entertainment, and profit that brought the music into being and that has troubled its history ever since. Phillips found his man, of course, and over the next two decades many other white musicians and producers followed in Presley's blue-suede footsteps, becoming rich doing covers or imitations of songs composed and first recorded by black men and women. Their success depended not just on their own energy and talent but on the de facto segregation of American radio and on the widespread racism—passive when it was not active—of many of the white youths who constituted the immense and hugely profitable audience for this new musical form.

The birth of rock 'n' roll out of the blues is attended, therefore, by a kind of original sin, fairly called "appropriation," "exploitation," and "theft." But accurate as they may be, these terms tend to predispose us to oversimplify the reasons why it drew so heavily on the sound and structure of the blues. According to most accounts, white youth liked the blues sound merely because they associated it with African American styles of resistance to white middle-class values. These accounts tend to be highly metaphorical, eschewing musicological analysis in favor of vague allusions to "rhythm," "energy," "realism," and the like. A critic as astute as Simon Frith, for example, writes that "Rock 'n' roll

faith is faith in the music's black elements, in its sense of performance, its physical energy, its directness, its vocal and rhythmic techniques." But surely a Beethoven symphony or a Strauss
waltz offers plenty of "physical energy," while country music,
klezmer, and polka all provide a dynamic "sense of performance"
and very danceable "rhythmic techniques." Why wasn't the music
of white youth based on those musical forms? Likewise, in his
beautiful tribute to blues and country music musicians, *Feel Like
Going Home,* Peter Guralnick writes that "there are lots of reasons why blues should attract a white audience," and he goes on
to list them. First, "there was the whole elaborate mythology"
of the Negro that was so appealing to young whites. Second, the
blues was "a perfect vehicle for our romanticism" because of its
"exotic nature, the vagueness of its associations." Third, there was
the intimacy of the music; "it was undeniably personal music."
Fourth, and "most of all," there was what Guralnick calls its "vi-
tality":

> I knew it immediately, I still hear it today. And while I have gone
> on to any number of ancillary enthusiasms, it remains central in
> my life. For lesser attachments there are always explanations, but
> blues appealed to something deep-seated and permanent in my-
> self, it just sounded right to me.

But surely numerous other musical forms available to white youth
were "exotic," "personal," and "vital." Why did we find the blues
in particular so compelling, so urgently "right"? Without denying
that the white assimilation of the blues was indeed exploitative and
unfair, and without suggesting that drama and fantasy play no part
in white enthusiasm for the blues, I want to explore the other side
of this relationship through a question seldom, if ever, asked: what
might young whites of the 1950s and '60s have had *in common*
with black blues audiences that made the blues form work so well
for them both?

In the opening chapter of *The Souls of Black Folk,* W. E. B.
Du Bois writes that when he was a young boy living in Great
Barrington, Massachusetts, he had the experience of discovering

his blackness through his discovery of what that blackness could mean to his white schoolmates. It seems that a sudden craze for fancy calling cards swept through the little school he attended. Children bought packets of the cards for ten cents, perhaps wrote their name and address on them, and then exchanged them with each other, as kids more recently have exchanged baseball cards or pogs. All went well for this little boy until abruptly, with no warning or explanation, a tall new girl refused his card, "refused it peremptorily, with a glance." As Du Bois goes on to describe the experience in one of the most famous passages of his book:

> Then it dawned upon me with a certain suddenness that I was different from the others; or like, mayhap, in heart and life and longing, but shut out from their world by a vast veil. I had thereafter no desire to tear down that veil, to creep through; I held all beyond it in common contempt, and lived above it in a region of blue sky and great wandering shadows.

This is hardly the most disturbing story in the history of African Americans after the Civil War, but it succinctly condenses a predicament in which virtually all African Americans found themselves— a predicament Du Bois called "double consciousness." The abolition of slavery made suddenly clear that every black individual had to deal with the invasion of personal identity by the racial stereotype invented by whites. One could not simply "be one's self." Even to choose to ignore the stereotypes was to accept a choice predetermined by this condition. One was forced to fend off or embrace, accept, deny, or reinvent the meanings of one's blackness. As James Weldon Johnson put it in 1912: "this is the dwarfing, warping, distorting influence which operates on each and every coloured man in the United States. He is forced to take his outlook on all things, not from his point of view as a citizen, or a man, or even a human being, but from the viewpoint of a *coloured* man." This was the predicament, wrote Du Bois, "of always looking at one's self through the eyes of others, of measuring one's soul by the tape of a world that looks on in amused contempt and pity."

Compounding the problem of double consciousness was the peculiar and bitterly disappointing nature of emancipation. During the decades in which they created and elaborated the blues tradition, African Americans experienced the passage from slavery to freedom as both a cosmic absolute, like the creation of something out of nothing, and a historical botch, compromised and blurred. On the one hand they were free, "free at last," and compared to their experience of three hundred years of slavery this new condition looked and felt like a new way of being in the world. On the other hand, for many slaves life actually worsened after the end of Reconstruction. Technically invited to join as citizens the nation that had enslaved them, they found themselves more cut off from white Americans than ever before. Legally, they were now citizens of the United States; throughout the South (at least), they were deprived of the rights and privileges of citizenship. Released from slavery into new possibilities of self-realization, many found that their racial identity worked even more strongly than before to curtail realization of their individuality. These conditions were not uniformly imposed on all African Americans. Differences of location, class, and gender gave varying inflections to them. But underlying all differences was the fundamentally common form of being in-between, of feeling what a historian has more recently called the "explosive combination of promise and disappointment that constituted freedom for African Americans."

These closely related dualisms—of being free yet unfree, of being released into new possibilities of individuality yet more deeply tied to community identity than ever before, of feeling happy and feeling unspeakably low, of transcendence and immobility, of connection and isolation, of being both inside and outside, of possessing a dynamic and powerful sense of self while experiencing that self as, in part, a construction of others—called out for a cultural form that could do them justice. That form was the blues, a musical form that sounded "right" because it so powerfully expressed what its audience was *feeling*.

In using a word like "express," though, we have to bear in mind that the blues (like all forms of music) are a force, not a mirror. They do much more than merely "reflect" certain historical conditions. They change conditions. They are dynamic. They do work for the people who listen to them. They give people a way to work through their responses to those conditions, a working through that is not necessarily conscious and analytical but more likely felt, experienced within the body and its tides of emotions and attitudes. We seldom adjust to the world by having particular thoughts about it. We adjust by shifting our inward posture, by experimenting, say, with a rush of anger that circulates within us until the outer world provides an occasion that calls it forth. We adjust by allowing ourselves to feel in a way that is at once intense and removed, or distanced, from "real" feelings. This is the way we feel within the frame provided by an aesthetic experience. It is here, within this house—in this case the house of the blues—that we move from room to room and look from window after window, becoming now this person, now that person, inwardly shaping and reshaping ourselves as we search for an attitude, or a stance, or an action that will make our conditions better or more bearable. This is the work we hear in every twist and turn and soaring note and walking bass-line of the blues.

Obviously, my life as a white kid in the '50s was worlds apart from that of a black sharecropper in the '20s or a black steel-worker in the '50s. But I think Du Bois's words are nonetheless a strikingly apt description of the condition of white teenagers of the '50s and '60s. We, too, seemed to have no true self-consciousness insofar as we had to borrow so much of that consciousness from the regard of others around us. We, too, were in-between: outsiders and insiders, free yet unfree, moving toward something new yet stuck inexplicably in what we'd always been. And if we think of "loneliness" as a complex cluster of emotions—as the desire to preserve the self *from* others expressed as a willingness to dwell in the longing *for* another—we can begin to see how the white middle-class teenager, too, "ever feels his two-ness, . . . two souls, two thoughts, two unreconciled strivings," how he, too, lives in "a world which yields him no true self-consciousness, but only lets him see himself through the revelation" of others around him.

It seems to me likely, then, that I and other white teens responded to the *sound* of the blues because that sound was uniquely able to express—and help us deal with—our own kind of double consciousness, our own way of being both insiders and outsiders. The fact that white kids didn't simply listen to the blues but sought energetically to learn to play the blues suggests to me that much more was at stake there than simply riling our parents or even searching for a musical space outside our own culture. In some way, the blues must have *spoken* to us, must have delivered some of their meanings to us. And I think this is why its basic structure of sound-created feelings was absorbed wholesale into so much '60s rock, not just through covers of blues classics by white bands but also through hundreds of original compositions that we didn't even know were blues songs—from Bob Dylan's "Rainy Day Woman #12 & 35" to the Beatles' "Revolution."

When I first heard the blues, their sound—quite apart from their lyrics—said something to me, reached me in a way no other music had. When I heard a song like "Hoochie Coochie Man" or listened to a rock song based on the blues form, what I heard without hearing, what I knew without knowing, was more complex than most historians of rock have allowed for. Although I could gain no access to the specific conditions being dramatized by the lyrics of blues songs, the *sound* of the blues, the *form* of the blues, was reaching me and speaking to me all the time because it musicked what I was feeling and gave me a structure through which to deal with the world I found myself in. (See appendix 2 for a detailed discussion of the workings of the blues form.)

"Blues Power!" shouts blues guitarist Albert King to an audience composed mainly of white kids at the Fillmore Auditorium in San Francisco. Twelve years have passed since Elvis released his version of "Hound Dog." It is June 26, 1968. "Some people get the reds, the pinks, the yellows," King tells the crowd, "but deep down they're all the good old country blues." Three days ago the Vietnam War became the longest war in the nation's history—and it would grind on for three more years. By June 26, the Beatles had been in their Abbey Road studio for over three weeks working on "Revolution" (a twelve-bar blues) and other songs of what would become *The White Album*. It is twenty days after Robert F. Kennedy's assassination in Los Angeles, fifty days after the Paris police stormed the

Sorbonne and began the events still known as "Mai" or "Soixante-huite" in France, sixty-three days after students at Columbia began their strike, and eighty-two days after Martin Luther King, Jr., fell backward on the balcony of the Lorraine Motel outside of Memphis, Tennessee. This was the spring also of the Soviet invasion of Czechoslovakia and of student uprisings in Berlin, Prague, Mexico, and Japan. It is the spring I will graduate from high school. It is the spring Charles Manson and his family of twelve move into Beach Boy Dennis Wilson's home at 14400 Sunset Boulevard. It is also the spring the Black Panthers emerge as a major force in Oakland (just a few miles from the Fillmore) and spread quickly across the nation. It is in this context that King's celebration of "blues power" seems deliberately to claim that the force of this particular cultural form is as great, if not greater, than any that could be mustered by mere political means.

For more than a decade, young whites had heard the blues indirectly, listening to Elvis, Jerry Lee Lewis, and Carl Perkins, and many less famous imitators and appropriators of the blues. Slowly they had come to know the timbre and textures of black voices, first through Fats Domino and Ray Charles, then through Motown and soul. Much more quickly they had become attuned to the sound of English voices—those of the Stones and the Beatles especially—doing covers of such blues as "Little Red Rooster," "King Bee," "Around and Around," and "You Can't Catch Me." In Detroit that very spring the MC5 had given their now-legendary Grande Ballroom concerts, performing "Stormy Monday Blues," Albert King's "Bad Sign," and Screamin' Jay Hawkins's "I Put a Spell on You" (along with Dylan's bluesy "Ballad of a Thin Man," three songs in homage to Pharoah Sanders, John Coltrane, and Archie Shepp, and a tune called "Come Together," the title of which John Lennon appropriated for his *Abbey Road* song, which begins with a paraphrase of Chuck Berry's "You Can't Catch Me"). In the Bay Area, white kids had been able to hear Albert Collins, Junior Wells, Big Mama Thornton, and Buddy Guy sharing the bill with the likes of Country Joe and the Fish, the Incredible String Band, the Sons of Champlain, and Rain. Through the resurgence of folk music, white youth had been introduced to the voice and sound of living relics of the old country blues traditions, men like Mississippi John Hurt, Josh White, Lightnin' Hopkins, and Sonny Terry and Brownie McGhee. By 1968, many thousands of white kids were not only unconsciously absorbing some of the moods and structures of the blues through rock 'n' roll but also knowingly wanting to hear more of the actual music itself.

In Cambridge, you could hear great blues at Joe's Place in Inman Square. In Berkeley, you could go to the Loading Zone. And later that summer, in Ann Arbor, John Sinclair and other devotees of the blues would put on the first Ann Arbor Blues Festival, at which a mainly white audience heard (among others) J. B. Hutto, Junior Wells, Luther Allison, Howlin' Wolf, Muddy Waters, Big Joe Williams, T-Bone Walker, Big Mama Thornton, Mississippi Fred McDowell, Lightnin' Hopkins, Freddie King, B. B. King, and Son House. White American kids in huge numbers had finally worked their way upstream to the source and found of their music: to the blues. Over the span of those twelve years, it was this blues—the blues as a culture's active response to its circumstances—that was selectively absorbed into the rock 'n' roll created by and for young white people. Not just its exoticism to whites, not just the lure of a forbidden negritude, and certainly not just its alleged wildness or sexuality, but the cultural *power* of this cultural form—power to express and to explore the condition of double consciousness— was seized upon, made use of, and adapted by white musicians and their audience. It's the power you can still hear in Janis Joplin singing "Ball and Chain," Jim Morrison singing "Roadhouse Blues," the Stones playing "Midnight Rambler," Jimi Hendrix singing "Voodoo Chile," or Dylan pounding out "Ballad of a Thin Man."

Did anyone know this at the time? Probably not. Writing in the late 1960s, rock critic Burton H. Wolfe could *hear* the blues in the music of the Grateful Dead, but like most other critics and historians of rock then (and since that time) he wasn't ready to *think* about what the blues were doing there. His description is typically vivid but superficial:

> The Dead's music, when all other analyses are thrown in as quali-
> fications, is primarily an imitation of Negro blues. The style of

singing is guttural, down and dirty; and the diction is that of Negro slang: "Ah luv you, babuh." That, plus the fact that the music drowns out the words, is why middle-class white people have such a difficult time understanding what the Dead are singing. You have to be a hippy, Negro, or drug addict. The Dead's music is the very heart of acid rock. . . . Its basic purposes are to blow the mind and provide action sound for dancing.

Somehow Wolfe moves from the blues to acid rock as if the fusion of these two forms needed no explanation: somehow blacks, hippies, and drug addicts (was the elision meant to be funny or was it just unconscious racism?) all have one simple thing in common—a need to "blow the mind" and get some "action sound for dancing."

The more complex truth is that when I and John Cunnick and hundreds of thousands of other white rock fans in the '60s did "a Master's Voice thing" and listened to music like that of the Dead for hours on end, a crucial element of what we listened for was the expressive wisdom of the blues. We heard much more than a fantasy of a life more real and more cool than ours. We heard sounds and rhythms that cast our feelings of loneliness—of subjectivity and unreality—into forms that were visible to our mind's eye. By giving ourselves to the shapes of these sounds, to the movement of these rhythms, we rehearsed repeatedly the predicament of being both insiders and outsiders, of fearing our loneliness and needing it, of depending on others to construct a self yet fleeing from others in order to make our own self out of nothing.

But our music worked on and through the predicament of our loneliness and our double consciousness without raising that predicament to the level *of* consciousness. For that is not how music works. It works in what I would call the vague space between sensation and consciousness. Because it has form, and because its forms respond to specific cultural needs, music is not mere sensation; it is *formed* sensation. Yet because it works with nonverbal materials, with what often feels like the very stuff of our feelings, music is not exactly translatable into words. Strictly speaking, it does not make sense. This is why Cunnick and his friends, and I and my friends, felt we were risking something, felt we were staking our sanity on the experience of living to music. We could not explain it to outsiders, but we confirmed it for each other just by being there, just by listening so attentively. We were discovering what the blues had for decades offered to African Americans: a medium in which the inner and outer changed places, in which private misery became public ritual, in which loneliness seemed to go beyond itself by so intensely being itself. The blues had power indeed. And so, in turn, did rock.

CHAPTER 3

"Something's Happening Here"

The Fusion of Rock and Psychedelics

In my earlier poems I told you, as precisely and eloquently as I knew how, about something; in the more recent poems something is happening, something has happened to me and, if I have been a good parent to the poem, something will happen to you who read it.

—Adrienne Rich (1964)

On August 30, 1964, a Sunday, Manhattan lay swathed in the heat of a summer afternoon. In their air-conditioned luxury suite high above the intersection of Park Avenue and 59th Street, the Beatles could hear the faint screams of fans who had gathered reverently on the sidewalks around the Delmonico Hotel, hoping to catch a glimpse of Paul, George, John, or Ringo peering from behind a curtain. Those screams had rung in the Beatles' ears for seven months as the cresting wave of Beatlemania rose higher and higher with no end yet in sight. In April the top five places in *Billboard Magazine*'s Top One Hundred chart were Beatles songs. On August 12, the film *A Hard Day's Night* had opened in more than 500 theaters nationwide, earning more than $1.3 million its first week and making Beatlemania a performance for millions of fans to watch and join vicariously. In late August the Beatles had five singles on the American charts and were winding up a triumphal coast-to-coast concert tour of the United States. Now, as they rested from their performance at the Forest Hills Tennis Stadium the night before, they talked to their guest, Bob Dylan, who had driven down from Woodstock to see them. Without fanfare, Dylan pulled a couple of joints from his pocket, put a match to the twisted end of one, and passed it over. For the first time ever, the Beatles were about to get high.

This was, without doubt, one of the most consequential moments in the history of twentieth-century American popular culture. But it was also just five guys getting stoned. It was the birth of a cultural sensibility that would one day colorize Pleasantville, but was also the first shot fired in the War on Drugs. Within a year, Dylan would release *Bringing It All Back Home* and *Highway 61 Revisited,* albums that introduced many thousands of American teenagers to his peculiarly mordant version of the psychedelic sensibility and forever altered the ambitions of rock 'n' roll. More slowly and more elaborately, and ultimately reaching a far wider audience, the Beatles would follow the path marked out by getting high, an experience Paul McCartney called "really thinking for the first time." Over the course of the next two years, long before most American teenagers of the '60s had even heard of, much less taken, psychedelics, millions would find themselves stumbling after the Beatles as they raced from the innocent enthusiasms of *Beatles for Sale* to Lennon's murky encouragement to turn off their minds, relax, and float downstream. By 1969, according to a Gallup survey of fifty-seven college campuses, 31 percent of students said they had smoked pot, and between 10 and 15 percent had experimented with LSD. That is, at least 10 to 12 million smoked marijuana and between 1 and 2 million dropped acid. (As noted earlier, the '60s are still with us: in 1997, 49.6 percent of high school seniors said they had smoked pot, while 13.6 percent said they had taken acid.) But the long-term cultural consequences of this moment in history cannot be measured simply in terms of such numbers. Rock 'n' roll brought psychedelics into popular culture even for the millions of Americans who never knew what marijuana smelled like. For better and for worse, the fusion of rock and psychedelics helped change fashion, art, politics, and social attitudes about everything from sex to schooling.

But changed them how? The largest and wealthiest and best-educated generational cohort in American history stood on the brink of maturity with rock music pounding in its veins and power at its fingertips. The blues, albeit in diluted form, gave much of this power. (Of the twelve songs the Beatles routinely played on this concert tour, five were unmistakably blues-based: "Twist and Shout," "You Can't Do That," "Roll Over Beethoven," "I Want to Hold Your Hand," and "Long Tall Sally.") But now these millions of kids were about to lay their hands on another power, a power the historian of the '60s approaches with some trepidation be-cause two dominant cultural attitudes toward psychedelics work in tandem to repress serious thinking about them. On the one hand, there is fear and distrust: psychedelics are lumped together with all other drugs, including heroin, cocaine, crack cocaine, and amphetamines. All are the same and all are evil. On the other hand, there is a bemused and knowing sophistication: psyche-delics are merely psychochemical entertainment. They're just fun. *Groovy, man.*

The truth lies somewhere between these two takes. Psychedelics are powerful. Psychedelics are distinctive. As research in the fields of psychopharmacology, religion, and anthropology makes perfectly clear, psychedelics *do* something no other drugs can, and that mysterious *something* lies very close to the human sense of wonder that is formalized in the world's religions. When psychedelics are taken out of specific cultural practices and rituals and disseminated indiscriminately to adolescents coming of age in a modern (or postmodern) world, consequences will follow. Half the difficulty of understanding those consequences is to get past today's prevailing attitudes of fear and dismissal and to take seriously the experiences of getting high and tripping. No account of the '60s or of rock music in the '60s can afford to evade this swampy issue. At the same time, no historian of the period can risk venturing into it without making clear at the outset that discussion does not mean endorsement or, worse, a foggy nostalgia.

In the Sunday *New York Times* that was delivered to their door that morning, an innocent, prepsychedelic *Times*, the Beatles might have read about the riot that had occurred Friday night in Philadelphia's north side. A full-page spread of photos showed burned-out shop fronts and black men and women surrounding a beleaguered police car. On the next page Governor Ross Barnett of Mississippi vowed to "deter integration of schools in Mississippi," while in a nearby column Princeton University proudly announced that "at least 13 Negroes," rather than the usual one to five, would be in its arriving freshman class. (Which among Princeton's exclusive eating clubs were those thirteen blacks asked to join?)

In Connecticut, the *Times* reported, a new Pesticide Control Board, "established largely as a result of the Rachel Carson book, 'Silent Spring,'" had recommended that the state ban the use of DDT. According to another article "the blue whale, the biggest animal in the world, is believed to be close to extinction." A British scientist was quoted as saying that "conservation of whales has failed . . . because, like other life resources, the whale belongs to no one and therefore it is in no one's direct interest to look after them." In Houston, a "reproduction expert" named Professor Erwin O. Strassman informed the world that in women "the bigger the brain, the smaller the breasts, and vice versa. . . . There is a basic antagonism between intelligence and the reproductive system of infertile women." Why are smart women "denied this privilege" of having children? "In some instances," claimed Strassman, "it is their own fault. I am referring to those who marry late [because] they want to finish their education. They hate to give up their careers."

Meanwhile, and perhaps not coincidentally, Beatlemania raged on around the Delmonico. That morning's paper described the "more than 1,000 teen-age girls" who "stood behind police barricades on the east side of the avenue shrieking like starlings as a deployment of 40 foot patrolmen and a dozen mounted policemen struggled to keep order." The *Times* review of the Beatles' Saturday evening concert at Forest Hills echoed the refrain:

> An overflow audience of more than 15,000 persons, mostly teenage girls, shrieked their approval. They continued their frenzied, nearly hysterical screaming as the quartet sang a number of their fabulously successful hits. It was virtually impossible to hear the singing over the shrieking, which often reached the threshold of pain.

And the not-yet-hip *Times* reporter (Robert Shelton) went on to fret that

> the Beatles have created a monster in their audience. If they have concern for anything but the money they are earning, they had better concern themselves with controlling their audiences before this contrived hysteria reaches uncontrollable proportions.

Those shrieks were a sign that something "uncontrollable"— some "monster"—was about to terrorize the nation. So was the

pungent smoke curling up from the joint Dylan had just lit inside a New York luxury hotel. Something was happening here . . .
but no one knew exactly what. The American white middle class,
soon to be dubbed "Mr. Jones" by Dylan, was complacently confident in itself, its power, and its future, for there seemed to be
no limit to what its America could achieve. It had won two wars
and put a man in space. The gross national product had averaged
5 percent annual growth for more than thirteen years, and the
real income of the average American worker had risen steadily
for more than a decade. Clearly, things were getting better all the
time. Compared to his counterpart in the mid-1950s, Mr. Jones
could afford to welcome change but only because he was certain
that the rational, technical, disinterested minds of business, government, and academy could control the scope and force of that
change.

Yet this very faith in progress and rationality produced a
countercurrent that licked at its foundations. The book at the top
of the *Times* best-seller list that Sunday, John Le Carré's *The Spy
Who Came in from the Cold,* invited Americans to ponder the Kafkaesque amorality of the Cold War. Standing in the Berlin rain with
the collar of his trench coat turned up, Leamas was a hero whose
inner dignity appealed to countless commuters waiting on the platform for their train to take them home to the suburbs. As these
Americans benefited from their position in an order that was systematically standardizing the home, the workplace, the school, and
the market, their appetite for romance and risk grew stronger year
by year. Some of this need was met by the Kennedy mystique, especially after his death. (The best-seller list this week included *Tribute
to John F. Kennedy* and *The Kennedy Wit.*) Readers flirted with the
likelihood of nuclear war when they read *Fail-safe* and with the
possibility of a military coup deposing the president when they
read *Seven Days in May.* They drank Veuve Cliquot champagne
with James Bond and drove off in his restored Bentley to do battle
with the nefarious agents of S.M.E.R.S.H. At its fringes, this romance of risk shaded into a newly acceptable pornography. *Candy*
was on the best-seller list that day and titillated thousands of readers with descriptions of Candy's "lithe round body arching upward,

hips circling slowly, mouth wet, nipples taut, her teeny piping clitoris distended and throbbing" as she cried "Your *hump* . . . GIVE ME YOUR HUMP!" to a deranged hunchback beating her with a coat hanger. Meanwhile, just down the list a few notches, Mary McCarthy's *The Group* frankly described a woman's first attempt to insert a diaphragm: "the slippery thing, all covered with jelly, jumped out of her grasp and shot across the room." *Nipples. Clitoris.* Such words had never been spoken so publicly before, and their utterance was a sign—like Dylan's joint—of a new inclination to experiment with forbidden pleasures and risky subjects. Something was happening here. Dangers and delightful transgressions beckoned.

And so did something else. On the best-seller list that week were two books about white racism (*Crisis in Black and White* and *Mississippi: The Closed Society*) and two exposés of the massive federal and corporate espionage presence in American life (*The Invisible Government* and *The Naked Society*). Echoing David Riesman's worries about the disappearance of privacy and the erosion of self in America, the author of *The Naked Society* wrote that "it is increasingly assumed that the past and present of all of us—virtually every aspect of our lives—must be an open book; and that all such information about us can be not only put into files but merchandised freely. Business empires are being built on this merchandising of information about people's private lives. The expectation that one has a right to be let alone—the whole idea that privacy is a right worth cherishing—seems to be evaporating among large segments of our population."

As these tiny doubts about the American way of life seeped into the consciousness of the white middle class, they were shockingly reinforced by a sudden renewal of African American rage that, after two decades of relative quiescence, flared up again in cities up and down the East Coast. Suddenly Mr. Jones found it more difficult to ignore that the entire postwar boom had simply swept around, or papered over, the conditions of millions of blacks hemmed in by white racism. The liberal, technocratic approach to national problems had had little impact on the historical legacy of slavery or on the contemporary fact of white racism. Meanwhile, the word "Vietnam" was appearing with increasing frequency in the news, sometimes accompanied by yet more doubts: was this a winnable war? was it a rational war? On August 30, 1964, with only 17,000 U.S. troops stationed in Vietnam at a cost of only $2 million a day, the war was still just a faraway skirmish with recalcitrant peasants duped by communist insurgents. But President Lyndon Johnson had gotten Congress to pass the Gulf of Tonkin Resolution just two weeks earlier, and in an article titled "New Crisis in Vietnam Poses Large Questions for U.S.," the *Times* that Sunday worried that

> the awesome, and perhaps invincible, problem of inspiring a disintegrating society to pursue with determination a patriotic defensive war is facing the United States in Vietnam. . . . The underlying fact that has been brought home to U.S. policy-makers this week with the latest Saigon political crisis was that successful war can hardly be fought in the vacuum of a society that no longer seems to care about winning and that, out of the frustration of many war years, seems to be turning on itself in fratricidal fury.

This was the America—confident, stable, risk-taking, with tiny fissures of doubt opening here and there—in which the Beatles, for the first time, got high. In which McCartney, according to a firsthand account of the afternoon, "seems to have had an out-of-body experience"; he "declared that he was '*really* thinking' for the first time and ordered road manager Mal Evans to write down everything he said."

Really thinking meant what? This is a question about the effects of psychedelics, but it is also a question about the needs of the young people who found in them something (*what* is exactly the question) that would help them get by. "There's no question," remembers writer Annie Gottlieb, "that the shift from alcohol to grass and acid manifested an enormous break in sensibility between us and our parents." But what exactly was the nature of this new sensibility? What explains the difference between Frank Sinatra singing subtle and sophisticated lyrics by Cole Porter and Bob Dylan delivering this caustic attack (in the form of a thirteen-bar blues) on the hapless Mr. Jones?

> *You raise up your hand*
> *And you ask, "Is this where it is?"*
> *And somebody points to you and says*
> *"It's his."*
> *And you say, "What's mine?"*
> *And somebody else says, "Where what is?"*
> *And you say, "Oh, my God*
> *Am I here all alone?"*

From the moment the Beatles smoked pot and started "really thinking for the first time," they joined Dylan in creating an entirely new kind of popular music—popular music saturated with an intense awareness of itself, of its paradoxical cultural functions, and of the relationship, at once symbolic and intimate, between rock performers and the rock audience. Suddenly, rock would strive to be adequate not just to the angst of teenage romance but to a world composed of blue whales near extinction, police cars overturned by antiracist anger, sex experts pontificating on breasts and brains, Vietnamese Buddhists and Catholics fighting one another in Saigon, tired American policymakers driving home from the Pentagon on an August afternoon, DDT settling in clouds over American lawns, policemen on horseback struggling to maintain order against a mob of shrieking starlings, *The Naked Society* lying next to *Candy* on a bedside table, the muffled sound of traffic, the thrum of air conditioning pulling power from a distant nuclear plant, and deep down in the heart of Texas President Lyndon Baines Johnson folksily defending his recent decision to send planes over the Gulf of Tonkin with the fateful lie that would cost so many lives: "We let them know that we were prepared to back it up, and we did back it up. We said to them you must leave your neighbors in peace and you mustn't shoot at American destroyers without expecting a reply."

Something was happening here . . . but what?

Tim Leary's more reputable predecessor in drug experimentation at Harvard was William James, a space cowboy in his time but now firmly enshrined in the canon, with volumes of his own in The Library of America. So it's from him that we draw an account of the psychedelic experience that places us safely beyond the glare of D.A.R.E.'s disapprobation. "One conclusion . . . forced upon my mind at that time," he wrote about a nitrous oxide trip,

> is that our normal waking consciousness, rational consciousness as we call it, is but one special type of consciousness, whilst all about it, parted from it by the filmiest of screens, there lie potential forms of consciousness entirely different. . . . No account of the universe in its totality can be final which leaves these other forms of consciousness quite disregarded. How to regard them is the question—for they are so discontinuous with ordinary consciousness. Yet they may determine attitudes though they cannot furnish formulas, and open a region though they fail to give a map.

James's words point to the fact (and problem) that the psychedelic experience is not so much an object of knowledge as an alternative form of consciousness that is *entirely different* from that rational mode through which we customarily believe that we know the things we know. For this reason, an account of the psychedelic experience is more difficult than, say, an account of an especially elusive life form dwelling at the bottom of the ocean. The psychedelic experience, itself a way of knowing, rises up as an alternative to, not as an object within the purview of, our usual ways of knowing. To reduce it to an object that can be known is to lose sight of it altogether.

As a psychologist and as a philosopher, then, James wrestled with precisely the problem we face now regarding the place of these drugs in recent history. No account of the universe *or of history* can be "final" if it "leaves these other forms of consciousness quite disregarded." But how to regard them is indeed the question. They are *so discontinuous with ordinary consciousness* and with ordinary time. How do we knit the two together? Should we? Would we be wiser to understand this discontinuity as an absolute fact? But what does it mean to understand history, and what can history be, if it acknowledges from the outset the existence of such fissures and breaks in the topography of experience?

One path through these questions begins with James's observation that a key aspect of the psychedelic experience is the feeling that this experience lies adjacent to everyday experience, "parted from it by the filmiest of screens." In other words, in spite of a power that has no counterpart in the everyday, the psychedelic experience is not exotic or distant but close and present. It is always there, though we seldom find the requisite stimulus that will deliver us into it. This aspect of the experience, what we might call its *nearness,* signals that these other modes of consciousness belong to us and we to them. Their nearness indicates that they are our birthright. To discover that, with just the slightest stimulus, one can stand within these streams of a different way of thinking and of feeling the world is to become aware of what James called the world's radical pluralism. The experience of stepping into a new framework of vision, into an alternative way of being in the world, is an unimaginably powerful confirmation of the view that "stability is not natural." Even today, so many years later, I can remember how the objects within my field of vision could occupy that field in a startlingly active way. Tripping, I don't just see the piece of paper that lies on my desk. All my senses are engaged with it at once. The paper lays hold of my attention and, as I behold, it performs a sensuous dance that discloses its intimate relationships with its surround. Looking closely, I see that a million threads of light are what make it up, and another million weave it into the background from which it stands forth, like a figure in a carpet. As I push away from the desk, it becomes thick and muscular in its self-assertion. And that very movement helps me see the *activity* of the desk itself, the rivers of grain flowing beneath the sheet of paper that now seems to float, caressed, on the back of this older brother whose parents, too, once stood in a forest, their leaves caressed by the breeze that carried the news from branch to branch.

Brought *into* the world's radical pluralism, the user of psychedelics can respond in any number of ways—from ecstasy to terror—but what underlies any and all responses is a profound redefinition of the relation of one's self to the world. *Your inside is out, and your outside is in.* This feeling of being brought *into* life, of experiencing one's self as a part of the manifold streams of existence, was commonly understood as an experience of the divine. Tim Leary made this claim ad nauseum. So did many others. "God is in everything," declared Paul in a 1967 interview. "God is in the space between us. God is in the table in front of you." Psychedelics could also bring one nearer to others, breaking down the walls that seemed to separate one's own consciousness from the consciousness of both strangers and friends, and thereby intensifying and validating the "other-directed" perspective. One user recalled that acid "has really affected the way I feel about human communication. . . . On acid I realized that you can jump those boundaries without intruding. You can enter someone else's sphere, and they can enter yours."

If there's something all too "like wow man" about this experience, there's nonetheless something appealing about it—and consistently appealing, for more than thirty years now, to the middle-class adolescent psyche. Submerged *in* the pluralism of the fluid world, no longer presuming to stand above it and no longer troubled by the seeming "unreality" of the social construction that has fixed this world in place, the user of psychedelics experiences nearness as a sensual delight, a loving touch. The feeling of being part of a more liquid world is a discovery that each and every cell across the entire surface of your body has a being of its own and is reaching out and responding to the feel of the surrounding world. As a tree is made up of innumerable branches and leaves, so "you" are made up of millions of cooperating units, each of which, in turn, is made up of its millions of parts. When your self is dissolved into these parts, the barrier of the ego falling away, you are integrated with the fragmented whole. And yet, you are not quite one with it either. Psychedelics often give a playful distance *from* the world even as they seem to bring one nearer to what is hidden *in* the world. You still feel your own distinctiveness—and may feel it more intensely than ever—but now it is not qualitatively different from that of a leaf among the leaves of a tree or that of a mote of dust in a swirling column of light. Loneliness is utterly banished. You at last shrug off the burden of human consciousness that seems to obtrude between you and all the universe. You see that we are not one *with* but one *among* the many. As Charles Perry wrote in one of the best accounts we have of the psychedelic experience:

> LSD and mescaline suppress the mind's ability to discriminate according to levels of importance—the kind of thing that allows a mother at a noisy party to hear the sound of her baby crying upstairs—and to form persisting notions about reality based on them. This faculty causes us to focus on one thing and ignore many others. Eventually, whatever we are familiar with tends to become mere background. . . . A chair becomes just a chair, something about which we have nothing more to learn. As adults we do not see a chair with the same intensity with which we examined one when we were children.

Suppressing our inclination to discriminate and focus, psychedelics strip away the crust of habit. We see again as a child sees. Not a sequence of isolated perceptions muffled and dulled by reason and inference, but one fabric of still sharp and undiscriminated phenomena that surround and include us.

Yet, as psychedelics reveal the hidden and very near fluidity and pluralism of existence, they also call attention to one's customary inattention, one's habitual dullness to the movement of distinct particulars interacting with each other and presenting what there is to be seen by the eye that can see. One comes to feel that sobriety (or whatever else we might call the condition of being "straight") is not a clear window that shows us the world as it really is nor are psychedelics necessarily a deplorable distortion of reality. One begins to suspect that we have all lost the ability to dwell in chaos and to see things as they are because we have been trained to do so by our education, by our parents, by our culture—all of which have conspired to persuade us that there is only *one* world, a fixed world, a stable world. And if that world seems oppressively "unreal" to youth, psychedelics offer a way not just to escape, which suggests flight into unreality, but to return home to the way the world really is. "Up until LSD," George Harrison remarked, "I never realized that there was anything beyond this normal waking state of consciousness. But all the pressure was such that, as Bob Dylan said, 'There must be some way out of here.'" The power of psychedelics to release users from this *here*—from their inherited history and their cultural training—is why they appealed with such force to the youth of the '60s. Psychedelics offered a vision that uniquely met the needs of young persons looking for confirmation of their adolescent vision of instability and for a radical reconfiguration of the relation of their self to the world. James's "filmy screen" became for these kids a cognitive counterpart to Du Bois's "veil," which, he claimed, gave African Americans "second sight" because it allowed them to see what those within a circle (whites) see as well as what only those who stand outside the circle (blacks) can see. Psychedelics likewise reinforced and reified the adolescent's doubled perspective as insider and outsider.

Yet this is still only half the story. The other half is rock. Together, psychedelics and music achieve a stunning synergy because music, too, is felt as something very near to us and at the same time as a world that is quite distinct from the world mapped by vision and touch. Poet Paul Valéry has written of going into a music hall with its hubbub of noises—people coughing, chairs scraping, the murmur of conversation—and experiencing its transformation into a "musical universe" the moment a musician starts to play an instrument. Suzanne Langer, likewise, has written of music as a "kingdom": as we step into it, "the mirror of the world, the horizon of the human domain, and all tangible realities are gone." And in a much grimmer setting, Bruce Jackson speculates in his book about Texas prison work songs that these "change the nature of work by putting the work into the workers' framework rather than the guards'. By incorporating the work with their song, . . . [the convicts] make it *theirs* in a way it otherwise is not." All these metaphors call to mind Baraka's description of the blues as an "area" created by blacks within white American culture. All of these writers are pointing to our sense that music creates an ontological framework, or world, independent of the everyday yet present beside it, and requiring only the slightest stimulus (a voice raised in song, the vibration of a guitar string) to call it into being.

Music feels very near to us also because we experience it so manifestly *within* ourselves. When we look at a painting or a play or a movie, the act of seeing is one in which we are inevitably required to deal with the distance or space that lies between us and the object we behold. We must map our visual field and establish relations (nearer, farther, smaller, larger) of the objects within it because these are not given immediately by sense impressions. Even reading requires translation from letter to word to image. Music, by contrast, is experienced as immediate. We might know perfectly well that it originates at a distance—across the room, perhaps—but we still experience it as contiguous with ourselves, as pressing upon us; it has already entered the canals of our ears and penetrated to our brain. No void or empty space lies between us and it. Music is in us, its rhythms an echo or objectification of the rhythmic qualities of our embodied life: of the heart beating, of the lungs expanding and contracting, of the legs walking.

But music not only annihilates the space that lies between us and it, it also establishes a feeling of space *inside* us, and when it opens up this space, it enlarges us. We feel that only a force intimate with and even coextensive with our self could accomplish this enlargement, and when we behold the existence of space within ourselves, our relationship to spatiality itself changes. Space is no longer an absence, or void, between us and the objects around us. Space is our familiar. Space is what we ourselves enclose. Our self, we see, is not a dense, inner kernel of compacted identity but more like a membrane, the filmiest of screens between the space within and the space without. It is a meeting place, a crossroads, where the inside meets the outside.

The closely related phenomenologies of music and psychedelics help explain, I think, why millions of young people in the '60s turned to these experiences as a way to work through and beyond their conditions. Historian Todd Gitlin has written about how in groups . . . we would sit around, listening, awed, all sensation, to Dylan's or somebody else's images bursting one out of the other like Roman candles, [and] while we jabbered and giggled at anything at all ("Can you dig it?"), the afternoon and evening seeming to stretch, the present liquidly filling all time past and time future, not just the words but the spaces between notes saturated by significance.

Similarly, as quoted on page 1 of this book, John Cunnick, a writer for the underground Seattle *Helix,* wrote:

I wake up in the morning, roll a joint, and do a Master's Voice thing in front of the speakers for a couple of hours; *then* I go outside. Music defines a total environment. . . . Straight musicians understand that kind of involvement, of course; but you can't really communicate to the outside how a hundred thousand children of muzak freaks . . . who in most cases never bother to study or even think about music, are involved in a single art form to the point where they virtually stake their entire sanity on it. Go to a house and someone hands you a joint in front of a record player, and it's assumed . . . that you are going to sit for a couple of hours, not talking, hardly moving, *living* to music.

Along with Gitlin, Cunnick, and their friends, several million in the '60s rock audience fused blues-based music with psychedelics. Repeatedly. Either experience revealed in its own way the always-present but hidden pluralism of the world, confirming the teenager's intuition that her parents' espousal of rules and norms was "just a lie." Together they worked even more powerfully. By dissolving the barriers between self and world, they undid the tension between the "other-directed" self who depended on the affirmation of others and the "inner-directed" self who sought to escape from the web of social relations, to find some kind of way out of here. In other words, music and psychedelics allowed the young to have it both ways. They took kids out of the conventional world structured by parents, away from the expectant gaze of others, but instead of delivering them into a void of loneliness they dropped them in a world radiant with connections and community, saturated with significance. Listening to music, stoned or tripping, the youth of the rock audience saw their intersubjective connections with others in a new way—not as an oppression that eroded their "real" self but as a manifestation of the cosmic or ontological interconnectedness of all things. Music thus seemed to initiate and instruct them in a vision. As Sandy Darlington put it in the *San Francisco Express Times:* "Week after week we go inside the music, and as they play and we listen and dance, the questions and ideas slowly germinate in our minds like seeds. . . . This music is more than entertainment. It describes and helps us define a way of life we believe in."

In an unusually thoughtful analysis of rock published in 1970, English professor Benjamin DeMott argued that middle-class kids were into rock and psychedelics because these allowed them to inhabit two worlds simultaneously: the physical and the mental, the meaningless and the meaningful. The pounding rhythms of rock encouraged them to surrender their egos to tides of selflessness and mindlessness, while intelligent rock lyrics (Beatles, Dylan, the Doors) allowed them to retain and exercise their critical faculties. But to DeMott, the "quasi-religious force" of rock was alarming: when kids succumb to "their relish for a thunderous, enveloping, self-shattering moment wherein the capacity for evaluating an otherness is itself rocked and shaken," they will lose "a civilized value now beleaguered on many fronts." What value? "Just conceivably, nothing less than that of the self itself."

DeMott was one of the few intellectuals of the time to take rock and psychedelics seriously, and he clearly grasped the fact that the rock of the '60s was distinctive—not just loud but loud and thoughtful; not just exuberant but exuberant and searching. But DeMott remained firmly stuck in his own generation's perspective when he drew so sharp a line between self and selflessness. I, like many of the young persons DeMott taught in the '60s, would have loved to possess his sure sense of self and his sophisticated appreciation of the ways selfhood has been constructed, complicated, and threatened throughout history. But that confidence eluded me: "the self itself" had already flown the coop. I experienced firsthand, as the very condition of existence, an emptiness of self DeMott seemed to have known about but could set aside whenever he wished to. For me and my friends, rock did not *cause* a loss of self. Rock was an expression of such loss; rock was a way of working through that loss.

For if memory serves me well, the fusion of rock and psychedelics worked on the problem of loneliness not just by offering nearness, pluralism, and intimacy as antidotes to the unreality of a stable world and the burden of other-directedness but by presenting an intensification of loneliness, or emptiness, for aesthetic contemplation. It is crucial to bear in mind that loneliness was not just a condition to be avoided; it was a survival strategy. It made sense to feel lonely in the new dwelling of the postmodern world because, paradoxically, the apparent authenticity of that emotion— loneliness was the only thing one could count on as being real— made it seem such promising material with which to fabricate a more satisfyingly authentic, self-possessing self. White middle-class youth may have read (with DeMott even) all of F. Scott Fitzgerald's books, but they were terrified that the "I" who read them really had no identity, no inner stuffing, no soul. I and my friends desperately ransacked the world and the past—blues, black argot, Indian mysticism, Edwardian fashion, Native American shamanism—for material with which to fill and dress the void we felt ourselves to be, always knowing that there was something ugly about this frenzied acquisitiveness. As Buffy St. Marie scolded us in the *East Village Other:* "The Indian has one thing left: his soul. The hippies are after the Indian's soul. They're vampire children of their parents. I call them soul suckers." Rock itself was just such a vampire feeding on the blues. But we in the rock audience placed what little faith we had in what felt like our *own* cultural creation, which was rock 'n' roll infused by psychedelics, because this fusion exquisitely dramatized our plight, powerfully meeting what Marin called the "adolescent demand" for "life on a grand scale, in a grand style." Rock somehow promised to make something out of nothing simply by expressing the feelings of the self that feels it is no self. The blues, too, had offered their audience this power to make something out of nothing, a promise captured in the words "the blues ain't nothin' but . . ." The phrase coined by the rock audience made the same point: "I know that it's only rock 'n' roll, but . . ."

And so millions ached ecstatically as Dylan sang about going to Desolation Row, the '60s counterpart to Heartbreak Hotel. They were themselves the "Miss Lonely" who was on her own, no direction home, a complete unknown, like a rolling stone. They went en masse to Strawberry Fields—you know, the place where nothing is real, and where it's getting hard to be someone, but it all works out (at least I think it's not too bad). For if there was pain, there was also bliss in the surrender to the rock vision. One side of *Sgt. Pepper's* is the void: the four thousand holes in Blackburn, Lancashire. The other side is joy: the girl with kaleidoscope eyes. Van Morrison's man from across the road with the sunshine in his eyes.

Ah—the sheer exhilaration of that plunge into the waters of a fluid world on the other side of conventionality. From the banks of the river that wends through "Tomorrow Never Knows" burst unrecognizable sounds of the life that is hidden behind the foliage. One finds oneself the companion of Rimbaud as he surrenders to the perilous delights of "Le bateau ivre." This is Allen Ginsberg's "American river" of "illuminations," "breakthroughs," and "epiphanies"—"Real holy laughter in the river! They saw it all! The wild eyes! The holy yells! They bade farewell! They jumped off the roof! to solitude! waving! carrying flowers! Down to the river! into the street!" This is also the river that flows more deliberately, guided by historical experience and cultural memory, through Aretha Franklin's "A Change Is Gonna Come." It is Joni Mitchell's voice singing *I wish I had a river / That I could skate away on.* If you *picture yourself on a boat on a river,* it will carry you through Van Morrison's "The Water" (*let it run all over me*) to Bruce Springsteen's "The River." It is the very river Norman Mailer heard in Lincoln Park, Chicago, on the eve of the Democratic National Convention—the river of psychedelicized rock 'n' roll. It flowed out of the blues, its seething energies fed by the bursting hearts of millions of teenagers who had never even thought about the blues. Immersed in the "electro-mechanical climax of the age," feeding it with their adulation and ennui, these kids knew that their senses had been stripped, their hands couldn't feel to grip, and they were ready to go anywhere, do anything, become anyone. They wanted rock and psychedelics to take them there.

But was there, in fact, a there there? As DeMott either knew or intuited, this power came with a price tag. Nearness can also be a source of fear, of "freaking out," for with the loss of boundaries comes the confirmation that the "self" may not exist at all once the walls surrounding it have crumbled. One hears words in one's head and does not know for sure if one is talking aloud or merely thinking. And one starts to wonder, if the world really is this near and this rich, then why the concealment? Is there trickery afoot? *As you stare into the vacuum of his eyes,* does your comrade on this trip turn out to be a demon? "I went into the bedroom with my girlfriend," recalls Jeff Maron, "and I was lying on the bed, and I looked at the wall and I saw through the wall. I saw the people who were in the next room, and they started to expand into the face of every single person I had ever known in my life. And they all started to come toward me, and as they came toward me they started to congeal into this ball of white light. And I knew that the minute it would touch me, I would be absorbed by it, and I'd become light. And I said, 'Fuck, I'm not ready for this.'" *I'm going back to New York City, I do believe I've had enough.*

No one was ready for it. No one was ready for the loss of pre-psychedelic innocence, for the fall into what Jimi Hendrix called "being experienced." *Oh, Mama, can this really be the end?* The cunning with which the Trickster duped me was truly diabolical. First I'd believed in ordinary consciousness. Then I believed in psychedelic consciousness. But now I understood, too late, that "consciousness" itself exists only in the hypothetical way that "causality" and "time" exist—as necessary, but unwarrantable, inferences from chaos. Shreds of such thinking trailed behind me as I underwent the real fall, the free fall, the downward slide, the *helter skelter.* The extremity of terror verged weirdly on exhilaration as I hurtled downward to the possibility, or inevitability, of my own nonbeing. *She's coming down fast!* As veil after veil of illusion flew past, as the Trickster created and destroyed with ever-increasing speed the screens of appearance through which I crashed, I understood that divine knowledge leads only to this: the knowledge that nothing is. That Nothing reigns supreme. Terrified, and struggling helplessly to brake my fall toward total ego dissolution, I knew I could never get back to where I once belonged. Sane or insane, I would have to look at the world through a tripper's eyes and live in this hell of Nothing forever.

The famous "death of the ego" was experienced sooner or later by anyone who tripped—and some trippers never recovered from this experience, never regained their precarious grasp of the "normal" way of being in the world. Psychedelics, even mirthful marijuana, are dangerous drugs, taking you to strange places where railway men might drink up your blood like wine. Yet precisely because it was so terrifying, for those who did survive it the death of ego was a tempering experience. It was a vision quest in which the seeker, having passed through a hellfire that annihilates the ego, emerged on the far side more reconciled to the fate of being without a self. The tripper saw that this is how it is: *no one* has a genuine self, and everyone must somehow go on nonetheless. So Riesman's "terror of loneliness" could also become ecstasy when you realized that, in the last analysis, the social self could never comprehend the cosmic self. You were always *in* and *near,* but you were at the same time always *free* because the world's radical pluralism was an automatic guarantee of your autonomy. There was nothing noble about lounging all afternoon in a suburban rec room and feeling that life sucked. But there was (and still is) something mythic about dropping acid and descending into a maelstrom where the nameless, nagging insecurities of the everyday become tempests and nebulae in the void of inner space.

This is why the insight into the world's instability provided by pot, acid, and rock had political consequences even while it failed to specify a particular political agenda. After getting high or tripping, '60s users realized that their belief in a core self was naïve, that their faith in stability was foolish, and so they were fully prepared to see through *everything,* including truth, justice, and the

American way. Acid and pot seemed to corroborate their adolescent certainty that they knew, saw, and understood an inner emptiness adults pretended was replete with meaning. What users had earlier felt as an unconscious suspicion or intuition—*that was just a lie*—became, when high or tripping, a verity. Yet it seemed that the deeper loss was their parents'. For while psychedelics corroborated the social self's fear of its own contingency, its dependence on the gaze of others, they also revealed a world saturated with significance. They revealed potential forms of consciousness in which the empty self was a sufficient space to dwell in, and in which the other-directed self was cosmically connected. And since the nearness of the psychedelic outlook—its presence there on the other side of that filmy screen—made it appear a mere extension of their own adolescence, or what sociologist Kenneth Keniston called their "postmodern style," the youth of the '60s looked with contempt and pity at their elders. Adults had simply chickened out. They had fled from the radical pluralism their own adolescence had revealed to them and had silently conspired to believe in a stable self and a fixed reality that no longer existed, if, in fact, they ever had. By choosing the martini not the joint, they had chosen to lie to themselves, and it was hard to forgive them for that.

Today, public discourse has become dogmatically cynical, advertising cunningly self-knowing, and rock music unambiguously ironic precisely in order to guard against this accusation: when a culture admits to itself that it's always lying, the discovery of deceit means nothing, provokes no anger, and has no consequences. But in the '60s, this trick had not been learned. Psychedelics confirmed the crucial adolescent accusation just at the moment when public figures were being caught telling enormous lies to others and to themselves: *We said to them you must leave your neighbors in peace.* Psychedelics and politics thus ran together in one strand, both of them dramatically confirming the adolescent's conviction that grown-ups are by choice deceitful, that culture is fundamentally false, and that rebellion is therefore an existential right, even a duty. Everywhere you looked, you saw that *something was happening.*

As the shadows lengthened in the streets below, as the shrieks of their patient, loyal fans grew dimmer and faded at last into the evening swell of traffic. As the sun reddened in the western sky, as the lights came on in windows across the way. As Dylan rose and stretched. As the Beatles said good-bye to him, laughed and looked at one another, looked again: what lay in waiting there? What surmises folded in the glance, what glints and gleams of a different future?

CHAPTER 4

"I Was Alone, I Took a Ride"

Revolver, Revolution, Technology

O to break loose, like the chinook
salmon jumping and falling back,
nosing up the impossible
stone and bone-crushing waterfall—
raw-jawed, weak-fleshed there, stopped by ten
steps of the roaring ladder, and then
to clear the top on the last try,
alive enough to spawn and die.

—Robert Lowell (1967)

Armed with pot and acid, fortified by the expressive wisdom of the blues, their way of seeing the world confirmed by powers that had simply fallen into their hands, the youth of the rock culture were ready for the next step. *To break loose,* as Lowell put it. *To go anywhere,* as Dylan sang. Less through determination than through drift, less through individual agency than because they were driven by adolescent vehemence, they were able to imagine themselves surpassing the limits, the invisible givens that clutch and hold us each in place. And because they were able to find confirmation of their resolve in each other's eyes, they believed they had pierced the filmy veil spun by convention and rediscovered the nearness of Being and the manifold possibilities of consciousness. "Between every human consciousness and the rest of the world," they might have read in one of Aldous Huxley's popular accounts of tripping, "stands an invisible fence, a network of traditional thinking-and-feeling patterns, of secondhand notions that have turned into axioms, of ancient slogans revered as divine revelations." Listening to rock, tripping on acid, they seemed to crash through those barricades and touch the reverse side of the weave, beyond words, beyond culture, beyond history. There they could see, as R. D. Laing declared, that "the fountain has not played itself out, the frame still shines, the river still flows, the spring still bubbles forth, the light has not faded."

Decades later, we are quite persuaded that we know better. To the contemporary historian, it seems obvious that when '60s youth imagined they were carving out a space for themselves within the culture at large, experiencing their music as an act of rebellion, breaking through to the *other side,* they were actually acquiescing in a capitalist process that was molding them to become consumers obsessed with consumer choices. To be Beatles fans, not Stones fans. To love Joni Mitchell not Judy Collins, or Bob Dylan not Donovan. All these turned out to be pseudo-choices "in a world of pettiness constructed by adults."

To this analysis, the '60s youth has a blunt answer: that's not how I *feel*. It's not a sophisticated reply, to be sure, but it does offer a foundation on which an argument of some complexity can be built. That argument would begin by pointing out that all people, in all historical periods, have had to exercise their choices within a field of possibilities. The Elizabethan playgoer who chose to see Shakespeare not Jonson was no freer, in an absolute sense, than the teenager flipping through record racks and choosing the Kinks not the Who. Not knowing with certainty whether we truly are free, what matters is whether we *feel* free. And keenly sensitive to the hypocrisy of adults, the '60s youth would be quick to point out that the unstated predicate in most theorizing about pop culture is that the theory itself has a purchase on the truth that is unavailable to those who are still locked within the system being discussed. But where is the warrant for such an assumption? Who can be sure that social theorizing and critical discourse are not themselves as controlled by capitalism as rock is? And that intellectuals who imagine that they can see what others remain blind to are not themselves caught up in a "world of pettiness"? No absolute assurance is available, of course. A critic's confidence must finally come to rest on the way he or she *experiences* the relation between the world and thinking. And I would hazard the guess that the most crucial component of that experience is surprise. We are seldom persuaded by our analysis of a situation if it does not surprise us. That tingle is what tells us that we may have ventured beyond the bounds of what we've been scripted to think and caught hold of a sliver of truth we had previously conspired, along with everyone else, to hide from ourselves.

So let's allow ourselves the possibility of being surprised, which is also the possibility of being afraid, as Mr. Jones must have been when he came face-to-face with sword-swallowers and one-eyed midgets. What if our conviction that "history goes all the way down"—that it structures all we are and can be—is not the acceptance of instability and contingency that we like to think it is but rather a defense against the more terrifying possibility that there are regions history cannot reach and shape? Against what R. D. Laing called "It":

> between us and It, there is a veil which is more like fifty feet of
> solid concrete. . . . Intellectually, emotionally, interpersonally,

organizationally, intuitively, theoretically, we have to blast our
way through the solid wall, even if at the risk of chaos, madness
and death.

The waterfalls, as Lowell observed, are stone- and bone-crushing,
not just beautiful. The intensification of life that living to music
produced was the pursuit of breaking loose *even if at the risk of
chaos, madness, and death.* To sanction an adolescent vehemence
that cuts through the lies of culture and steps into that region beyond the veil is to legitimate madness and mysticism and to affirm
the belief that instability is more natural than stability. If it is also
a blind surrender to capitalism, in which after all, everything that
is solid melts into air, it is nonetheless a capitalism that surprises
(what would the Beatles do next?) and in so doing contains (in
both senses of the word) the possibilities of its own undoing.

In other words, when remembering the '60s we must bear in
mind that if we approach the rock culture only through the question of its political value, we will fail to gain real access to it. That
culture understood itself as going beyond the terms of political debate and discourse. It was playing, as Wittgenstein would have put
it, a different language game. It was concerned above all to enlarge
the possibilities of existence, to create a social order more tolerant
of alternative visions of reality. It was in essence anarchistic—
owned by neither Left nor Right—because for better or worse it
was hellbent on undoing the very distinctions between these. If
you see life as a knot of contradictions so intense that *there's no
success like failure, and failure's no success at all,* you can't easily establish criteria by which to evaluate political ideas and policies. If
you need a dumptruck to unload your head, all you can do is keep
going one step further, to wherever your momentum takes you—
behind the veil to It. As one underground newspaper said: "DRUGS
BREAK PATTERNS, that's all they do. When patterns are broken,
new worlds CAN emerge. They may be better or worse (good or
bad trip) but they are new." They surprise us. And that is the sole
warrant of their value.

The lure of this kind of experience, with all its joys and risks,
was musicked by countless rock songs of the '60s. Unfortunately,
the most famous of these is "Break on Through" by the Doors, a

lifeless cliché from the moment it was released, a blunt affirmation but nothing more. It might be more surprising and useful to begin with a song by Led Zeppelin, their 1968 arrangement of the traditional "Babe I'm Gonna Leave You." Historians of the '60s who have caught hold of the terms "breakthrough" and "breakdown" have tended to arrange them in a neat linear sequence—from Woodstock to Altamont, or from the Summer of Love to the Chicago Convention. But at the time, as this and many other songs of the '60s show, these two states were inseparable, concurrent, interpenetrating each other and forming one feeling-state.

Stripped away from Led Zeppelin's massive sound dynamics (in this debut album they are introducing the heavy-metal aesthetic), the song's lyrics are trite:

> *Babe*
> *Baby baby*
> *I'm gonna leave you*
> *I said baby*
> *You know I'm gonna leave you*
> *Leave you in the summertime*
> *Leave you when the summer comes around.*

This is, on the surface, a typical masculine celebration of the right to leave any relationship in order to "ramble" and be free. But sharper feelings are at work elsewhere—above all in the contrast between the delicate acoustic guitar melody that opens the song and the downward-driving heavy-metal rhythm figure that breaks the song apart after the first stanza, sounds that musick both the triumph *and* the melancholy that accompany one's passage into another mode of consciousness. This psychedelic reference is made explicit midway through the song, when we are lifted upward on a whooshing column of unidentifiable sounds that derive from the Beatles' "A Day in the Life." Within the frame of these sounds, the *Babe* Robert Plant sings to is not just a girlfriend who must be left because the urge to ramble has seized him. She is ordinary life as well, a world he loves but which he must leave in order to get over there, to the other side, to the fountain, to "It." Plant's gorgeous legato delivery of

Babe babe babe babe babe baby baby I'm gonna leave you

becomes a primal scream that poignantly evokes the pain of falling into ecstatic vision and psychedelic experience. The person who has seen the mysteries, or just tripped, can never return to the world as it used to be. He, or she, is an exile forever now, cut off from the simple comfort and complacence in which those who have never glimpsed another reality dwell.

But "Babe I'm Gonna Leave You" can be heard also as an envoi not to commonplace reality that has been left behind but to the new world that has been discovered. "People coming down from LSD," recalled Charles Perry, "often feel that they have been unfairly cast out of a state of mind that is their birthright." In this hearing, Plant's "Babe" is the vision itself—the Beatles' girl with the sun in her eyes, Dylan's Johanna, or his sad-eyed lady of the lowlands. The sadness we hear now is the grief that accompanies the inevitable *return* from splendor to mundanity after what Shelley called the "transitory brightness" of the mystical moment.

"Babe I'm Gonna Leave You" reinforces the ambiguity produced by its sounds when Plant improvises with the lyrics. First, he sings that the need to ramble is calling him to "go away"; later, he sings:

I can hear it callin' me the way it used to do,
I can hear it callin' me back home.

"Home" and "away" can be the same place, I think, only when "home" is understood to be the extraordinary at-oneness with the world experienced long ago by the child before he or she became absorbed in the static reality constructed by culture. To go back to that home, back to that presocial innocence of an undivided self, we have to go away from society into a primordial loneliness. Joni Mitchell sings that we have to get ourselves back to the garden, The Band sing that they want to get back to Miss Fannie; on *Abbey Road,* the Beatles will conclude it's impossible *to get back home—* that the curse of modernity is to make the best of what we have.

Like these and many other '60s songs, "Babe I'm Gonna Leave You" is faithful to the double nature of the breakthrough experience. Grief and exultation were the twin poles, the two emotions that structured the inner life of this '60s. One knew that the world would never be the same, that one would never be completely at home in the world again; from now on one would always see the world from one remove, from the other side of the veil "away," because the trip to "It" on the other side had permanently altered one's way of being in the world, one's stance—or (who knows?) one's cerebral cortex, one's DNA. Yet the trip that exiled one from the world was also an adventure that returned one to a different, maybe more ancient, home. And it was exciting, dramatic. The tripper became an Orpheus who had journeyed to an underworld that lay behind the papier-mâché of middle-class split-levels, lawns, and shopping centers. The tripper had authority because he had *been there* and glimpsed alternatives. The tripper had seen life from both sides now.

If we don't count the Holy Modal Rounders' 1964 cover of Leadbelly's "Hesitation Blues" (to which they add a verse about "the psychedelic blues"), the very first pop songs to give voice to the complexities of the breakthrough experience were the final three cuts on the Beatles' *Revolver*. Released in the United States on August 8, 1966, two years after their meeting in the Delmonico with Dylan, the album appeared at least a year *before* psychedelics irrupted into American youth culture. The vast majority of young listeners heard *Revolver* with prepsychedelic innocence, and it sounded bizarre. More bizarre by far than *Rubber Soul*. As they gazed at Klaus Voorman's cover art—in which small photos and drawings of the Beatles emerge from the tangled, spaghetti-like hair of four larger renderings of the Beatles' head—they heard music that required them to learn a new way of listening, to develop a new kind of taste. (Only the fact that the Beatles had already proven themselves could persuade their fans to make an effort so contradictory to pop culture's customary work of creating a familiar, frictionless world.) *Revolver* seemed to draw them out of the home of rock and take them away somewhere else. But where? That was the question one half-consciously pondered as one drifted downstream on the album's current of intriguing sound.

George Harrison's "I Want to Tell You" is about desire, an "I want" song that seems deliberately to invoke some of the Beatles' earliest hits—"I Want to Hold Your Hand," "Tell Me Why," "She Loves You"—but only in order to emphasize the surprising

differences between itself and them. For what desire reaches for
here is not the warm young body at the dance. Instead, it wants
to *tell us,* to get through, to break the codes and the bullshit, to
make genuine contact. Following in the footsteps of such songs as
"Michelle" and "Here, There and Everywhere," this song carried its
listeners even farther into some place new and very strange, where
they heard Harrison sing

> *Sometimes I wish I knew you well*
> *Then I could speak my mind and tell you,*
> *Maybe you'd understand.*

Understand what? What does Harrison *mean* by "It's only me, it's
not my mind, that is confusing things"? And what's the *difference*
between "me" and "my mind"? I was sixteen years old as I thought
about these questions, sitting through long hot summer afternoons
in the air-conditioned family room of our neighbors, the Bakers,
whose daughter Marian inexplicably allowed me to court her. We
stared for hours at the album cover, meeting the eyes that looked
back at us from the tangle of hair. Harrison seemed to imply that
he knew what is confusing things, and yet he said quite plainly that
he couldn't get the message across: I want to, *but.* And this unsatisfied desire seemed to press against the surface of conventional pop
sound, distorting it, blurring it, melting it into weird textures and
contours. The song sounded as though it were actually disintegrating as it moved from the relatively familiar sounds and images of
the first stanza to the chanted *I've got time* tapering to a drawn-out
wail or prayer—*tiiiiimmme*—at the end.

What Harrison wants so much to tell us, as most Beatles fans
would understand when they heard *Sgt. Pepper's* a year later, is that
it's possible to go to a state of mind where the source of everyday
confusion becomes visible. From where he stands and chants, with
all the time in the world because he has slipped outside of time,
Harrison can see very clearly what is confusing things. It's the claim
of everyday consciousness, the standard against which all other
forms of consciousness are judged. This claim, so carefully shaped
and tended by our culture, causes confusion because it is a lie.
Everyday consciousness cannot understand or even describe many

other states of mind and being—reveries and dreams, fits of pas-
sionate love or anger, and in particular the inherent mysticism of
the adolescent as he or she charts the murky waters between childhood and maturity. You are confused, the song seems to say, not
because you are stupid or defective but because society will not
honor the vision that your age has blessed you with, Cassandras
all. The song cannot say this directly in words (*all those words just
seem to slip away*), perhaps because words are suspect, servants of
society, traitors. So Harrison sings that he *wants* to tell us (just as
Lennon will later sing that he *would love* to turn us on, not that he
has or will or can). And because words fail, he relies on sound—
on playing with sound—to get his message through. As he dis-
solves the conventional in the uncanny, he makes the uncanny not
just bearable but right; he establishes the possibility of other aural
codes, other ways of listening, other desires and satisfactions. And
so his music *does* tell us. It says: not one, but many.

With its chorus of brass instruments shouting out their support
for the lyrics, Paul McCartney's "Got to Get You into My Life" has
been aptly described as an absorption, or imitation, of the Motown
sound he had heard in such pop hits as "Baby Love" and "I Hear
a Symphony." But surely John Lennon was right when he suggested
that McCartney wanted to use that sound to convey something utterly unconventional: his earliest experiences with LSD.

> *I was alone, I took a ride*
> *I didn't know what I would find there.*
> *Another road where maybe I*
> *Could find another kind of mind there.*
> *Ooo, did I suddenly see you?*
> *Ooo, did I tell you I need you,*
> *Every single day of my life?*

As I listen to these words today, decades after I first heard them,
I half-wonder if I haven't just made the song up—it so willingly
represents what I have described as a journey from loneliness (*I
was alone*) toward a reconfigured sense of self (*another kind of mind*).
The song is obviously about a vision (*did I suddenly see you?*) and
about the bliss of that experience (McCartney's sweet little *ooo*s).

But what it's most concerned with is a particular urgency, the singer's urgent desire to connect his vision with *every single day* of his life by communicating it to others. To his audience.

In other words, McCartney isn't satisfied to be a solitary, misunderstood mystic. He's a showman to the core, not a shaman, and like George Harrison he wants to tell us, to share the vision with us. It's as if he can't believe in it himself unless others join him and confirm it and thereby legitimate it. His shouted "*Got* to get you into my life," coming to us with the spiritual intensity of gospel and soul, is the musical equivalent of R. D. Laing's belief that "we *have* to blast our way through the solid wall" to the other side of consciousness. Supported by a choir of horns, this voice demands the most radical freedom imaginable. Yet it also demands *our* understanding. Breaking through requires getting through.

As would soon become plain, so much of the ecstasy and urgency of the '60s arose from this need to take the private experience of breakthrough and go public with it. One felt that the only way society could be revolutionized into a culture more hospitable to the visionary experience was by getting everyone into each other's lives. By getting everyone to connect, to come together, to get it together—even if that just meant sitting around getting stoned with each other and hearing (so we thought) the *same thing,* the same complex and untranslatable message in the music we listened to. "And we of the community," to quote Sandy Darlington again, "gather there to listen and dance. . . . Week after week we go inside the music, and as they play and we listen and dance, the questions and ideas slowly germinate in our minds like seeds: this is our school, our summit conference." The adolescent who looks back at me from those years urgently wanted to make public connection and community at the lonely crossroads of the most private experiences—there where he felt the rush of a psychedelic breakthrough, there where he heard the most amazing blend of power and nuance in the riff of an electric guitar.

But why? Why wasn't he content with bliss in solitude or with the underground bravery of the Beats? The answer might be that he and his friends were already too deeply structured by a predisposition to consider the views and feelings of others. We were already so fully shaped, that is, by what Riesman so clumsily called "other-directedness," that we weren't content to wrap ourselves in mystic reverie. We wanted company. We wanted *approval*. And so, for reasons less blameworthy than the metaphor suggests, we wanted to eat our acid and have it, too. We wanted the transgressive experience of breakthrough, but we also wanted to publicize it and legitimate it. We wanted an underground, but we wanted to publish it in so-called underground newspapers that could be picked up on any street corner. We wanted, in short, that absurd paradox: a counterculture.

But the absurdity of the paradox, or the futility of that hope, does not entitle or require us to simply dismiss it today. Quite the contrary. By following an essentially paradoxical logic wherever it might lead them, the advocates of this vision were exhibiting a kind of courage—the courage to criticize their conditions from within them. Unlike the theorists of both the Old and the New Left, the vehement adolescent did not pretend that intellectual analysis could deliver him from the contradictions of his historical situation. At some gut level, the adolescent understood that a pervasive sense of unreality and an imprisoning subjectivity were immutable facts about existence in America in the late twentieth century. The question the adolescent posed was not "How can we create a different world?" but "How can we dwell in this world with an intensity sufficient to turn it inside out, to show that it's a facade, and that behind it lies chaos, instability, madness, freedom, death?" And that willingness to use the materials provided by one's conditions in order to break through to the reverse side of those conditions was epitomized most compellingly by the rock audience's medium of self-expression: *electric* music.

The culminating song of this suite, John Lennon's "Tomorrow Never Knows," is regarded by many critics as the most important rock song of the decade. The dean of Beatles scholars, Mark Lewisohn, calls it a "masterpiece" that marked "a *quantum jump* not only into tomorrow, but next week." Ian MacDonald writes that it "introduced LSD and Leary's psychedelic revolution to the young of the Western world, becoming one of the most socially influential records the Beatles ever made." Willfred Mellers regards it as a "consummation" of themes inherent in the Beatles' work from the very beginning. All true. Yet we must also remember that to the millions

of young persons who, innocent of Leary and LSD, eagerly unwrapped the new Beatles album and sat back to see where it would
take them, "Tomorrow Never Knows" was an enigma they would
understand only gradually, through many listenings and over many
months. They heard it first and foremost as a place to dwell, not
as an answer or a deliverance.

Those yelps! Those cries! Incredibly far-away and compressed
almost beyond recognition, Lennon's voice emerges from this
thicket of incomprehensible noise to address, directly, his listeners.
He tells them to

> **Turn off your mind**
> > *relax*
> > > **and float downstream,**
>
> **It is not dying.**
> **It is not dying.**

How utterly strange this sounded to the ears of teenagers expecting
their pop music to be about romance. Not for one millisecond does
this song pretend to be part of the everyday world, an extension
of the continuum in which its teenage audience lived and in which
they had been listening, just a few years earlier, to tunes like
"Johnny Angel" and "I Want to Hold Your Hand." (And to which
they continued listening: "Red Rubber Ball," "Bus Stop," and "See
You in September" were all big hits that summer.) Both Harrison
and McCartney had used the stock conventions of pop music to
advance a psychedelic message. Lennon went further. No tele-
phones ring unanswered in this song, no lovers go on dates, no
dance band plays past midnight. Instantly and unapologetically the
song projects itself from some otherworldly location and insists that
if we want to get it we have to go to it. Eventually one would learn
that the lyrics were borrowed from *The Tibetan Book of the Dead*,
excerpts of which Lennon had read in Leary's *The Psychedelic Experience* and later tape-recorded to guide himself through an early
acid trip. But at the time, in August 1966, only a handful within
the immense Beatles audience had any inkling of the actual facts
and chemical substances. All the rest heard strangeness, un-
diluted and outrageous strangeness, as Lennon's otherworldly and
inhuman voice began intoning lines like

That you may see the meaning of within.
It is Being.
It is Being.

Mark Lewisohn and Ian MacDonald have provided wonderfully detailed accounts of the studio techniques developed by the Beatles, Geoff Emerick, and George Martin to produce a song that sounds, as Tim Riley says, "as though it's touching down from a different galaxy." Lewisohn writes:

> No John Lennon vocal had ever sounded like *that* before. *That* was the sound of a voice being fed through a revolving Leslie speaker inside a Hammond organ. Organ notes played through it are given the Hammond swirling effect; voices put through it emerge in much the same way. "It actually meant breaking into the circuitry," says Emerick. "I remember the surprise on our faces when the voice came out of the speaker. It was one of sheer amazement. After that they wanted *everything* shoved through the Leslie: pianos, guitars, drums, vocals, you name it!"

This song also introduced the use of tape loops, which are made "by removing the erase head of a machine and then recording over and over on the same piece of tape." MacDonald tells us that:

> There were five in all, each running on an auxiliary deck fed onto the multitrack through the Studio 2 desk and mixed live: (1) a "seagull"/"Red Indian" effect (actually McCartney laughing) made, like most of the other loops, by superimposition and acceleration (0:07); (2) an orchestral chord of B flat major (0:10); (3) a Melletron played on its flute setting (0:22); (4) another Melletron oscillating in 6/8 from B flat to C on its string setting (0:38); and (5) a rising scalar phrase on a sitar, recorded with heavy saturation and acceleration (0:56). The most salient of these are (5), which forms the first four bars of the central instrumental break and subsequently dominates the rest of the track and (3) which, working in cross-rhythm, invites the audience to lose its time-sense in a brilliantly authentic evocation of the LSD experience. (The second half of the instrumental break consists of parts of McCartney's guitar solo for "Taxman" slowed down a tone, cut up, and run backwards.)

Why? Why did the Beatles become obsessed with the possibility of taking available technology and effectually subverting it, ripping it apart and making it do things it was never intended for? The Leslie effect, we are told, was created when John said, "I want to sound as though I'm the Dalai Lama singing from the highest mountain top." But this is just a metaphor. Lennon and his mates were searching for a *sound,* and they didn't know what it was until they found it. ("I remember the surprise on our faces when the voice came out of the speaker.") It is recognizably a *technological* sound; no one would mistake it for the natural voice of a Dalai Lama chanting in the clear air of a Tibetan mountaintop. The sound of this song and of so much of *Revolver* wreaks havoc with the distinction between the natural and the artificial. It is a "mind-bending" sound because it invites the listener to enter an acoustic universe in which familiar signposts of authenticity have been deliberately removed. Nothing straightforwardly refers to anything one can recognize. The totality of sound is not intended to evoke four young flesh-and-blood Beatles with their actual fingers playing real guitars and their Beatle-booted feet keeping time on the dusty floor of a dance-band stage. The album did not so much invite its still-innocent audience to "lose its time-sense in a brilliantly authentic evocation of the LSD experience" as offer extended immersion in denaturalized sound. It is a denaturalization made all the more intense and perplexing because the subjects being denaturalized are the Beatles themselves: not strangers, but familiars, not distant and indifferent pop stars, but young men known individually by their fans, known as persons involved in a relationship with their audience: John, Paul, George, and Ringo. Why did the Beatles, and their audience, go for this sound?

The reason, I think, had been carried within rock music from its inception; it was implicit in the decision to *electrify* music and to make the *electric* guitar the centerpiece of the rock sound. ("The sound," observed Ralph Gleason, "is the sound of the electronic age. A dissent from older forms.") But under the spell of psychedelics, first Dylan, then the Beatles, then Jimi Hendrix, all began consciously to explore and exploit the electrical essence of their music, the electric ladyland that rock music carried its audience into. The challenge their rock accepted was to overcome technology, to humanize technology, to demonstrate that the kinds of truth-telling possessed by music could be turned upon technology and renew it.

At just about the time rock was born, but with no interest in its existence, the German philosopher Martin Heidegger wrote his famous meditation on the nature of technology, "The Question Concerning Technology." Heidegger was struggling to invent a richer vocabulary in which to think about what technology is, what relation it has to the human spirit, and how the future of that relationship might be guided toward better outcomes. The problem was difficult, he thought, because technology was not all bad. Indeed, it expressed a long-standing and on the whole admirable human impulse to bring the truth of Being out of what Heidegger called its "concealment." But Heidegger believed that Being came out of concealment only because it *called* humans to bring it forth. Humans, in turn, should acknowledge and reverence this invitation extended to them; never should they presume to think that they alone, through autonomous acts of Faustian will, had managed to wrest truth out where they could see it and control it. But that denial of an interactive, interdependent relationship with Being was precisely what technology, especially after Auschwitz and Hiroshima, had come to express.

Now, Heidegger's question concerning technology is also a question concerning the electronics of rock 'n' roll. Heidegger ends his essay on a hopeful note, wondering whether the reverential revealing made possible by the arts could somehow redeem and renew the hubristic revealing undertaken by technology. Heidegger hints that the answer is yes: since the deepest impulse behind technology is to experience Being—not to control matter but to come into the presence of truth—it is just possible that humans might win their way back to an awareness of Being's concealedness and to thankfulness for Being's self-revelations. Technology renewed by art could make this possible. But the stakes are high. For if the opposite occurred, if art were to wind up enslaving itself to technology, humans would lose their last and best hope for dwelling in a world still enchanted and radiant with meaning.

Revolver only asks the questions raised by Heidegger. It does not answer them. The sixteen-year-old who spent hours and hours absorbing the words and sounds of *Revolver* spent hours and hours in a borderland where technology and mystery seemed to be allies, not enemies. But who could know for sure? The unearthly sounds that *Revolver* released into the world were at once the antithesis of the human and a provocative indication of the *mysterium tremendum*. They allowed the imagination to traverse the netscape of a future in which biology and technology would come full circle and touch. The sounds of *Revolver* emptied the old container of pop music, but the metallic remains were revealed to be rich, textured, intriguing, appropriate. As they took their audience through a radically defamiliarized acoustic universe, these sounds were essentially *questioning* sounds. They kept forcing their audience to ask: what is this I'm listening to?

About a year later, in a free-associative, probably stoned conversation with a reporter for *International Times* (known familiarly as *IT*), Paul McCartney showed that he was quite conscious of the questions concerning electronic music, defamiliarization, and personal identity. McCartney at this moment was beside himself with excitement. It seemed to him that everything he had been learning through psychedelics and meditation could be made available, through music, to millions upon millions of Beatles fans—if he and the other Beatles were careful not to go too far too fast. "I'm trying to take people with me," he says, but "I don't want to be shouting to people 'Listen, listen, I've found it! Listen, this is where it's at!' and everyone going 'Oh fuck off, you fucking crank,' because I see the potentiality in them as well, not just in myself." The way to reach them is through music, especially electronic music, which seems to be "the next move" because "there's a lot of good new sounds to be listened to in it." But McCartney, astute showman that he is, knows that electronic music is risky: "if the music itself is going to jump about five miles ahead, then everyone's going to be left with this gap of five miles that they've all got to cross." Nonetheless, this is the risk the Beatles took, especially on songs like "Tomorrow Never Knows." (On an outtake of "A Day in the Life" released on *The Beatles Anthology,* McCartney is heard to say: "The worst thing about doing something like this is people get a bit suspicious. Like, 'Come on, what are you up to?'")

The root problem, the twenty-five-year-old McCartney sagely explains, is that we all tend to dismiss whatever is unfamiliar.

"That's the first mistake, and that's the big mistake everyone makes, to immediately discount anything that they don't understand." For McCartney, this defensiveness is the original sin because it is a distrust of existence itself. Once we accept the claim implicitly advanced by our parents and culture—that only those things that fit into the design as we now understand it can be thought of as "real"—we have begun the long slide downward toward a life of self-imprisonment in suburban "unreality." This is why the most important thing a popular artist can do is confront an audience with strangeness and at the same time lead them through the experience of that defamiliarity until they can accept it. The Beatles' defamiliarization of the world is like tripping on music instead of on acid, McCartney seems to suggest. "The most important thing to say to people is, It isn't necessarily so, what you believe. You must see that whatever you believe in isn't necessarily the truth, because the fact that it could be right or wrong is also infinite, that's the point of it. The whole being fluid and changing all the time and evolving." *Very strange.*

Thus emerged the new morality: the categorical moral imperative to notice the radical discontinuity in each instant of life. To be aware of the gaps of light and shade between every blade of grass on the shimmering lawn. It was the morality of doubt. Of questioning. As Aldo Giunta wrote in *The East Village Other* in October 1966, "There is an essential dichotomy of moralities in America, on the one hand of Caesar (*where Caesar commands, we obey*), and on the other of the truly modern, flexible man (*I will not, until I have questioned.*)" Hippies, wrote Ralph Gleason in *Evergreen Review* in September 1967, "are not just dropping out into Limbo or Nirvana. They are building a new set of values, a new structure, a new society." Most obviously, the hippies are "attacking the very principle upon which this society is built: It is more sacred to make money than to be a good man." At a deeper level, the hippy is simply committed to the authority of the individual vision. Do your own thing. All of existence is a game, "changing all the time and evolving," and no one vision of it should preempt or silence others.

If living like what Hendrix called a "Highway Chile" sounds dangerously irresponsible today, it also sounds decidedly postmodern. For what it means is that we can never know which of our many selves is, finally, authoritative, since none of them is essential. All we can do is keep on going, with our flaming hair blowing in the wind. McCartney stumbles through this problem when he says that virtually all the people he meets in a day "are acting in some way." Their belief in one narrow band of the spectrum of existence, to the exclusion of all others, has forced them to play roles, to live hypocrisies, to act. "And of course I'm acting, all the time," McCartney admits. "But at least I'm making a serious effort not to act now, realizing that most of my acting is to no avail anyway."

But if not acting means spontaneously being yourself somehow rather than picking and sticking to a particular role, if it means seeing "that everything is beautiful and everything is great and fine," then deliberate choice becomes undesirable. Indeed, if *everything* is fine, then hypocrisy is fine, too, and so is acting, and so is "the fantastically abstract way of living that people have got into without realizing it." Eventually, if you wander far enough down this path, you have to conclude *that nothing is real, there's nothing to get hung about.* Why, then, play one note rather than another? Why is one musical decision better than another? Why is one self more real than any other? While McCartney was ready to don the vestments of a pop guru, he was unprepared to answer such questions. "To really try and sort it out in a year is too big a project," he confesses. "So at the moment I'm just trying to operate within the new frame of reference but not pushing it. Because to push it would be to alienate myself completely from everything. It would really make me into a very sort of strange being, as far as other people were concerned."

As far as a lot of people were concerned, this "very strange sort of being" was what the Beatles had already turned themselves into—and had been ever since they gazed out from under lank and graying locks on the cover of *Rubber Soul.* The sounds and voices on *Revolver* were even stranger. The Beatles seemed to be giving up the illusion of their individual personhood and dissolving in the electronic maelstrom of their music. Yet despite McCartney's worries, their audience was certainly going with them. The audience found something deeply appealing not just in Harrison's broadening of the meaning of communication, not just in the urgency with which McCartney wanted to blend private mysticism with public celebration, and not just in the album's interrogation of the values of technology. They were drawn as well by the album's foray into depersonalization. They were drawn to the possibility of experiencing, in sound, a self that was not a self. They were discovering the possibility of a *sound* that, even more compellingly than the electric guitar and Elvis's voice, corresponded with and expressed their inner condition of loneliness, their desire for a self that was not a social self, their willingness to destroy the social and experience themselves, if need be, as mere nothing, as a blank— *complete evaporation to the core.*

Very soon, many Beatles fans would start taking the psychedelics the Beatles had been experimenting with. When we did, we would experience this intensification of loneliness as something even more powerful than rock by itself. For psychedelics also gave a profoundly impersonal experience. As Huxley observed in a talk delivered to the first American symposium on psychedelic substances (held in Atlantic City on May 12, 1955),

> the most striking feature [of the mescaline experience], stressed emphatically by all who have gone through it, is its profound impersonality. The classic mescaline experience is not of consciously or unconsciously remembered events, does not concern itself with early traumas, and is not, in most cases, tinged by anxiety and fear. It is as though those who were going through it had been transported to some remote, non-personal region of the mind.

But even before we smoked pot or dropped acid, we could experience such impersonality just by listening to *Revolver*. "Tomorrow Never Knows" especially carried us again and again to "some remote, non-personal region of the mind," to a new kind of Heartbreak Hotel where we heard the colors of our dreams and felt a strange new ease in our loneliness. The Beatles made *Being* feel right even for their fans who never experimented with psychedelics. Their music made it okay to be what you felt you were anyway: a person without distinctive personhood, a self without singular substance.

Revolver—a disk that pivots round the spindle of a turntable, a pistol that recalls Mao's definition of power, and a prescient foreshadowing of the word by which the '60s would claim a place in history: revolution. *Revolver* became the number-one selling album in England on August 13 and in the United States on September 10, 1966.

FEELIN'
GROOVY

FREE
ACID
LICK
HERE

LOVE
L'AMOUR
IS
EST
OUGHT POUR
YOU
ALS
NEE
VOU
LIE

CHAPTER 5

"Never Do See Any Other Way"

Sgt. Pepper's Lonely Hearts Club Band

Politics has the function of bringing people out of isolation and into community, thus being a necessary, though not sufficient, means of finding meaning in personal life.

—The Port Huron Statement (1962)

We're as much influenced by everybody else as they are by us, if they are. It's just all a part of the big thing. I give to you and you give to me and it goes like that into the music you know.

—George Harrison (1967)

On March 17, 1967, eight weeks before the release of *Sgt. Pepper's,* Jimi Hendrix's "Purple Haze" hit the airwaves in England. It entered the charts at #39, soared up to #3, and stayed on the charts for fourteen weeks, selling more than 100,000 copies. With uncharacteristic coyness, Hendrix always denied that the song had anything to do with drugs. "The key to the meaning of the song lies in the line, 'That girl put a spell on me,'" he told an interviewer. "It's nothing to do with drugs. It's about this guy, this girl turned this cat on, and he doesn't know if it's bad or good, that's all, and he doesn't know if it's tomorrow or just the end of time."

No one in his audience was convinced, of course, any more than Beatles fans were persuaded later by John Lennon's claim that "Lucy in the Sky with Diamonds" had nothing to do with LSD. In the seven months since the release of *Revolver,* rock culture had become thoroughly psychedelicized, especially in London, San Francisco, and New York. Who could hear the words of "Purple Haze," not to mention its *sound,* and not think they described an acid trip?

> *Purple haze all in my brain,*
> *Lately things just don't seem the same.*
> *Actin' funny, but I don't know why,*
> *'Scuse me while I kiss the sky.*

The perception that the world was suddenly and inexplicably changed (*Lately things just don't seem the same*) had become the touchstone of the emerging counterculture. The Beatles had already sung about being alone and taking a ride to another kind of mind; on *Sgt. Pepper's* they would sing about having a smoke and going into a dream, or about someone being *suddenly* there at the turnstile. The Stones, taking the phrase from Dylan, would merrily confess that *something happened* to them yesterday, but exactly what they couldn't say—either because words failed or because the law forbade them. By the spring of 1967, huge numbers of youth were in the know. The radical and often frightening instability of existence had become cause for celebration, the basis of a self-identifying culture of heads, freaks, hippies, and students who asked each other, with a silent glance, *are you experienced?*

Combining an utterly authentic blues sound with a psychedelic willingness to explore all the possibilities of electric music, Jimi's first album was a perfect vehicle for the expression of this new sensibility. He did not have the advantage enjoyed by the Beatles, who could launch their experimental music from a platform of solid fan support. His music was every bit as difficult as theirs, and maybe more so. Yet *Are You Experienced?*, released on May 12 in England and on August 26 in the United States, rose quickly to the #2 spot (just under *Sgt. Pepper's*) and stayed on the charts for some 33 weeks. In the United States it went to the #5 spot and remained on the charts for 106 weeks—more than two years.

Only one song on the album ("Red House") is formally a blues, but the imprint of Hendrix's three years as a blues and R&B guitarist is unmistakably present on virtually every number. "Hey Joe," as Hendrix later said, "is a blues arrangement of a cowboy song that's about a hundred years old." He described "Stone Free" as "blues and rock and whatever else happens." "Manic Depression" has been rightly described as "a 12-bar blues flipped upside-down." But these more obvious examples don't adequately convey how deeply bluesy this first album is. Hendrix returns again and again to the blues idiom, throwing in blues licks and chord changes that ballast his most exuberant experiments in electronics with the centripetal return home that characterizes the blues. Just as the blues help ground and validate the experimentalism of jazz, so they work in Jimi's music to restrain and give credibility to the feedback-fuzz of technologized fantasy that was immediately recognized as the sound of acid expanding to fill the cerebral cortex of the tripper.

Part of the appeal of his music (and of The Who's and Cream's) may have come from a kind of cultural chauvinism; I sometimes suspect that white kids, including myself, heard in his music not just the absorption of blues they heard in all rock but a going-beyond or trumping of the blues, a radical revision of the blues into an idiom—the psychedelic—they could claim as their own.

But it's more likely that what we heard in Hendrix—and saw in his person—was an African American validation. It was almost as if Muddy Waters himself had given his blessing and his blues to white kids and their culture of loneliness. (Hendrix's bass guitarist Noel Redding previously played for a group called "The Lonely Ones.")

For behind Hendrix's Highway Chile, soon to become Voodoo Chile, lies a long tradition of blues declarative of personal identity, a tradition that received definitive expression in (among other songs) Muddy Waters's "Hoochie Coochie Man" and Ruby Smith's "Fruit Cakin' Mama." (See appendix 2 for a full discussion of these songs.) But while Hendrix draws at every moment on this blues tradition, he moves away from what Ralph Ellison called its balanced tensions between "the comic and the tragic aspects of life" and instead walks resolutely in the direction of tragedy alone, urging his audience to go with him. While in "Hoochie Coochie Man" Muddy Waters defiantly announces that he is "here"—*Everybody knows I'm here*—"here" is just where Hendrix refuses to remain. *Walk on, brother*, he urges. *Don't let no one stop you.* Hendrix wants to go further, to go out of history, to go to a utopia that is truly no place. *Got to, got to, got to get away.* While in a Hendrix song we hear the most complete translation of the blues sound to the needs of his white middle-class audience, we don't quite hear the blues themselves— or if we do, it is a new kind of blues, what he called "a today's kind of blues." Hendrix isn't Albert King or Muddy Waters. He is "Jimi," who has self-consciously swerved out of the blues path in order to commit himself to his own style; his clothes, hair, hats, bandannas, rings, voice, Fender Stratocaster, and Marshall amps all express his unwavering determination to take that style as far as it can go.

Like Dylan, that is, Hendrix is ready to go anywhere. He approaches the structure of a song from the outside, picking it apart piece by piece, and in the end demonstrating that there is no *inside* to this song (or indeed to anything). Everything is projection from an absence, with no solid point of origin. Everything is flight, a leap outward. Or descent, a sinking downward. Hendrix gives full measure to the risks and the costs of his ambition when he sings *Don't know if I'm coming up or down* or when he goes the distance in his solo on "Manic Depression." On more than one song he invites his listeners to join him on the bottom, beneath the ocean, and in those moods he sees the place as a wonderful shelter, a return to primordial silences, an ecstatic calm. As a writer for the underground paper *The Sun* put it: Hendrix takes "you further and further into your mind so that the totality of what you are hearing is too great to really understand . . . but compels you to just feel."

Even while he took full advantage of all the resources of the blues, Hendrix shared the Beatles' interest in developing original *electronic* sounds that could map the seam between this world and others. There's no way for the historian to describe those sounds, if only because Hendrix invented so many of them. But an energy many of them shared was unmistakably sexual. With the possible exception of Santana, no '60s band came closer than The Jimi Hendrix Experience to creating the sound of sexual desire. ("I'm sitting here listening to 'Foxy Lady,'" wrote rock critic Terri Sutton in 1989, "which I consider one of the most erotic songs ever written.") The chords and rhythms of songs like "Foxy Lady" or "Fire" made all earlier efforts to create a purely and fiercely sexual sound—from Presley's "All Shook Up" through Tommy James's "Hanky Panky"— seem anemic. But sex itself was not really what Hendrix's vision was about. On "Manic Depression" he sings *You can make love or break love, it's all the same.* And later he would comment: "You'll always have cats to stand up there and sing you pretty songs. We're just going to another vein of it, just translating it into our own image. 'Cause what I was trying to do, like was a today's type of blues. Like 'Manic Depression' is a story about a cat wishing he could make love to music, instead of the same old everyday woman."

In Hendrix's music, sex was always a breaking loose. But to work, sex had to be broken free of romance and love and domesticity, just as music had to be broken free of convention and channeled through the unpredictable pathways taken by heavily juiced electrons. "Heavy rock," wrote a reviewer of Hendrix for *Old Mole,* "is rebellion and disgust. It is a plea against loneliness, people reaching out over personal isolation barriers. It is raw sex." Only when we understand "loneliness" not as romantic lovelorn sadness but as a complex, self-contradictory, and often angry attitude toward all of life can we see how "disgust" and "raw sex" are a kind of answer to it. Hendrix's phrase "make love to music" is another version of John Cunnick's "living to music." For Hendrix and his audience, music and raw sex were not just a way to get out there: if you did them right, they *were* the out there. Jimi's rock was more than a "plea." It was the energy of desire itself, and it swept him out to sea, *far out,* over the edge. Like the tripper who went from one to two to four or more tabs of acid, Jimi's music insistently expressed a willingness to court a reality that at once annihilated and affirmed his own.

This was, in essence, a tragic attitude, if by the word we mean a refusal to reconcile oneself with existence as one finds it, a determination to supersede the visible and invisible limits life imposes on us all. Like Jim Morrison and Janis Joplin, but with infinitely more ability as a musician, Hendrix approached his music with a ferocity that was uncompromising, determined, rebellious. While his showmanship was gaudy, a comic put-on and a mocking put-down of conventions, his music was essentially tragic. In song after song on *Are You Experienced?* he recommits himself to the break-through experience, to going beyond, getting out of what he dismisses as *your little world.* He is the "Highway Chile" who, with his guitar strapped across his back, has *left the world behind.* He mocks those who would *put him on a chain; they must be insane.* He insists on being *stone free to ride the breeze, stone free to do what I please.* Sometimes he deflects criticism with a laugh that is not really a joke: when people claim that the perpetually mobile Highway Chile is *a tramp,* he replies *I know it goes deeper than that.* It goes deeper because it goes all the way down into the restless, fluid nature of existence itself. More often, Hendrix scripts himself as a sorcerer who can conjure up a sound so powerful, so menacing—think of the opening chords to "Purple Haze"—that it says, in effect, "I'll break through or die trying." And that willingness to be sacrificed is what his audience loved to hear in his music (and in the lyrics of the Doors and in the fraying vocal chords of Janis Joplin). They wanted their music to take them, vicariously, to IT—even at the risk of madness, chaos, and death.

But the tragic attitude, while indispensable, was not the dominant mode of the new counterculture. When Hendrix poked fun at cats who "stand up there and sing you pretty songs," he was very likely thinking of the four moptops themselves, incarnated now as the Lonely Hearts Club Band, standing up in front of an adoring "lovely audience" (in the aural universe of the album, not in life, where they had ceased performing years earlier) while Billie Shears (a.k.a. Ringo Starr, born Richard Starkey) mocked Shakespearean tragedy as he asked the spectators to lend him their ears while he sang them a song. We can't know why the Beatles were so able to musick a comedic attitude to life, but the contrasting yet cooperative personalities of Lennon and McCartney, complemented later by George Harrison, probably had a lot to do with it. They balanced each other, and in the balancing of their competitive, often conflicting personalities, they were forced to forge excellence through compromise, and thereby urged reconciliation with history not rebellion, love not raw sex.

Love, love, love, they sang in the summer of 1967, creating what would be the anthem and the symbol and the actual epicenter of this cultural moment. *Love is all there is,* they sang, and that simple or simplistic message was instantly convincing to their millions of fans. Here, at last, was the answer to loneliness. The timid self that had to hide behind its loneliness in order to preserve itself as a self, this fragile waif was suddenly allowed to step forward into the sunlight, to come out of hiding, to celebrate itself and its needs and its desires. There was a wonderful feeling of *release.* Balloons rose into the sky.

Taken out of context of their music as a whole, the Beatles' claim that *love is all there is* sounds stupidly naïve. Wasn't this the era (isn't it still?) of Auschwitz and Hiroshima, Vietnam, Westmoreland's napalm, Oswald's bullets, Bull Connor's fire hoses and police dogs? But to hear only the lighthearted joie de vivre of their pronouncement is like remembering "Strawberry Fields Forever" only by its title, forgetting the wistful, defeated sound of Lennon's voice and the bitter humor of *It's all right—that is, I think it's not too bad.* A melancholy shadow falls across almost every song on *Sgt. Pepper's.* Only grudgingly and cautiously can one *admit it's getting better, a little better, all the time,* and even then a qualification pokes fun at this optimism: *can't get no worse.* When one looks out at the world, one sees that *everything is closed, it's like a ruin.* One sees the *space between us all,* not to mention the four thousand holes in Blackburn, Lancashire.

In fact, the entire psychedelic infatuation with love, expressed as pink and blue and lime-green uniforms, as flowers, intensity, and delight, grew out of the soil of the Beatles' freshly dug grave. The vision of love in *Sgt. Pepper's* was credible to their audience only because it was deepened by these shadows, only because its final song ("A Day in the Life") gave such magisterial utterance to the void of meaninglessness that love must dare to redeem. It was not a simple vision, because the '60s were not a simple moment. When the Beatles sang that "love is all there is," they did not mean that love is here now, within our grasp, the solution to all problems. Rather, as Richard Poirier observed back in 1967, they were acknowledging that "'Love' remains the great unfulfilled need, and the historical evidence for this is endless musical compositions about it."

> Lennon and McCartney's recognition through music that the "need" for love is historical and recurrent is communicated to the listener by instrumental and vocal allusions to earlier material. The historical allusiveness is at the outset smart-alecky— the song opens with the French National Anthem—passes through the Chaplin echo, if that's what it is, to various echoes of the blues, and boogie-woogie, all of them in the mere shadings of the background, until at the end the song itself seems to be swept up and dispersed within the musical history of which it is a part and of the electronics by which that history has been made available.

And just as "All You Need Is Love" refers to many songs of the past, including the Beatles' own "She Loves You," so the cover of *Sgt. Pepper's* brings a motley crew of celebrities into a moment that contains both past and present. The circle of mourners who surround the Lonely Hearts Club Band at the side of the Beatles' grave are celebrants who have gathered, as in the last act of a comedy, to set aside their differences and affirm a compact of reconciliation.

With rich historical allusiveness, the album's music and its graphics required listeners to locate themselves in a flow of time, to experience themselves living in a drama shared by other generations.

Sgt. Pepper's was in this sense the opposite of utopian. It did give its audience a place to be, a cultural space in which to dwell, but that space was firmly centered in history, not in a "no-place" beyond it. The Beatles' *feel* for history, conveyed as much through their music as their lyrics, obliged them to be more worldly than revolutionary, more witty than angry, more comedic than tragic. They sang that things were getting better all the time. That the leaks were being fixed, the cracks being mended, and the world being made whole again. We're learning that we're all one and that life goes on within us and without us—*within* us as the force that drives us, *without* us as the force that encompasses us and sustains itself long after we have disappeared. Small, mortal, and insignificant, we shouldn't take ourselves quite so seriously. It *doesn't really matter if we're wrong or right, where we belong is right*—here in this fleeting moment of history that we share together. Since it's all a *show,* no need to be so vehement. *Sit back and let the evening go.* Come to the circus we've created for you, a circus made of electronic sounds, the sound of trained horses prancing 'round the ring, the sound of your own chatter as the band tunes its instruments, the sound of your applause. Come home with us. *We'd love to take you*—not to Heartbreak Hotel this time, not *away,* but *home,* for yes, there is a home for you in the world. It's not the home she's leaving after living alone for so many years. It's *our* home, the home you share with your friends, the home we can all still be in—if you just say the word—when we're *sixty-four.* But of course *that* world is *this* world. There's no difference. You'll have to wake up, get out of bed, go off to a boring job, have a cup of coffee, a smoke, and . . . dream your way to the sun-drenched park where the *girl with kaleidoscope eyes* is waiting for you, there by the turnstile.

In comedy, performance takes precedence over authenticity. This is why there are so many cases of mistaken identity, cross-dressing, and masquerade in Shakespeare's comedies. While the tragic hero insists on the uncompromising essentiality of his character, an essentiality that requires him to do what he must, whatever the cost, the figures in a comedy experience themselves and the world by taking on and performing different identities. Always committed to change and self-transformation, the Beatles went one step further on *Sgt. Pepper's* by feigning their own demise and re-creating themselves as the Lonely Hearts Club Band. They took loneliness and made it a performance.

Of course, Elvis Presley, Lesley Gore, the Beach Boys, Pat Boone, and the Stones all performed loneliness by acting it out or displaying it in the songs they sang. That's what their audiences wanted them to do. But the Beatles actually stepped out of the frame in which all other singers had performed; they doubled themselves and became an audience for their own performance. When they sang *We hope you will enjoy the show* and *You go to a show, you hope she goes* and then *We hope you have enjoyed the show,* they underscored the performed comedy in which they and their audience participated. When they sang most of "She's Leaving Home" from the viewpoint of the parents whom they satirized (*never a thought for ourselves* is the credo of the other-directed society) and yet showed compassion for (*Love is the one thing that money can't buy*), they performed the wisdom of comic reconciliation. When they sang of the nursemaid by the roundabout that *though she feels as if she's in a play, she is anyway,* they were turning their audience on to this comedic way of thinking about themselves. The joke about the nursemaid applies as well to us. Thinking that we are in a play, like knowing that we are only dreaming, is usually a reliable indicator that in fact we are *not* in a play or in a dream. We have simply chosen to take part for a while in a play; we are performing Hamlet but we do not think we have become Hamlet. But the Beatles suggest that even though we feel safeguarded by this notion, safeguarded by a distinction between the reality in which our real self dwells and the play in which we temporarily perform, there is in fact no such distinction. We are in a play anyway.

In other words, self-consciousness does not automatically protect us by removing us from where we are. Yet the subtle consolation of this comic vision is that self-consciousness does not separate us from reality either. Watching ourselves perform ourselves does not mean that the watcher in us stands outside the circle, on the other side of a veil. The vision from the other side of the veil reveals that there are no sides, no inside, no outside. Everything is a play. As Harrison struggled to say in an interview:

> There's something happening. If everybody could just get into it, great, they'd all smile and all dress up. Yes—that'd be good. "The world is a stage." Well, he was right, because we're Beatles, and it's a little scene and we're playing and we're pretending to be Beatles, like Harold Wilson pretending to be Prime Minister.

Lennon makes essentially the same point when he sings:

> *Always know sometime I think it's me*
> *But you know I know that it's a dream.*

We live, that is, a double consciousness—one in which "knowing" merges with just "thinking" (sometimes) that we are authentically ourselves, a genuine "me," while also knowing that it's all a "dream." Not an "unreal" dream. Not "just" a dream. But Lennon also reminds us that the comic is not to be confused with the funny. *Let me take you there,* he sings, as if from inside a lost childhood, *'cause I'm going to* . . . And as one went there one knew that the spirit of the song was right, that it was right to be sad. We feel joy as we join these others who feel likewise, but we know that this joy is always a sadness at the same time. Because the sky is blue, it makes us cry. We know that sadness goes with our loneliness, and we can hear that sadness in the first three bars of "Lovely Rita" and in the twelve bars of Lennon sighing *I* or *Ai* or *Ahh* just before *I'd love to turn you on* in "A Day in the Life." This knowledge is what gives the reprise of "Sgt. Pepper's Lonely Hearts Club Band" such power. It's a determined, courageous reaffirmation—like Elvis's renewed attack in "Heartbreak Hotel." We hope you have enjoyed the show. We're sorry but it's time to go. Look for . . . she's gone. This knowledge of futility is what made the Beatles' community so precious and so fragile, and it's what made their hopefulness so compelling.

Was it sad or brave or just foolish that "underground" was the name given to that place where the community gathered? In 1967 a writer for the Cambridge (Mass.) *Avatar* wrote:

Who is the Underground?

You are, if you think, dream, work, and build towards the improvements and changes in your life, your social and personal environments, towards the expectations of a better existence.

Optimism is always pathetic in retrospect, just as cynicism is bankrupt to those who hope. The hopefulness of this '60s can seem so foolish, and so painful, to those who have had to harvest the disappointments of subsequent decades. Today, as rock critic Simon Frith observed, "The exhilaration, the sense of change and purpose, the emotional underpinnings of the *experience* of liberation are dismissed as fraudulent because of what happened next— just as the genuinely disruptive ideological effects of our drug use in the '60s are concealed by blanket references to drugs' 'inevitable' evil consequences." But I trust that by now my readers will believe with me that the optimism of this '60s was neither glib nor unconscious of all the reasons to despair. Hope, for the writers and publishers of these underground papers, was an act of daring because there were never sufficient grounds for hope. Hope could never hope to be more than a self-fulfilling prophecy.

Warren Steel, writing in the *Avatar* in September of that year, compared the hopefulness of rock 'n' roll with the despair expressed by "serious" avant-garde music: "Hope. Our new music reflects the hope of enlightenment, hope of achieving beauty in a technological age, instead of the despair and confusion which led to the 'spaceman music' [e.g., of Cage and Stockhausen]." And for a brief while, the Beatles were fully prepared to invest their immense credibility in the effort to sustain this hope. Interviewed in January of 1967, Paul McCartney said:

I don't believe that it ends with our Western logical thought, it can't do, because that's so messed up anyway, most of it, that you've got to allow for the possibility of there being a lot, lot more than we know about. To bang one note on the piano, instead of trying to put millions of notes into it, and just to take the one note of the piano and listen to it, shows you what there is in one note. There's so much going on in one note, but you never listen to it!

Again, it is the *nearness* of Being—just there beyond the filmy screen—that helps make hope possible. All you have to do is *listen to it*. If you listen to musicians who are discovering that *one note* can expand into a universe of sound, you have a chance of crossing over to an alternative reality, *beyond Western logical thought,* where hope is earned rather than denied. Paul continues:

> Of course it will take a bit of training. But the good thing about it is that if you are prepared to accept that things are not just broad and wide, they're infinitely broad and wide, then there's a great amount to be done. And the change-over—it can be done. It just takes a bit of time, but it will be done, I think.

It can be done. *It will be done.* This hope is made possible by the discovery of pluralism, which tells us that the logic that had led to Auschwitz, Hiroshima, the silent spring, the Vietnam War, and institutionalized racial oppression was not the only game in town. Once you discover that *things are infinitely broad and wide,* the way a single piano note can resonate like a full orchestra, then you can see that there is plenty of room for new attitudes, different perspectives, including visions energized by optimism.

This comic vision lent itself perfectly to the needs of an audience that wanted to explore the ins and outs of love *and* confusion. As the Beatles moved from album to album, style to style, mask to mask, the only constant was their mischievous self-consciousness that they were all and none of these. (*I am the Walrus. The Walrus was Paul.*) They celebrated communication even as they acknowledged its limits. (*You never give me your pillow, you only give me your situation.*) They combined an absolute reality of identity with a mobility through identities. (*You say yes, I say no, you say stop, I say go, go, go . . .*) In songs and interviews, they repeatedly made clear that no one moment would fix and freeze them, least of all the media, over whom they would always triumph. They would always win because they played by a different set of rules. Their own. ("I know I'm going to need a new set of rules," said McCartney, "and the new set of rules have got to include the rule that there aren't any rules.") And so the Beatles won. But in the very moment of their reconciliation with loneliness and despair, their celebrants (Beatles fans all) had to admit that if reconciliation did not mean submission, it did not mean victory either. It meant acceptance.

So the note of triumph and celebration we hear in the reprise brings Sgt. Pepper's show to an end—but then we discover that *the Beatles'* show goes on, into "A Day in the Life." This shift from inside to outside, from fantasy to frame, once again reminds us of our doubleness, of the way we're inside and outside, within and without at the same time. "A Day in the Life" testifies that the comedic vision is not easy. It must be won and sustained in the face of everything we confront in modern life, in the news we read, in the films we see. There are 4,000 individual reasons to despair, and encompassing them all is the biggest reason of all—the possibility that the *show* means nothing, that *we* mean nothing, that nihilism is after all the right response to the way the world, or cosmos, is. (Yet even here, right in the middle of Lennon's pessimistic confession, an alarm clock rings, the bourgois self leaps into action, and McCartney's optimism comes back into play.) The blank face of existence is the grand backdrop to comedy, and to remind us of that the Beatles give Lennon's despair the last word, or almost the last word. For down comes the crashing chord that shows us "how much there is in just one note," the one note that, like comedy, encompasses so many notes, so many truths. And as their final word the Beatles chant with mock dementia, twelve times, *Never do see any other way.* As if to say, this way, the comedic way, is the right way.

Two paragraphs of Dotson Rader's luminous and poignant memoir of the Columbia takeover convey this mood better than any other words I know; they also remind us that student politics in the '60s were always energized by this paradoxical blend of giddy hope and adolescent angst. After barricading themselves inside a building and steeling themselves for an onslaught of police, Rader and his comrades get the news that negotiations will continue, that the dreaded bust is not (yet) under way:

> The whole commune was relieved that the bastards had given us more time. And, at the same moment, we were proud of ourselves because no one had walked out, no one had pan-

icked. We had stayed solid. The barricade was taken off the passage window. The singing and dancing started. Someone got a guitar and sat down on the second floor landing and we sang Bob Dylan's "It's All Right, Ma." Students sat on the steps before him like a tiered choir and sang along: *though the masters make the rules for the wisemen and the fools, I got nothing, Ma, to live up to.*

About an hour later a bagpiper came into the building and we joined hands in a long chain and danced behind him, snaking through the building, up and down the stairs, playing, shouting happily, singing about how we weren't going to study war no more. And later still I stood with Frank on the balcony beside the red flag in the coolness of that lovely night and tore sheets of paper and threw them down in lieu of rice on the couple who had been married that night in one of the liberated buildings and were walking toward us, now under the balcony, now on the lawn, candles in their hands, a wedding party of tired professors, flower children, and red-banded communards dancing behind them singing. We raised our arms and shouted out into the night: "We've won! We've won!"

If the Revolution looked at times like a high school production of *Romeo and Juliet,* no one knew better than the participants how absurd their ambitions were, how fleeting their victory, how fragile their community. Joe Cocker's tortured yet exhilarating version of "With a Little Help from My Friends" musicked the feelings of everyone who knew that any second now the girl with the sun in her eyes would be gone. Just as the student revolution could hope for nothing purer and better than this moment on the balcony, just hours before the police did move in, so comedy could be no more than a staying action against resurgent loneliness. Cocker's cover begins with a typically *white*-rock guitar solo, an abstract, acid-influenced expression of the cold spaces from which one hopes to be rescued by one's friends. But this sound is soon warmed and vivified by Cocker's voice (itself a tribute to the even warmer tones of Ray Charles's voice) and by the reassuring sweetness of a gospel organ and choir. The song then becomes dramatically African American in its feel, a dynamic call-and-response between the agonized (yet determined) Cocker and the encouraging (yet wistful) choir. *Do you need anybody?* they ask. *I need somebody to love,* he replies. And in his tones one hears the deepest need of the culture of his audience breathed forth with an almost unbearable intensity. The rich layering of musical resources—Joe Cocker doing Ray Charles doing Sgt. Pepper's Lonely Hearts Club Band who were actually the Beatles who were almost always doing some version of black music even as they quoted Shakespeare's *Julius Caesar*—gathers power and builds momentum. Toward the end of the song Cocker allows himself to go as far into the heart of his condition as Elvis had in "Heartbreak Hotel," but instead of crooning he simply screams—screams his pain at such length, and in a way so naked and unaestheticized that even Ray Charles might have sat back in wonder—and when the gospel choir kicks in with *High with a little help from my friends!* Cocker's listeners were lifted up along with him, redeemed by the assurances of community and connection even while the thrust of Cocker's song underscored how fragile and vulnerable they actually felt.

Thirty years ago it was as if rock had tapped into a wellspring where Being gushed forth in a play of light and sound that was free and unnamed and not yet frozen into the forms that history and culture demand. It was as if one knew that the wisest cultures find a way to preserve the knowledge of this fountain, an esoteric knowledge hidden from ordinary sight, and it was as if rock was the way *our* culture had found, entrusting a cohort of vagabond misfits with this light of the ages. It was as if the mutability of Dylan and the Beatles—every album so utterly different from the last—was the very sign of their faithfulness to this mission. It was *not* as if rock "saved." It was not as if salvation were a possibility. Most people in the rock audience knew that they were *stuck inside of Mobile with the Memphis blues again,* and they preferred to stay stuck than to move on schedule along the planned trajectory of *Twenty years of school* to the *day shift* where *the heart attack machine is strapped across your back, and then the kerosene.* It was not as if they had a story they could believe in, with delay and crisis and resolution, but rather as if they had stepped through the sheen of the waterfall to behold nothing that could be named, nothing that one could carry back, but just a promise, a possibility, a mystery that helped them turn the tables on their culture. It became suddenly clear that what our culture says to us, and the very terms in which despair and hope are called for and called forth, are mere details, scintilla, motes, specks—not illusions absolutely, but illusory when we take them for what they claim to be, namely the totality of what can be "real." Rock insisted that meaning emerges only when we have dispensed with the narrative of coherence.

But another '60s voice was skeptical. John Wolfe, also writing in 1967 (in Philadelphia's *Distant Drummer*), argued that the Beatles' celebration of love and communication ignored the need for concealment that any genuine counterculture requires:

> There can be no revolution when *Life* turns its cameras on the newest underground five minutes after it has been formed. With instant communication there can be no secrecy; with no secrecy there can be no effect. . . . It may be that Dylan has found the only solution—by dropping out completely to his Woodstock tomb he has remained pure.

Is Wolfe correct? When young people got stoned together and listened to the Beatles *communicate* with them and validate their sense that they were a community, was that listening predicated on the very modernity that has eviscerated the self in the first place? Was the communication celebrated by the Beatles and their fans just a supreme instance of the reach of capitalism and technology into everyday life?

As I look back decades later, what's so striking about the '60s is that these questions were raised all the time, not least within rock music itself. Voices spoke up on each side, some favoring the esoteric, others the erotic. All through the '60s, the Beatles were engaged in a kind of cultural call-and-response with the Stones, whose harder music kept reminding one that the Beatles' belief in communication seemed to slight the fact that communication is always mediated and distorted (if not undone entirely) by power. In song after song—"Play with Fire," "Cool, Calm, and Collected," "Yesterday's Papers," "Under My Thumb," "Paint It Black," "Stray Cat Blues"—the Stones systematically attacked the Beatles' romanticism in general and their kinder, gentler style of masculinity in particular. As Alan Beckett wrote in the *New Left Review* in 1968:

the danger in work like much of The Beatles' is the tendency towards manic denial that there can be anything difficult in relationships—anything that cannot be achieved immediately and magically. In their typically arrogant and narcissistic themes, the Stones are providing criticism of this kind of facile intimacy.

The culture founded on rock was relentlessly critical of itself. When The Who released *The Who Sell Out,* in which "real" songs are interspersed with parodic advertisements, their audience was fully prepared to get the joke. They already knew that rock culture was what is now called a "commodity culture," and that by publicizing their values in the marketplace they risked losing whatever force rock's critique of capitalism carried. When the Beatles sang *Boy, you're gonna carry that weight, carry that weight a long time* and punctuated the message with the sound of trumpets and the return of *You never give me your pillow* as a refrain, they put this consciousness into sound. The *weight* is the weight of a kind of awareness— consciousness that consciousness itself both connects and separates us from existence. It's similar to what Keats called "the burthen of the mystery," and what the Port Huron Statement called "the pressure of complexity upon the emptiness of life." And yet, even as rock fans admitted to themselves that the mystery was "so heavy," that the burden of their self-consciousness was almost unendurable, they continued to celebrate their creation of a community that was constituted by this consciousness. For better or worse, it was there, in the streets.

When the Grateful Dead told their listeners *to come hear Uncle John's band,* they were inviting one to step into the mystery—and not alone, but as part of a community. When Van Morrison sang about the caravan that was on its way *into the mystic,* one knew that the caravan was composed of oneself and all those who were listening to that song. When the Beatles seemed to sum everything up on the end of *Abbey Road* by singing that *in the end, the love you take is equal to the love you make,* they were urging their fans to commit themselves to sustaining this fragile mood. And thus it did seem as if a multitude of persons were involved collectively in the making of a new cultural space that would be hospitable to the breakthrough experience. It was as if a synthesis of private ecstasy and social energy had been achieved. That synthesis was named by the word love. Behind the filmy veil, at the very place where Being comes into the being that we can experience at all, it comes as a gift, as the miracle of something rather than nothing, and as a gift it bespeaks love. It comes as the girl with kaleidoscope eyes, who will urge you, if you listen carefully, *Never do see any other way*. Love is all there is, therefore. And since human love is just a manifestation of cosmic love, all you need is love, therefore. All together now, therefore. For just a moment, it all seemed so simple, so clear, so right.

CHAPTER 6

"Evil" Is "Live" Spelled Backwards

The Radical Self in
Highway 61 Revisited and
The White Album

Evil is "live" spelled backwards. It
centers around the id. Dark seat of
inner drives. And the forces exist or
are created and if you perceive
them fuck epistemology and dig it.
And call them demons or powers no
matter, it's just like an LSD vision
anyway so what difference does it
make . . . because you're dealing
with an elemental force that you
can use or can destroy you and if
you become nonfunctional what difference does it make if you're crazy
or possessed and if you can use it
what difference does it make if it's
Lucifer himself or the unholy force
of your will.

—Deday LaRene (1969)

"**O**h God, no, please don't! Oh, God, no, don't, don't, don't . . ." If Tim Ireland, supervising a children's camp-out on the night of August 9, 1969, had been able to follow the distant sound of the man's voice through the shrubs and stunted pines and over the chaste lawns of Beverly Hills back to its source down the driveway at 10050 Cielo Drive, through the open door, turning right past two blue trunks toward the living room, where a huge American flag covered a couch, he might have seen the first blow knock the pregnant woman to her knees, the knives rising and falling in the delicate hands of three teenage girls, rising and falling into the prone body, killing past death. But the act had no witnesses except the victims and their killers. Only they knew that the *helter skelter* had begun. That it was *coming down fast.*

Helter skelter was the vision of a dedicated Beatles fan, a bizarre turn in the already twisted history of whites and blacks in America, a vision filtered through the blues into the music of the Liverpool Lads and thence into the LSD-saturated mind of Charles Manson, who heard in *The White Album* what every attentive Beatles fan found there: a message, an authorization, an affirmation of one's understanding of the '60s. Manson's own version of the vision was that African Americans would soon rise up like blackbirds and though their wings were broken, learn to fly. They would slaughter all the whites, those *little piggies,* but when they had seized control of the nation they would discover that they needed white expertise after all. At which point Manson and his family would emerge from hiding to lead them. Of course, this prophecy had not been vouchsafed to everyone. Just to a chosen few: John, Paul, George, Ringo—and Charlie. Dig, the Beatles were *communicating* it man, and if you dropped acid and smoked pot and listened carefully to the words of *The White Album,* you would hear it too. Leslie Van Houton, Patricia Krenwinkel, and Susan Atkins had heard it. As their knives rose and fell, rose and fell, the songs of *The White Album* surged through their veins and the screams of their victims blended with the shrieks of Beatlemania.

Manson was insane, but he was also representative. When *everything connects,* the vision can be one of joy or terror. Both possibilities lived side by side in the '60s. Bummers and Bliss. Madness and Ecstasy. Evil and Love. Evil was in the air partly because everything seemed to happen under a mushroom cloud, the stench of Auschwitz in the nostrils, the snarl of police dogs in the ears. But evil was also in the sensibility of the counterculture because the psychedelic experience of radical pluralism so often includes a rendezvous with the devil. Not just the occasional bummer, but even the normal trip could reveal that malignant power was as much at home in Being as happiness and love and peace. If acid and pot were nothing but tangerine trees and marmalade skies, marijuana would probably be legal by now and LSD might be. But at the very moment these compounds disclose the miracle of light and leaf to the tripping eye, they also disclose a horror that comes and goes, nodding and winking, just there behind the lattice of the primal elements into which the social construction of reality has temporarily dissolved. When you break on through to the other side, be prepared to meet something you hadn't quite reckoned on. As Aldous Huxley observed during his very first trip: "If you started the wrong way, everything that happened would be proof of the conspiracy against you. . . . You couldn't draw a breath without knowing it was part of the plot."

So '60s rock was often about magic, voodoo, surrenders to Dionysian amorality, and pacts with the devil, about the terrors of psychedelia and the pleasures of paranoia. Bob Dylan made this territory his own as early as 1964, with *Bringing It All Back Home* and *Highway 61 Revisited.* Then the Rolling Stones and the Doors led one to the fissure where the Beatles' field of poppies gaped open to reveal a darker underworld ruled by death and evil. There one heard, as the supreme testament, the cry of Hendrix's Stratocaster. And by the end of the decade, even the Beatles had been there too, with "Yer Blues," "Piggies," and "Helter Skelter" painting frescoes on the walls of Manson's tortured psyche. The question posed by these and many other rock musicians was the question that troubled the cohort they played to: is the discovery of alternative realities entirely benign and helpful? Or is it, as so many scriptures and folktales warn, the unearthing of something fundamentally malign at the very heart of things? Is the devil just a bugaboo meant to frighten good citizens away from the fountain of esoteric knowledge? Or does civilization require its excessive modes of vigilant repression in order to keep an essential wickedness from bursting loose into the world?

Not that "evil" has to be the name for this force. In The Band's "The Weight," we hear from a man who has pulled into a town called Nazareth feeling *half past dead* and hoping to find a place to rest and recover from his journey. What he finds instead is a mocking wheel of eternal return. Each and every encounter with the inhabitants of this town turns back upon him, leaving him saddled with a weight he can't get out from. The figures he meets—Luke, Carmen, Chester—are comical; they don't burden him with snapshots of napalmed Vietnamese villagers or news of a bombing in Birmingham. But they seem to be incarnations of a single power, dream representations of an inescapable reality, and they mesh together in one purpose: to burden him, to weigh him down, to absorb him in this nightmarish landscape. Again and again, he cries out for relief:

> *Take a load off Fanny,*
> *Take a load for free;*
> *Take a load off Fanny,*
> *And-and-and—*
> *She put the load right on me.*

This burden was nothing, of course, compared to the things being carried by an infantryman slogging at that moment through the mud of Vietnam. Few white kids in college between 1964 and 1972 suffered real hardship. Instead, they had to grope through the fog of a baffling plurality, where they encountered an inscrutable figure who, like history, always managed to get the last word:

> *Crazy Chester followed me*
> *And he caught me in the fog;*
> *He said I will fix your rack*

If you'll take Jack my dog.
I said, wait a minute Chester,
You know I'm a peaceful man.
He said, that's okay, boy,
Won't you feed him when you can.

It was the Rolling Stones, as Alan Beckett pointed out, who most consistently voiced the counterculture's realization that alternative realities include evil and violence, not just flower-power. But when the Stones musicked this misgiving, their rock expressed anger, not caution. They responded to evil with much more rage than regret. "Street Fighting Man," "Jumping Jack Flash," "Sympathy for the Devil," and "Gimme Shelter" all respond to the discovery of evil with rock that is a kind of marching music—a call to arms or, rather, to high drama. It has often been said that the Stones wrote the soundtrack for the rock culture's fantasy of revolution. But it is worth remembering that their songs are not exhortations to go out and *do* something, much less to join the forces of progressivist virtue so that capitalist evil may be defeated. Instead, the Stones musicked something much more like a frustrated child's fury, a pissed-off *why the fuck does it have to be this way?* attitude that pushed to the fore in the mid-'60s. Even while one felt the rage of a street-fighting man, one knew full well that street fighting was not the release one sought, the deliverance longed for in "I Shall Be Released." The enemy was not a gang or even a cop; it was existence itself. It was the riddling trickster who keeps asking you to guess his name while teasing you with the knowledge that the devil is behind your own eyelids. It was all too concise and too clear that you were part of a problem. That the enemy was within you, not just without you.

Even when political discourse was given new life and scope by the New Left, it could not encompass or articulate this cohort's terrifying sense that the worm of evil lay coiled within them. "Evil," wrote Deday LaRene in the essay on the Stones quoted on page 123, "is 'live' spelled backwards." Although it could not be named by a political word, this essentially paranoid and apolitical vision of rock and psychedelics—*fuck epistemology and dig it—*

breathed intense energies into the radical student movements of
the late '60s because it confirmed what so many already felt. When
you feel that your inmost self is actually a plaything dancing in the
gaze of those outside you, you're already just a step away, a *kiss
away,* from paranoia. And when you get caught up in a political
struggle against a system that has already worked its way deep inside you, that struggle is necessarily self-destructive, an attack on
yourself. Psychedelics and rock reaffirmed this bizarre meshing of
inside and outside, self and system, making it impossible to confine
evil to any one side or to tell the difference between *Lucifer* and
one's *own will.* Or between Ronald Reagan saying "If it takes a
bloodbath, let's get it over with," and Mark Rudd declaring "It must
be a wonderful feeling to kill a pig or blow up a building." *You're
dealing with an elemental force that you can use or can destroy you.*
You'll never know which, so *what difference does it make?* It is
here—where the vision of existence as a profound instability looks
liberating at one moment, then suddenly malevolent the next—
that '60s rock and '60s politics flowed into each other.

Yet because these complex feelings are seldom named by conventional politics and political language, they have been omitted
from the picture of the '60s given to us by historians concerned
with the New Left and other political movements. After all, how
could a serious scholar of politics and power take seriously such
notions as evil, ontological instability, *an elemental force that you
can use or can destroy you?* If memory has a path back to those
feelings, it makes its way through the sound of rock and the veil
of psychedelics, back to the afternoon of July 25, 1965, when Bob
Dylan took the stage at the Newport Folk Festival and declared in
music that the old politics was gone and something new and
strange was about to take its place.

✇

If, as Judith Shklar has suggested, a "liberal" is someone who
thinks that cruelty is the worst thing people do to each other, then

the early Bob Dylan was a classic liberal. More than any other popular singer of the early '60s, he forced his audience to look squarely
at the ways we are cruel to each other, whether it be the fun of
killing Emmett Till or the indifferent curiosity of people stepping
around the dead body of a street person or the callous greed of
arms manufacturers profiting from war. In "A Hard Rain's Gonna
Fall," Dylan vows that he will never stop telling and speaking and
breathing the truth about human cruelties:

> *I'll walk to the depths of the deepest black forest,*
> *Where the people are many and their hands are all empty,*
> *Where the pellets of poison are flooding their waters,*
> *Where the home in the valley meets the damp dirty prison,*
> *Where the executioner's face is always well hidden,*
> *Where hunger is ugly, where souls are forgotten,*
> *Where black is the color, where none is the number,*
> *And I'll tell it and think it and speak it and breathe it,*
> *And reflect it from the mountain so all souls can see it,*
> *Then I'll stand on the ocean until I start sinkin',*
> *But I'll know my song well before I start singin'.*

But Dylan changed abruptly. He turned, as the title of his next
album announced, to "another side" of himself. He quit playing
the role of Old Testament prophet—investigative reporter who will
reflect evil from the mountains *so all souls can see it.* He plunged
inward, into the nightmare visions of his own psyche, his "thought-
dreams" as he called them. Soon afterward, he went electric, horri-
fying and scandalizing the fans of folk music who had assumed he
shared their antipathy not just to human cruelty but to modernity. To go electric, to start playing rock, was to turn one's back on
the primitive and authentic "folk" who preserved an earth-centered
ethos against the soul-killing onslaught of modernity. It was to join
the enemy.

This metamorphosis was misunderstood at the time and I think
it continues to be, even by most of Dylan's defenders. Dylan's
change was less a rejection of folk per se than a turn from a mainly
Appalachian-ballad style of folk music to the folk music of Chicago:
electric blues. It was not so much a calculated move to garner a

larger audience as a popular artist's instinct to stay a step *ahead* of them. Dylan turned to a strongly blues-based rock because he felt that the condition named by rock—what he too would call "loneliness"—was personally more compelling and disturbing than political injustices he had witnessed. And according to Bob Spitz, the most astute chronicler of Dylan's life, there is little doubt that this sudden and radical change of focus was prompted by Dylan's discovery of LSD in the spring of 1964. It was an experience, oft-repeated, that transformed his music. He spent the next months writing many of the songs that appeared on *Bringing It All Back Home* and *Highway 61 Revisited,* and the following summer he introduced them to a startled, hostile audience at the Newport Folk Festival.

If Dylan's decision to go electric looked at the time like a renunciation of politics and a shameless embrace of modernity, what's clearer today is that Dylan was just using his acid trips to move in the direction of a *different style* of politics: not the liberal politics of the older generation but a radical politics that was as much an attack on the self as a critique of society, more an expression of confusion in the face of ontological chaos than of determination in the face of injustice to others. In Dylan's music, we hear liberal politics conceived in terms of injustice done to others reimagined as a radical politics conceived in terms of one's own loneliness. We hear the confused inscape of individual character replace liberalism's neutral but empathic distributor of justice. This was in essence a politicization of the private sphere—making the personal political as feminists would teach people to say—and it meant that a turn *inward* was a turn toward, not away from, politics. (Just as he was living through this transformation himself, Dylan wrote in the liner notes for *Another Side*: "loneliness has clutched hands and squeezes you into wrongdoing others.") Starting at that concert in Newport, Dylan began to voice the feelings that three years later drew many young whites through the process of political radicalization, a process that manifested itself in many public political actions, from antiwar demonstrations to seizures of university buildings, but that had its origins in a private war against the liberal, lonely self, what Morris Dickstein called "a psychodrama of self-validation."

In one of the clearest statements of the difference between the old politics and the new, Greg Calvert, the national secretary of SDS in early 1967, formulated the distinction between liberal and radical in terms of the different ways they configured the relation between self and other. "Liberal consciousness is conscience translated into action for others," he wrote. But "radical or revolutionary consciousness . . . is the perception of *oneself* as unfree, as oppressed—and . . . leads to *the struggle for one's own freedom in unity with others who share the burden of oppression*." In other words, radical consciousness is the paradoxical fate of Riesman's other-directed self. Now it isn't enough to work for others as, say, Pete Seeger and other folksingers imagined themselves doing. Now one had to *become* the "other," to internalize and identify with him. Now the felt absence of a self within could be filled by the other whom one affiliated with.

As soon as we were persuaded that the system was hostile not just to black Americans and Vietnamese peasants but to ourselves personally, we became "radicals." To remain a passive accomplice of the system was to be a ghost, precisely the nonentity the system worked to produce; but to become a victim or, better yet, an enemy of the state was to be something solid and real, a target, a felt presence, a skull cracking beneath a policeman's stick. The liberal whose heart bled for others rather than himself was simply denying the fact that he had no self to be concerned about. The radical repossessed this self in the very act of admitting that he or she was oppressed—conflating the oppression of others with what Osha Neumann so honestly described as oppression by one's own subjectivity. Neumann's complaint about "unreality" became Mark Rudd's "I hate this weird liberal mass of nothingness." And so, as the scene of politics shifted to include the events of the inner life, an acid-fueled trip into the void of inner space where flowers bloomed beside rotting corpses made sense, made political sense, was a political act. And this is why the loneliness of millions of otherwise apathetic white kids fed into the liberationist politics of the New Left.

Bob Dylan's turn away from explicit protest to songs about the explosion of consciousness anticipated and then gave expression to this transformation of the liberal conscience concerned about

others into the radical "perception of *oneself* as unfree, as oppressed." More than any other album, *Highway 61 Revisited* was the
masterpiece that helped the counterculture deal with this transformation by putting it into music. Looking back now, it's hard to
believe that the Dylan who conceived of this album, who crafted
its distinctive sound, and who wrote the lyrics that still astonish
and disturb, was only twenty-three years old. (Twenty-four when
the album was released.) Yet this was his *sixth* album in three years,
and that depth of experience shows. On this, the second of his
electric albums, Dylan totally commits himself to the new medium
and demonstrates total mastery of it. Compared even to *Bringing It
All Back Home,* released in the same year, *Highway 61* has a sound
that is wonderfully full, lush in melody and harmonics yet rhythmi-
cally spare and hardbitten. From the opening three drumbeats of
"Like a Rolling Stone" to the raging sadness of the harmonica solo
that concludes "Desolation Row," the sound of the album is a gorgeous put-down of sentimentality. Dylan's band does much more
than just back his vocals. They deliver a music that matches the
lyrics in intensity and nuance, and it is obvious that Dylan himself
loves their sound. The engineering carefully adjusts Dylan's vocals
and harmonica so they are only slightly out in front of the other
musicians, and Dylan's arrangements give the band a great deal of
space in which to strut their stuff. Dylan himself is suddenly more
mature. His confidence in his vision and in his ability to convey
it is complete. His voice seems to drop down an octave, assuming
a smoky, reedy texture. Rightly proud of this voice, he *displays* it,
lingering over and drawing out all the long vowels, especially
the "o's" and the "a's." And it is on this album too that he carries
his harmonica style into entirely new territory, finding in that
tiny instrument the expressive power of an alto sax. (This harmonica sound is so much his own, and he does it so well, that
no one since has even tried to imitate it, much less to extend its
capabilities.)

   With all these resources at his command, what does Dylan have
to say? From beginning to end, the album presents a consistent
vision in which grief and rage merge to bear witness to evil. Many
individual lines and stanzas do not make conventional sense. Their

function is not to describe or explain evil (or anything else) but to open up a field in which the listener's attention is seized and dropped and held and released by possibilities of meaning that amuse and interest but do not quite come into being. These intriguing ciphers are held together by a filigree of lines and phrases that are piercingly lucid. Take, for example, the first three lines of this stanza from "Tombstone Blues":

> *The ghost of Belle Starr she hands down her wits*
> *To Jezebel the nun she violently knits*
> *A bald wig for Jack the Ripper who sits . . .*

The words hang together syntactically, and they convey a vague and disturbing sense of chaos and malignance at work. But we can't figure out who Belle Starr was, why this is her ghost, what it means to hand down one's wits, or how a wig could be bald. These units of the stanza are decipherable but incoherent—like a code we have not quite broken. Then comes the final line. While it does not suddenly pull to the surface a network of meaning that was hitherto concealed, it does bring the stanza down to a very specific and concrete point of reference, to the world Dylan's audience knew and loathed and feared:

> *A bald wig for Jack the Ripper who sits*
> *At the head of the chamber of commerce.*

Tunneling through the psyche rather than mounting a frontal attack with logical analysis, this stealthy assault on middle-class complacency was devastating and delightful as soon as we "got it."

Most stanzas work in similar fashion, but a few hang together more tightly. For example, *Where Ma Rainey and Beethoven once unwrapped their bed roll* does make a kind of sense: in what may be an oblique reference to Chuck Berry's "Roll Over Beethoven," Dylan suggests that great blues and great classical music could—and did—go to bed together. The next line—*Tuba players now rehearse around the flagpole*—suggests that those days have given way to bland music in the service of nationalism. And the next line—

And the National Bank at a profit sells road maps for the soul—carries forward the cynical analysis of music and nationalism and connects these with the way capitalism profits by repackaging and marketing the very meaning it has already sucked out of life. The final line drove like a spike through the hearts and minds of college students while at the same time delighting them, since it succinctly summarized their own feelings about their situation: *To the old folks home and the college.*

And onward the song drives, every line delivered rapid-fire. The band is cooking. The lyrics come and go more quickly than we can keep up; they force us to sharpen our wits and accelerate our cognitive apprehension of them. But because Dylan bites off his words and phrases, they are anything but evanescent or ephemeral. They come out compact, sharp-edged, forged. They have the inevitability of stones, of words of poetry. Dylan calls this song "Tombstone Blues," and although it does not conform to a standard blues form, it does use blues chords, and Mike Bloomfield, on guitar, lays down plenty of blues licks. *Highway 61 Revisited* is in fact Dylan's most consistently and self-consciously *blues*-sounding and *blues*-derived album. The album title itself refers to the interstate highway traveled by many African Americans on their way to Chicago from the Mississippi delta; the highway runs through Minnesota, where Dylan grew up, and thus is also his metaphorical link to the Delta Blues. The album is a revisiting of the *blues*—of the journey from the pastoral past into urban modernity. And the underlying blues feel of the album (strongest on "It Takes a Lot to Laugh, It Takes a Train to Cry," "From a Buick Six," and "Just Like Tom Thumb's Blues") helps hold it all together as a unified aesthetic experience despite the deliberate incoherence of the parts that constitute it.

Dylan's use of the blues here brings into aural play a whole universe of references and a musical system in support of the creation of something new: a self-conscious musicking of the double consciousness of white middle-class youth. You could call it "white boys' blues," and that would be true. But you would not want the dismissive tone of that description to block your access to, and appreciation of, what Dylan and his band are using the blues form to musick. I have called the album a merging of grief and rage in the act of bearing witness to the evil that is in the world and in one's self. That was, I think, its most important quality and contribution. The relatively conventional politics of the New Left, wrote David Lewis Stein in 1969, "had little meaning for kids who dropped out of university political science courses and were huddling on mattresses in chilly rooms smoking grass and dropping acid." And listening to *Highway 61 Revisited,* no doubt. The album gave us a sound that was commensurate with our feelings because the evil it depicts is not diagnosed or analyzed. It is just presented, and in a way that speaks to the insight of the adolescent who looks at the world from the other side of the filmy screen: evil is incomprehensible because it's everywhere, woven into the fabric of existence as tightly as one's own identity is knit into a system that drops napalm on people in order to free them. *God said to Abraham, "Kill me a son,"* Abe said, *"Man, you must be puttin' me on."* But no, God is not putting him on. He wants the killing to occur and he has a particular location in mind: down on Highway 61. The *rovin' gambler* of the last stanza of the title cut wants to stage *the next world war* as a spectator event. He finds a promoter who has *never engaged in this kind of thing before:*

> **But yes I think it can be very easily done:**
> **We'll just put some bleachers out in the sun**
> **And have it on Highway 61.**

What makes the album bearable is Dylan's mordant humor, blended equally of matzo and mojo. The sheer incomprehensibility of evil makes it absurd and therefore funny. Dylan's humor is a way of managing evil, of one-upping the devil. But while Dylan always gets the last word and the best word, he never quite triumphs. His bitterness enlists humor to sharpen his despair.

It is only with tongue in cheek, then, that Dylan feigns to wish that his words could offer some kind of solace, *could ease you and cool you and cease the pain of your useless and pointless knowledge,* and his withholding of condolence, his unremitting pitilessness, is the attitude that makes this music so effective. Those privileged white kids tucked safely into their dormitory rooms at night knew very well that they were utterly undeserving of pity. The scorn Dylan lashed us with was sweet. To pity us, to feel sorry for us because our privilege had granted us the curse of being the first to experience what was promised to every successful (that is, lucky) inhabitant of modernity—that would have demeaned us further. We knew that our only dignity and thus our only redemption was a complete negativity, unencumbered by pity or self-pity, an absolute zero. When Dylan slammed the slumming rich girl who threw the bums a dime in her prime, he was scourging us in his audience, too, and we responded with a rush of gratitude. "How does it *feel*," he asked, how does it *feel* to be in this paradoxical condition in which privilege is the gate to a new kind of hell? When we have really given up, says Dylan, when we have gotten to the point where we can mail postcards from Desolation Row instead of looking into it—that is, when we have totally *surrendered* to our despair—then we can "come see" him, then we can be with him, then we can be with each other.

The desire here is what Dylan elsewhere called *Looking for my double, seeking for—complete evaporation to the core.* Song after song seeks a willed extinguishing of every flicker of mental life. To be invisible, with no secrets to conceal, is to achieve some bare minimum, some absolute poverty, an evisceration of self so thorough that only these visions will remain when we have gone. For those of us who were undergoing the process of radicalization, who felt that our only chance of redemption or release was to go through the state of our own emptiness and out the other side—a move musicked by Dylan's decision to go electric and by the Beatles' decision to exploit technology—it felt good, it felt right to take drugs that carried the risk of self-annihilation. As we tumbled down the side of a ravine, falling from safe, distanced, middle-class awareness of wrongdoing *out there* to knowledge of something more terrifying *in here,* a figure loomed suddenly in front of us, and as we stared into the vacuum of his eyes we knew that he was in us because we belonged to him, that we were evil's victims and its perpetrators, and so we yearned for the understanding we found in "Like a Rolling Stone."

> *You said you'd never*
> *compromise*
> *With the mystery tramp, but now you*
> *realize*
> *He's not selling any alibis*
> *As you stare into the vacuum of his eyes*
> *And say*
> *do you want to*
> *make a deal?*

The mystery tramp has a long background. He is the Hoochie Coochie man in one incarnation, the Voodoo Chile in another, the satanic riddler who shrieks *Won't you guess my name?* in yet another. The white middle-class kid who thought she could face this reality without flinching has suddenly realized that she's dealing with powers far stronger than she had imagined. This is the power of evil but also of voodoo, and also of the shaman, and also of psychedelics. She realizes suddenly, and too late to go back, that once you have crossed a certain line there is no return to the innocence and comfort of the past. Dylan's songs mock the adolescent forward. There's no turning back now, so don't even look back. You have to press forward, into the vacuum, hoping . . . what?

Our paradoxical hope was that the acid bath of negativity would cleanse us of all our historical contaminations, including our racial and class privileges. (I was still a few years away from being shown and seeing my privileges as a male.) Only by reducing our own subjectivity to nothing could we free others and ourselves from its oppression. Only thus could we be reborn as that person fantasized by so many songs: the innocent apostle of love greeting life with a stoned smile, a peace sign, and unshorn hair. Back in the garden again, untouched by evil. Twenty acres on a hillside in Montague, four friends in an old farmhouse, cheap red wine, lentil soup, bread. Riding that easy chair, going nowhere.

But first we had to break through to the other side and stand with the oppressed of the world. We would become, as the first Yippie manifesto put it, "the delicate spores of the new fierceness that will change America." White students, claimed Shin'ya Ono of the Weathermen, had to face up to the fact that "their only choice is either joining the world revolution led by the blacks, the yellows, and the browns, or of being put down as US imperialist pigs by the people of the Third World." Very few white students actually went that far. Only a tiny handful joined the Weathermen militants who vaunted: "We are against everything that's 'good and decent' in honky America. We will burn and loot and destroy. We are the incubation of your mother's nightmare." But many of us could feel the rage and despair that sparked these words—a rage against the world and the machine and history and ourselves and the system, call it Maggie's farm, that had nurtured and corrupted us. If we didn't throw bombs, we could at least do what the first Yippie manifesto advised: we could "create our own reality."

In a series of brilliant articles for *Ramparts,* David Horowitz described how Columbia's Russian Institute had been initiated by a member of the OSS and how it was underwritten by a five-year start-up grant from the Rockefeller Foundation, whose director of social sciences (Schuyler Wallace) was a member of the Council on Foreign Relations (CFR), as were David, John, and Nelson Rockefeller. Moreover, Horowitz showed that the institute's second director (Philip Mosely) was a former State Department officer (and the brother-in-law of Bay of Pigs architect Richard Bissell), and that of the institute's five-man steering staff "four had been associated with the OSS or the State Department, three were in the CFR, and three were members of the upper-class Century Club (as were Schuyler Wallace and Allen Dulles, the OSS veteran who went on to head the CIA)." The links Horowitz and other Left journalists uncovered among universities and their research institutes, private foundations, the CIA and the State Department, and major U.S. corporations were spellbinding and Kafkaesque.

But the shock of such revelations was not that powerful men knew each other, went to the same prep schools, married into each other's families, and checked their coats at the same clubs: one already knew that. What chilled was the depth of the academy's subservience to research as a tool of policy—policy that was being established not in the light of public debate and elections but in the interlocking boardrooms of foundations and corporations. For this fact led to the conclusion that there was no such thing as a disinterested university, and without disinterest, there was no place for students to stand. No place to think or reflect—except Maggie's farm. The very privilege of having the time and space to think at all, whether about Heracleitus or Heidegger, black holes or DNA, was underwritten by the university's increasing dependence on its corporate and foundation benefactors. Like it or not, everyone with any privilege was implicated, part of the problem. This self-knowledge turned a screw inside, and something shifted, and the world looked different. This was *radicalization*.

In crash pads and dorm rooms, by the light of guttering candles or goosenecked desk lamps, with posters of Che and Janis taped to the walls and the smoke from a joint filling their lungs, Dylan's fans followed his music into a sustained aesthetic contemplation of this force whose name they could only guess. For what was it? A demonic impulse within humankind? A universe that is not just meaningless but malignant? No one name or formula would do, and this is where rock and psychedelics had the edge over formal philosophical or theological discourse. Acid and pot seemed to confirm that once you saw the world as it was, "everything that happened would be proof of the conspiracy against you." The sharp, hard images that come hurtling out of Dylan's songs made no sense yet they somehow connected; they seemed truer to the all-encompassing incoherence of this force than any systematic attempt to explain it, whether by Milton or Marx. And it was all coming down so heavy, so fast, so soon. We knew *too soon* that there was *no sense in trying* to understand—too soon because we felt too young to bear the burden of this knowledge, knowledge that made us somehow older than our prosperous, innocent parents.

In the brilliant, agonized chapters that conclude his history of the '60s, Todd Gitlin tries to understand why the New Left, in which he had played an important part, broke into factions and allowed the most extreme militant groups to set the tone and program of the Movement. His answer is a theory of what he calls "forced revolution": radicals became increasingly radical because they were trying to make a revolution happen among people who didn't want one. Students got the revolution under way, but the working class (which, the theory ran, suffered most from the Vietnam War and from capitalist oppression) never got on board. Hardhat construction workers baffled Marxist analysis by demonstrating *in favor* of the war, and the war went on, day after day, as though all the marches and mobilizations had meant nothing. It began to seem that ever more radical measures were required. So when Ronald Reagan declared: "If it takes a bloodbath, let's get it over with," the most radicalized students were willing to accept the challenge. "The real division," said one of them, "is not between people who support bombings and people who don't, but between people who will *do* them and people who are too hung up on their own privileges and security to take those risks." And so they kept pushing and pushing, and the harder they pushed the farther they distanced themselves from the "masses" in whose name they struggled.

But Gitlin himself is not quite satisfied with this explanation, for "there is still a missing link. . . . How exactly does one get from murky theory about the world revolution to blasting caps and roofing nails? Not just through wrongheaded political analysis. . . . It asks too much of a strictly political logic, either the Pentagon's or the Weathermen's, that it should explain the building of bombs whose use it is to kill civilians at random. Nor can individual biographies account for the way revolutionaries can shade into nihilism."

What Gitlin is reaching for is something that could be spoken within rock but not within traditional political discourse, or what he calls "strictly political logic." The youth in the Weathermen were just the extreme edge of a counterculture that, as a whole, was undergoing the process of radicalization and with it the profound interpenetration of self and evil that Dylan musicks on *Highway 61 Revisited.* If "individual biographies" are unable to "account for the way revolutionaries can shade into nihilism," it is because individual biographies are unlikely to see the phenomenon more broadly—as generational, as part of a large demographic group's confused struggle to resolve simultaneously the dilemma of modern selfhood and the omnipresence of evil. The New Left had to self-destruct because the enemy was ultimately one's self. The radical had to go all the way to blasting caps and roofing nails because, feeling nothing within, she had nothing to lose. Violent acts, like drugs, broke patterns. What emerged might be good or bad but at least it was new, and with that newness came the promise of innocence. As Jacob Brockman wrote in late 1968:

> By their refusal, their mischief, their infiltration, great numbers could begin to conceive of something more decent than submitting to the culture. There was that vague and fragile chance, and although I had contempt for much my generation spawned, I could not see another chance anywhere I looked.

Four years after Dylan released *Highway 61 Revisited,* the Beatles revisited this territory on *The White Album*—that blank space in which to dwell, that long double-album for the imagination to hide in and explore. But with a critical difference. If Dylan was caught up with the problem of evil, the Beatles, with the '60s at their backs, could feel this also as the problem of history. *The White Album* was a titanic, appropriately incoherent effort, at once exhausted and heroic, to come to grips with the shape and meaning (or meaninglessness) of the '60s and beyond that the horizon of human history as a whole. The Beatles' work on the album began soon after the assassinations of Martin Luther King, Jr., and Bobby Kennedy, in the climate of the takeover of Columbia, the events of Mai in Paris, and massive student unrest in Japan, Mexico, Czechoslovakia, and Germany. While the world caught fire around them, the Beatles worked furiously in their Abbey Road studios.

A glance at their production schedule gives some sense of the effort they put into this album.

May 31: 2:30 P.M. to midnight.
June 4: 2:30 P.M. to 1 A.M.
June 10: all afternoon.
June 11: 3 hours in the evening.
June 20: 7 P.M. to 3:30 A.M.
June 21: 2:30 P.M. to 3:30 A.M.
June 25: 2 P.M. to 8 P.M.

July 9: 2 hours at night.
July 10: 7 P.M. to 1:30 A.M.
July 11: 4 P.M. to 3:45 A.M.
July 15: 5 hours.

And on and on they went, logging in long hours from late spring to early fall. ("Ob-La-Di, Ob-La-Da"—that seemingly carefree jest—required fifty-seven hours of production time.) For the making of *The White Album* was an exhausting process of layering, juxtaposing, blending, mixing, dubbing, unraveling and reweaving in a relentless search for moments of serendipity. On July 16, their longtime engineer Geoff Emerick quit, later remarking that "I lost interest in the *White Album* because they were really arguing amongst themselves and swearing at each other." On August 22, Ringo quit the band—seriously quit—and had to be wooed back. George Harrison would later say that it was during the long, long summer of 1968 that "the rot had set in."

And yet, out of this mess, forged by the pressure of the times and the pressures of their own relationships with each other, the Beatles produced the first major postmodern work of popular culture. With thirty songs in no apparent order, combining the British folk ballad tradition, Victorian band music, country western, blues, heavy metal rock, and lullabies, it is an eclectic and incoherent collage, or bricolage. Intensely aware of its audience's hunger for interpretation, it teases them with a *glass onion*—with mystery made transparent—as John mockingly sings, *You've all heard Ob-La-Di-Bla-Da, but do you know where you are?* and *Well here's another clue for you all, the walrus was Paul.* One goes to wherever Lennon is as the eagle picks his eyes and the worm licks his bones while he too goes somewhere within the world of music, feeling *just like Dylan's Mr. Jones.* Yet the very next moment one sits in the open air beside a mountain stream and listens to *the pretty sound of music as she flies.* And was Charlie Manson completely wrong? What are the final thirty-seven bars of "Helter Skelter" "about" if not violence, history (returning), drugs, and death? Ringo's scream that he has blisters on his fingers transports one for a split second out of the world of fandom and into the recording studio, the space of production, the place where cigarettes are being smoked and tea is brewed and the music is being made, and then one hears the long long time of Harrison's search for his god, and the long long time of adolescent in-betweenness, and the long long time of an acid trip in its dying glow, and the long long time that was just then being laid to rest along with the hopes of *Sgt. Pepper's.* And this song, too, ends with a gnashing of chords, a chaos of moans. Referencing so much of the history of popular music, *The White Album* ridicules efforts to assemble that history into a sequenced story.

The Beatles are still committed to their essentially comedic vision (*Yeah, yeah, yeah*), but now it stands closer than ever to the abyss of irony. The colorful world of *Sgt. Pepper's* has shattered into millions of pieces, millions of steely guitar riffs. California surfers. The Cold War. The National Rifle Association. Coal mines in the north of England. Doomed country markets with the air of carnival. Laughter. Machine-gun fire. Bungalow Bill, synthesis of British imperialism and American manifest destiny. All the children sing! Playful, but nihilistic. Inclusive, but chaotic. *You become naked,* whispers Yoko, as a child babbles and cries on "Revolution 9." If we're supposed to cry in the face of history and make our mother sigh, doesn't that mean we have to be two persons at once—the child who rejects the world as it is (and cries) and the mother who's resigned to the world as it is, yet who can't help empathizing with her child (and sighs)? There, on that narrow line separating tragedy from irony, rejection from resignation, is the place of reconciliation where we have to take our stand. It is precisely where Harrison sits while his guitar gently weeps. It is exactly where Lennon is when he sings to the mother who abandoned him that half of what he says is meaningless, but he says it just to reach her. If there is any comedy here, it is the bitter comedy of Samuel Beckett writing, "I can't go on. I'll go on." It's the terrifying comedy of McCartney shouting that he gets to the bottom then goes back to the top of the slide and he turns and he goes for a ride, up and down, stuck in the playground of history, *Helter Skelter!*

But it is comedy nonetheless. For while the Beatles musick all the emotions that made violence and self-destruction so appealing, so right, so inevitable, they pull back at the last minute, at the very edge, and draw a distinction between themselves and the Mark Rudds in their audience. When it comes to revolution, to destruction, to minds that hate, to pictures of Chairman Mao ("Dare to struggle. Dare to win."), you can count them out. While Lennon's voice whispering *in . . . in* is his way of musicking how close he is to crossing a line, he will not, in the end, cross it. In this, their most explicit statement about politics, the Beatles stay committed to music, self-consciously emphasizing the musicality of their statement, of it being a musicking statement, folding in enough music history (the blues lick opening, the loving yet self-parodying *shoobedoowah, ooh shoobedoowah*) that one has to *hear* that history and therefore hear one's own embeddedness in history and therefore take the comic view that is wiser than the vacuous rhetoric of the Weathermen calling for blood.

The literature of mysticism consistently warns that any seeker who penetrates the veil of everyday existence will at first be assaulted by demons, terrors, and devils. These are the ego's guardians, the watchdogs and gargoyles who keep the self from straying beyond the bounds of a specific ego-identity. Mystical texts assure us that these horrors, too, are just illusions, part and parcel of the web of phantasms with which the ego ties itself to this world. In the '60s, many who took the psychedelic trip to the other side found themselves surrounded and engulfed by these spectral demons. But even when they were not high, they found themselves engulfed by horrors that were stubbornly real and frighteningly near. For a cohort of middle-class youth who were trying to find some way out of the trap of their history, the psychedelic apocalypse became one with the political revolution. So much of their music now told them that they'd never get out from under the weight their history had dropped on them. The summer of love notwithstanding, they could hardly evade the fact that the ultimate expression of evil, the Faustian worst that man could do, was now a real possibility. It was implicit in the mild thoughtlessness with which their fathers lived, drawing a salary from Dow Chemical or Chase Manhattan Bank. It flamed explicitly from a Zippo lighter in Vietnam. It stared back at them from the eyes of Charles Manson or from their own eyes in a mirror, tripping past midnight in a diner's restroom. Just four years earlier, *yeah, yeah, yeah,* they were taking to the dance floor because *something was happening.* Now they found that they could not, after all, escape from history. Nor could they make it. How, then, except with "Tombstone Blues" or "Yer Blues," could they name this condition—one in which the earth's most privileged cohort was also powerless, radicalized for nothing, fated to wait for decades on the watchtower, listening to the wind rise and watching the approach of two riders who knew their destiny yet would never, it seems, arrive?

"Our Incompleteness and Our Choices"

Forgetting the '60s and Remembering Them

Oedipa wondered whether, at the end of this (if it were supposed to end), she too might not be left with only compiled memories of clues, announcements, intimations, but never the central truth itself, which must somehow each time be too bright for her memory to hold.

—**Thomas Pynchon,**
The Crying of Lot 49

I sit on the floor tonight, remembering the '60s, listening to the three songs that conclude Jimi Hendrix's *Electric Ladyland:* "House Burning Down," "All Along the Watchtower," and "Voodoo Chile (Slight Return)." What I hear in them tonight is Jimi trying out three different responses to the news that "Evil is 'live' spelled backwards," to the realization that when "the very ontological foundations are shaken . . . there are no supports, nothing to cling to, except perhaps some fragments from the wreck." "House Burning Down" opens with a searing blues riff and goes on to narrate the discovery that "brothers" kill each other, destroy each other, burn down each other's houses, seemingly for no reason. Hendrix responds to this incomprehensible violence with bewildered pain—*I said, oh baby / Why did you burn your brother's house down?*—and closes the song with a solo that unmistakably mimics the sound of warplanes bombing and strafing the fields of Vietnam. Then, after the slightest pause, his music flows into the thundering chords that open his version of Dylan's "All Along the Watchtower," another meditation on the attitude we should take toward the evils—*businessmen they drink my wine, plowmen dig my earth*—that dominate the world. This song understands our temptation to respond ironically, to conclude that, after all, *life is but a joke,* but it urges us to go a step further:

> *But you and I we've been through that*
> *And this is not our fate*
> *So let us not talk falsely now*
> *The hour's getting late.*

By 1968 Dylan had concluded that inward-turning "thought-dreams" swathed in bitter irony would no longer suffice. But now he wasn't advocating a return to liberal politics either. So what should we do? Clearly, the stance we take toward evil matters. While the princes and ladies walk along the walls of the castle, oblivious of their peril, we the misfits, the joker and the thief, must do otherwise. But what? What must we do?

Dylan's song gives no answer, and in Hendrix's version the pain of our paralysis is sharpened by the apocalyptic winds struck from the cold strings of his guitar. Hendrix labored for weeks over the song, and one eyewitness recalls that he would "pop his head around the corner and say 'Was that alright? Are you sure?' I'd say 'yeah Jimi, that's great.' He'd say, 'well I'm gonna do another one,' and we'd keep doing tracks and each one would be better than the last one and he would never think that what he did was good enough." Hendrix playing Dylan represents the consummate fusion of the blues tradition with the psychedelicized hunger of white youth enmired in loneliness and looking for a new self, trapped in history and looking desperately *for some way out of here*. Attacking these problems with all the resources of the blues, while also intensifying the blues with the visionary hopefulness of psychedelics, Hendrix's "Watchtower" is a brilliant articulation of the agony of knowing and waiting, of being aware of the approaching thunderstorm and not knowing what to do about it. This may be why the song continues to be covered by rock bands from U2 to Dave Matthews. Teenagers still stand there on the watchtower and wait and wonder.

The final song on the album, "Voodoo Chile," turned out to be the last one recorded by The Jimi Hendrix Experience. The song appears on the album twice, and as the title of the second version ("Slight Return") suggests, we are supposed to hear it as a reprise and as a coda. Standing squarely in the tradition of "I am" blues songs like "Fruit Cakin' Mama" and "Hoochie Coochie Man," and working through the classic twelve-bar blues form, it announces the presence of Jimi's personal identity, his black identity, and his identity as a performer. Like these blues songs, it is also a celebration of *power*. Jimi is standing next to a mountain, but he can chop it down with the edge of his hand. He can pick up all the pieces and make an island. After all, he's a "voodoo chile," and the voodoo chile is neither paralyzed by indecision nor overwhelmed by the demons he encounters on his trip behind the veil. Using the force of his magic and his music, calling forth the mysteries of the psychedelic blues with a sorcerer's hand, he will shatter the mountain that looms over us and build us an island in the ocean, a place apart.

Here once again is the psychedelic, *electric* vision of modernity in which music creates a world within the world. In which acid-as-voodoo reveals that the void of self is a plenitude of colors, swirls, textures, possibilities. But Jimi knows that this vision is bound to upset some people; he knows he will *raise a little sand,* and his little chuckle here lets us know that this is comic understatement, a humorous but equally confident version of Muddy Waters's *I'm gonna mess with you.* If "House Burning Down" is an expression of the bewildered pain we feel when we become aware of evil, and if "Watchtower" places that awareness in anguished confrontation with its own inaction and impending doom, "Voodoo Chile" bluntly asserts (again) that psychedelic awareness can remake the world in innocence and create new grounds for hope and action.

But, like so many other songs of the '60s, "Voodoo Chile" is also a kind of farewell. Neither the Hoochie Coochie Man nor the Fruit Cakin' Mama worried that they might be annihilated by the power they tapped into. They expressed no consciousness or fear of their own mortality. One is a "man," the other is a "mama." But the voodoo *chile* knows that self-extinction is an intrinsic part of the performance he is enacting. The power he draws on to re-create the world is in large part the power of youth, of the adolescent vision into the unstable heart of things, and as he ages, this power will fade. And because this power is drawn as well from his willingness to break through to the other side, "to risk chaos, madness, and death," to come face to face with the evil in himself and in the world, he will probably never attain the solid maturity of Muddy Waters or Ruby Smith. He has crossed to the other side and laid his hands on powers that can, and will, eventually destroy him. He knows this and he conveys the premonition of his self-extinction not just here but in song after song, his guitar meditating, musing on his death. His final words (*Well, I'll say one last thing*) speak directly to his audience's willingness to remain true to his vision, to remember it, so they can join him there, on the other side of the veil that falls between life and death, between youth and maturity, and between two ways of seeing and being in the world:

> *I didn't mean to take up all your sweet time,*
> *I'll give it right back to you one of these days.*
> > *(ha ha ha)*
> *I said, I didn't mean to take up all your sweet time,*

I'll give it right back to you one of these days.
And if I don't meet you no more in this world,
Then I'll meet you in the next one, and don't be late.

Although no performer gave himself as fully to this sense of mortality as Jimi Hendrix, the music of the '60s consistently expressed a self-conscious foreboding that the end of the '60s was as certain as the end of youth. Jimi did not have to overdose on barbiturates and choke to death on his own vomit (September 18, 1970) for these lines to have the meaning they carry. Like the Beatles, he was looking ahead to his dissolution because it was prefigured in his music. *Will the wind ever remember, the names it has blown in the past?* The question Hendrix asks—as McCartney does in "When I'm Sixty-Four"—is whether his audience will join him there on the other side of the death that would also be the "end" of the '60s, the end of youth. He is singing, in other words, about memory and history.

Thirty years later, on his 1998 *Time Out of Mind,* Bob Dylan would wearily return to the same questions. The "time" that is "out of mind" now is the '60s, as the cover art, juxtaposing today's Dylan with the Dylan of *Bringing It All Back Home,* makes plain. The time is "out of mind" in two senses: it happened long, long ago, and it seems to have been shoved into the darkest corners of public memory. In the saddest voice he has yet uncovered, Dylan seems to be singing directly to his old audience, singing as a jilted lover might, reminding them that he's been faithful and asking why they haven't been. ("I'm under the impression," Dylan said in an interview that year, "that people aren't really paying attention to my records.") On "Dirt Road Blues"—that *blues* again—he recommits himself to the task he has always performed. He's going to *keep on walkin' 'til there's nothin' more to see.* As in "All Along the Watchtower," he will continue to confront our apocalyptic future: *it's not dark yet, but it's getting there.* Meanwhile, what about his old audience? Are we really listening to his songs? Are we still walking with him?

This is another way of asking not what the '60s meant, but what they mean. I began writing this book because it seemed to me that the '60s I knew best, a particular '60s, had been oversimplified and forgotten. This '60s was in experience a predicament. Like many others, I hungered for meaning and for a self that was more satisfying than the phantom I'd been given by my culture. Yet, again like many others, I also accepted the likelihood that no such meaning could be found, that the terms of existence had been radically altered by modernity, and that wisdom required me to accept, even embrace, the fate of a disenchanted world and a voided self. The modern world's hostility to an inner life with meaning and warmth seemed to be writ large in America's techno-mechanical war against Vietnam, in white America's blind unwillingness to see the humanity of black Americans, and in the subordination of learning and free inquiry to the needs of the military-industrial complex.

Essential to that '60s was the music in which I and my friends thought about and worked through this predicament—usually unconsciously, always at an aesthetic remove—trying to reconfigure it, to find a way out, to come to some peace. We did not think that the music was a solution. Not even the Beatles at their most giddily optimistic could offer us a simple triumph of connection over anomie, love over loneliness, peace over war. Every good rock musician emphasized now one, now another facet of this predicament, and the best of them made clear that each facet was just a part of a larger and more complex whole. The sound of my yearning for transcendence came through with aching clarity in "I Shall Be Released" or Neil Young's "Helpless" or Jefferson Airplane's "Somebody to Love" or Dylan's "I Want You" or his "I Dreamed I Saw Saint Augustine." The sound of a bemused and worldly acceptance came through in "The Weight" or the Beatles' "She's So Heavy" or the Stones' "You Can't Always Get What You Want." I seemed always to be in both places at the same time. And so did the people I knew and the many I did not know who sat and listened to such music with rapt attention. Both then and now, the question confronting us was: what do we *do* with our vision?

As a historian, I know that my generation was probably not the first to experience this predicament—indeed I wonder if there's a long-standing pattern of conflict between the dynamics of capitalism and the American construction of youth. I am thinking not only of the "lost generation" that came of age during and just after the First World War, not only of generation X and generation Next, but of young New Englanders in the 1840s. Emerson reflected on these early slackers in one of his lectures:

It is a sign of our times, conspicuous to the coarsest observer, that many intelligent and religious persons withdraw themselves from common labors and competitions of the market and the caucus. . . . When I asked them concerning their private experience, they answered somewhat in this wise: . . . mine is a certain brief experience, which surprised me in the highway or in the market, or in some place, at some time,—whether in the body or out of the body, God knoweth,—and made me aware that I had played the fool with fools all this time. . . . Well, in the space of an hour, probably, I was let down from this height; I was at my old tricks, the selfish member of a selfish society. My life is superficial, takes no root in the deep world; I ask, When shall I die, and be relieved of the responsibility of seeing an Universe which I do not use? I wish to exchange this flash-of-lightning faith for continuous daylight, this fever-glow for a benign climate.

In the 1840s, as in the 1960s, young people dropped out of the "common labors and competitions of the market" because they had been surprised by a private experience that they could not sustain and that left them once again selfish members of a selfish society.

Yet there is an important difference between the '60s and these other periods. In the '60s, the self-willed breakthrough to alternative states of consciousness (what Emerson here calls "flash-of-lightning faith") was much more widely publicized and consequently much more commonly experienced. When Ralph Waldo Emerson or William James or even Allen Ginsberg wrote about the private experience of breakthrough, their work was available to a relatively small circle of cognoscenti. When Virginia Woolf developed a prose style that conveyed these other states of consciousness with breathtaking force, she found an audience (small, cosmopolitan, educated) that understood and appreciated her achievement. But when Bob Dylan proclaimed with mocking good humor that "*Everybody* must get stoned" and proceeded to unfold songs that constructed a play-space for the altered consciousness, he reached an audience of tens of millions, and the vast majority of these were kids—teenagers, adolescents. The audience that gathered around the Beatles was even larger. In turn, this extraordinary publication of the breakthrough experience briefly created a wild paradox: it created a culture that defined itself as a "counter" culture, as a "benign climate" where the "flash-of-lightning" experiences of transcendence, flux, and radical self-redefinition were honored and sustained. As I have tried to show, I went into this culture with joy, but I also ran into a presence there that disturbed and frightened me. We could name that presence with a word like "evil" or "devil"; we could use the image of Dylan's "mystery tramp"; we could look into the eyes of Charles Manson. But in every case we would only be gesturing toward a ghost that is just as indescribable as the mystic's more joyful epiphany, as "the girl with the sun in her eyes" who is "gone" as soon as we look for her.

Does the ephemerality of the vision make it fundamentally apolitical, as most historians of the New Left think? Does the danger of breakthrough mean that it should be prohibited, as critics like Allan Bloom seem to suggest when they claim that Nuremberg and Woodstock were essentially the same? Emerson, Whitman, and Ginsberg all thought that keeping this knowledge hidden (in mystery, ritual, and the like) and controlled (by priesthood and professions) was fundamentally at odds with democracy. So, I think, did Bob Dylan. And so did the audience he played to. This is why the counterpart to the '60s effort to put democracy in the streets was the counterculture's push to put breakthrough, or vision, there. Not just the best minds of a generation, but *everybody* must get stoned.

In turn, though, the unprecedented publication of the breakthrough experience, which entailed an anarchistic antipathy to all cultural conventions, and to traditional politics of both Left and Right, helps explain the vehemence with which the '60s have been rejected and the diligence with which they are oversimplified and distorted. While the writers of the 1840s and of the 1920s have now been included in the mainstream of American culture, the radical vision of the '60s remains outside the pale of what can be accepted. Even Americans who lived through the '60s and remember them with respect are likely, in some recesses of memory, to be deeply afraid of them. I know I am.

But remember I must, if only in order to demur when Daniel Bell writes that "Beginning with the 'new sound' of the Beatles in

1964, rock reached such soaring crescendos that it was impossible to hear oneself think, and that may indeed have been its intention." Did Bell ever *listen* to the Beatles? Surely what was "new" about so much rock of the '60s—and especially about the music of the Beatles and Dylan—was that, while it gave the physical pleasure of being overwhelmed by large sound, it also invited one "to hear oneself think" and provided an aesthetic space in which thinking could take place. Bell likewise advances the broad claim (based solely on Susan Sontag's essay "Against Interpretation") that the "sensibility of the sixties" was hostile to interpretation. But surely the lyrics of '60s rock, and especially of Dylan and the Beatles, deliberately provoked their audience to wonder and discuss what they were "really about"—an interpretive activity still going strong, thirty years later, on the hundreds of Web sites devoted to their work. Bell, like so many observers of the decade, had trouble seeing its complexity and nuances partly because he was so *shocked* by one or more of its aspects, and partly because he wants so much to fit this complex decade into a rather simple narrative about the history of the last seventy years.

More recently, Francis Fukuyama has claimed that the '60s "counterculture worked . . . harm on the weakest members of American society." The '60s, he writes, were

> about breaking out of the stifling norms and taboos of mid-century America. The most visible manifestations were the loosening of moral restraints on sex and drugs. The rates of single-parent families and drug addiction were always higher within the black community than among whites, but the incidence of both began to skyrocket for African Americans only after the late 1960s.

I share some of Fukuyama's worries about the consequences of the counterculture, but is he really writing in good faith when he tries to pin the problems of "the black community" on hippies and radical chic? How can he so totally ignore that the late '60s were not just the peak of the counterculture but what economist Lester Thurow has described as "a surge in a long immobile glacier," a turning point at which "economic inequality started to rise," so that by the early 1990s, the share of wealth (more than 40 percent) held by the top 1 percent of the population was essentially double what it had been in the mid-1970s and back to where it was in the late 1920s, before the introduction of progressive taxation? Fukuyama turns a blind eye to these facts because he wants to pin the blame for the steady widening of the gap between the richest and all other Americans on the shibboleth of cultural radicalism.

But neoconservative historians and critics are not the only ones to engage in oversimplification that rubs out the complexity of the '60s counterculture. When we see today how extensively youth are exploited as a consumer market, it's easy to understand why cultural critics like Jacques Attali are skeptical about the critical capacities of rock. When we see that funky health-food stores have turned into nationwide businesses, we can understand why some Left historians have interpreted the disruptions of the '60s as a sweeping away of the detritus of early and precapitalist traditions in order to make space for the brave new world of the 1980s and '90s—a world in which "globalized" capitalism usurps local and even national autonomy, in which acquisitions and mergers take the place of manufacturing and public investment, and in which the proliferation of goods and markets makes consumerism a total way of life. Contemporary critics of the '60s like Thomas Frank are simply following in the footsteps of Regis Debray, who argued decades ago that the self-styled revolutionaries of the '60s were the dupes of this larger history: "What appeared to them to be constraints on their existence as individuals turned out to be, in the last analysis, constraints on the extension of the market across the whole field of social life." Christopher Lasch similarly, though much more willing to acknowledge the complexities of the '60s, nonetheless folds the history of that decade into his master narrative of America's march toward total narcissism and "the therapeutic sensibility."

As I've tried to show, none of these criticisms would have surprised the audience for '60s rock. By musicking the "explosive combination of promise and disappointment" that constituted youth in the '60s, rock voiced its own self-criticism from the beginning. Dylan especially dealt with the shadow, with the dark side of the breakthrough experience, with the corruption of love and the presence of evil within us, vomiting a flood of words that knew themselves to be ineluctably a part of the thing they hated. These *dis-illusioned words like bullets bark, as human gods aim for their mark,* and they offer as much solace as scab-picking. They give voice to that other side of the '60s, to a tough-minded clarity and cynicism that kept pace, step by step, with the dance of love and peace and flowers.

This is the voice we hear all through *Highway 61*. It's the voice we hear in a leaflet distributed in Haight-Ashbury by the Communication Company, warning that "Rape is as common as bullshit on Haight Street" and asking, "Does acid still have to be sold as hard as Madison Avenue still sells sex? What do these nice people mean by 'Love?'" Three thousand miles away, a writer for the *East Village Other* asks the same question: "Is love a fond hallucination remaining as a verbal residue after a brought-down acid consciousness—a memento mori? . . . What does it mean in tenements and brickpiles and police stations and racial antagonisms and among those who have no other choice but to be exploited?" And it's the voice of Joni Mitchell looking back at the '60s and sighing

> *Acid booze and ass*
> *Needles guns and grass*
> *Lots of laughs . . . lots of laughs.*

These voices of the rock culture were relentlessly self-critical because they knew themselves to be inextricably caught up in the dynamics of American society, constituted by its expectant gaze, a part of the problem until they became part of the solution. Young, yet fated to grow old.

Today, despite the prevalence of versions of the '60s that try to silence these voices, they can be heard in music that is still available to offer a more complex understanding. Sixties rock not only survives, it flourishes. Millions of younger Americans are listening to it. Every college campus today shelters a sizable subculture of guys with long hair, jeans, and flannel shirts and girls who go barefoot in India-print skirts; their style, speech, and gesture mimic with astonishing fidelity the style of the counterculture, which they can have seen only indirectly—on the jacket sleeves of old Neil Young albums or in videos of *Woodstock*. Meanwhile, many of the most popular bands of the 1990s (Dave Matthews, Phish, Smashing

Pumpkins, U2, Oasis, Nirvana) produced a sound that is sometimes startlingly '60s-like and even pays homage to '60s classics. These bands and their audiences are drawn to the resources of '60s rock because, in significant measure, they are dealing with the same issues. The Smashing Pumpkins, to take just one example, are as familiar with the inscape of the void (*the world is a vampire*) as Bob Dylan, and so, I suppose, is their audience. They sing out of the loneliness that was the condition of adolescents thirty and forty years ago, from the *nowhere* between childhood and a rotten maturity:

> *welcome to nowhere fast*
> *nothing here ever lasts*
> *nothing but memories of what never was*
> *we're nowhere, we're nowhere, we're nowhere to be*
> *nowhere, we're nowhere, we're nowhere to see*
> *living makes me sick*
> *so sick I wish I'd die*

But this despair is not the only note they hit. A filigree of psychedelic hope runs through their work—in the cover art of *Mellon Collie and the Infinite Sadness* and in lyrics like

> *and in my mind as I was floating*
> *far above the clouds*
> *some children laughed I'd fall for certain*
> *for thinking that I'd last forever*
> *but I knew exactly where I was*
> *and I knew the meaning of it all*
> *and I knew the distance to the sun*
> *and I knew the echo that is love*

So while Fukuyama and Debray and I squabble in the captain's tower, calypso singers laugh at us, and the music of the '60s goes right on evolving a memory of itself that is far more powerful and widespread than anything we might put in print, as the popularity of raves, trip hop, and acid jazz and the enduring meaningfulness of the word "psychedelic" all attest.

The '60s are not over for American culture. They might scarcely have begun. We are still asking what the vision was for. We are still coping with the consequences of a moment when the instability of the foundations was revealed, and celebrated. We are still wrestling with the sense of a beginning that may also be an ending— both tomorrow *and* the end of time. And we are trying to do so when the very notion of history itself may no longer make sense, or not the same sense anyway, because of what happened in the '60s. When Norman Mailer stood on the greensward near the Lincoln Memorial on the afternoon of August 21, 1967, observing the troops of the counterculture who had gathered to march on the Pentagon, he found himself reflecting on the way LSD seemed to be destroying history as thoroughly as technology was destroying nature:

> If nature was a veil whose tissue had been ripped by static, screams of jet motors, the highway grid of the suburbs, smog, defoliation, pollution of streams, overfertilization of earth, anti-fertilization of women, the radiation of two decades of near blind atomic busting, then perhaps the history of the past was another tissue, spiritual, no doubt, without physical embodiment, unless its embodiment was the cuneiform hieroglyphics of the chromosome (so much like primitive writing!) but that tissue of past history, whether traceable in the flesh, or merely palpable in the collective underworld of the dream, was nonetheless being bombed by the use of LSD as outrageously as the atoll of Eniwetok, Hiroshima, Nagasaki, and the scorched foliage of Vietnam.

I don't know if Mailer ever took LSD himself, but his notion that psychedelics were bombing the past has a certain intuitive force. What he's looking at as he muses are the clothes worn by his troops—buckskins, jeans, top hats, ponchos, army surplus jackets, turbans, capes, even a "knight unhorsed who stalked about in the weight of real armor"—and he interprets this indiscriminate indifference to sequence, order, chronology, and social position as an expression of what psychedelics had done to the historical imagination of these young persons. Bombed it to smithereens, so that the "history of the past was being exploded right into the present." Just as psychedelics reduced one's ability to organize perceptions according to categories of the more and less important, so they also annihilated one's ability to perceive history as an immutably ordered sequence of events receding endlessly into the past. Bombed by LSD, time loses coherence and depth. Events of both the past and the present become contemporaries, splashes of color on a two-dimensional plane—just as Poe and Marx take their places near Sonny Liston and Marilyn Monroe on the cover of *Sgt. Pepper's*. So if we seem to have freed ourselves from the idea that the past determines us simply by virtue of its coming earlier in a chain of causes and consequences, we may be newly confined in the claustrophobia of an eternal present that is always at the same time the past. This sense of history is even harder to escape. As Michael Herr wryly remarked after returning to the United States from Vietnam: "Those who remember the past are condemned to repeat it too, that's a little history joke."

You may never have taken LSD, but America has. And what Aldous Huxley wrote of the individual tripper—"the man who comes back through the Door in the Wall will never be quite the same as the man who went out"—is true of American culture as a whole. Which may be why Americans can't forget or expunge the '60s no matter how hard we try. All that business is unfinished within us. As W. S. Merwin has so beautifully put it:

> We know that age to be utterly beyond reach now, irretrievably a past, a period whose distance we already feel as though it had stretched into centuries, and yet it appears to us to be not only recent but present, still with us not as a memory but as a part of our unfinished days, a ground or backdrop before which we live. It could be said that we are haunted by it, which would suggest that that time was not done with in us, that what we saw and felt then is still part of our incompleteness and our choices.

If what Merwin means by "our choices" is the memory we collectively make of the '60s, and the use we make of that memory to guide our actions in the future, then we should begin by remembering that we do not come to these choices unprepared. As I've tried to show, rock of the '60s was deeply concerned with memory and history—and with how it would be remembered itself. Most famously, Don McLean's "American Pie," which was the #1 song for many weeks in 1972, offered its audience an extended meditation on the meaning of '60s rock and in particular on what McLean saw as the victory of the satanic vision over prepsychedelic innocence. Less obviously, Neil Young's *After the Gold Rush* (1971) brooded over the problem of reconciling one's self to the disintegration of the dream: *It's over,* mourned Young. *All things must pass,* sang George Harrison. Even back in 1967, on the cover of *Sgt. Pepper's,* wax effigies of the young Beatles gazed down at the flowers that marked their grave, while the Lonely Hearts Club Band, in full regalia and surrounded by the encouraging, knowing faces of their predecessors on the stage of popular culture, looked steadily into an endless vista of the future, meeting the eyes of all who would look back at them, withdrawing into the past even as they stood forth from it.

But it was Dylan, not surprisingly, who first folded this awareness of the transience of '60s popular culture and the ephemerality of youth into his songs. To those who listened carefully to "My Back Pages" back in 1964, the song's *Ah, but I was so much older then, I'm younger than that now* might have meant that the loss of youth's idealism is not a mark of growing up but of growing down, not of maturity but of regression. To those with more interest in irony and ambiguity, the lyrics might have suggested something quite different: that the idealist's first angry response to injustice is mistaken. That by trying to *rip down all hate* I may be promulgating another *half-wracked prejudice,* and that by simplistically seeing *life as black and white* I may be turning into my *enemy.* Perhaps only by moving beyond conventional stories and clear oppositions (*Good and bad, I define these terms / Quite clear, no doubt, somehow*) does one become truly oppositional, that is, "younger" rather than "older." Looking back from the postmodern cool of the new millennium, one hears in this song an adumbration of our skepticism toward claims that any truth can give us the foundations for our beliefs:

> *I dreamed*
> *Romantic facts of musketeers*
> *Foundationed deep, somehow*

Ah, but I was so much older then,
I'm younger than that now.

And if, as was most likely, one simply let the words and images flow through one's consciousness—*crimson flames, corpse evangelists, mongrel dogs, confusion boats*—one might have heard the refrain simply as an enigma, like a zen koan, to be absorbed and contemplated inwardly. If one dwelt within this paradox of becoming younger rather than older, and did not seek to decode or make sense of it, one might have dwelt within the unaccountability of time. It did not move straightforwardly from "before" to "after," or from "young" to "old," or from "the '60s" to "the '90s." Time was more like a house with many rooms: just as you never knew where you'd be, you never knew for sure when you'd be.

"Bob Dylan's Dream" (1963) and "Chimes of Freedom" (1964), too, are uncannily prescient about the problem of fixing in memory a moment dedicated to instability. In "Dream," Dylan sings that he fell asleep *on a train goin' west* and had *a dream that made me sad / Concerning myself and the first few friends I had.* The dream turns out to be a vision of the future, a future in which these friends lose touch with one another and lose the world they made, and held, in common:

As easy it was to tell black from white
It was all that easy to tell wrong from right.
And our choices were few and the thought never hit
That the one road we traveled would ever shatter and split.

In "Chimes of Freedom," Dylan and a friend (or friends) are surprised by a strange joy that comes in a powerful lightning and thunder storm. *As majestic bells of bolts struck shadows in the sounds,* these seemed to be *the chimes of freedom flashing.* The synesthetic fusion of sound and sight allows them to see and empathize with numerous victims of injustice and unfairness, from *refugees on the unarmed road of flight* to the *mistreated, mateless mother,* from the *mistitled prostitute* to the *countless confused, accused, misused, strung-out ones and worse.* But Dylan complicates the experience of this vision by introducing a note of premature loss, of anticipated nostalgia. Even though the song was released in 1964, its final verse reminds us, in case we had not noticed, that the events narrated in the song occurred in the *past*. He now *recalls* that vision, recalls how he and his companion were once exhilarated, *starry-eyed and laughin'* as they *listened one last time* and *watched with one last look, / Spellbound and swallowed 'til the tolling ended.* Just as the distinction between *home* and *away* blurs for the person who has tripped to the other side of the veil, so too does the distinction between past and future. The vision always knows its own ephemerality, what Emerson called its "flash-of-lightning faith," what Pynchon describes as a truth "too bright for . . . memory to hold." The knowledge of its imminent dispersal is present even when the vision waxes brightest. That bitter taste of that foreknowledge was present in the mouth of anyone who lived, no matter how spellbound and swallowed, in the '60s I have tried to write about. We always knew it would end because the music itself told us it would: *when the music's over, turn out the lights.*

So maybe it's fitting that this '60s hasn't been integrated into the nation's history. I don't believe strongly enough in the values of tradition or in the honesty of sweeping epics about "the American experience" to wish for the vision expressed by rock and psychedelics to be woven into a seamless story about national progress or national decline. The '60s I lived, and in particular my experience of altered states of consciousness, make wholehearted belief in such coherence impossible. I heard the sound of glass breaking too many times in *The White Album* to feel that we can ever put all the pieces back together again. And I also understand what Nietzsche meant when he remarked that "a historical phenomenon, completely understood and reduced to an item of knowledge, is, in relation to the man who knows it, dead." I don't want to comprehend the '60s and place them in the museum where infinity goes up on trial. I'd prefer to let this moment remain out there on what he calls "the earthly and darkened horizon that was the source of its power for history," even if that means waiting ourselves on the watchtower, waiting and watching while the wind begins to howl.

Yet I'm not content to sit by and watch as the '60s get reduced to a mere caricature. I believe that the best of the music of the '60s was as good, in its own way, as any art ever produced. It was good because it didn't oversimplify. It celebrated transcendence, but it also warned against the dangers of going too far and staying too long. It could be a loud and rhythmic invitation to surrender consciousness to sensation, but it richly used the resources of the blues to musick the double consciousness of its adolescent audience. It offered the feeling of community and solidarity that young people felt was missing from the American way of life, yet it also provided a refuge within which a young person could experience individual selfhood with a satisfaction not derived from the gaze of others. It painted bright pictures of the counterculture ("Penny Lane") and it provided bleak ones ("Desolation Row"). It expressed utopian hopes, but it infused and tempered these with historical self-consciousness.

This historical self-consciousness—which is consciousness of living in a *different kind* of history—is an essential aspect of what seems to me now to have been the enduring contribution of '60s rock: its comic vision of reconciliation. While the New Left was torn between a dream of seizing our place *in* history and a dream of revolution that would deliver us *from* history, rock offered a perspective that embraced both these desires and yet gave greater authority to the former. For the comic perspective, which sees us all as ineluctably enmeshed in history, ultimately subsumes the revolutionary utopian perspective simply by locating it in the ebb and flow of history's tides. The comedic perspective is inclusive, so it speaks of "coming together" and "getting together," while the utopian desire is a disjunctive and dismissive impulse to "get out of this place," to find "some kind of way out of here," to get "back to Miss Fanny." The vast field of '60s rock was able to include both these poles and everything between them—from conventional romance ("Bus Stop") to revolutionary arrogance ("God bless their pointy little heads"), from romantic musings on the death of youth ("I Don't Live Today") to celebrations of cosmic love ("May This Be Love"), from cynical critiques of consumer capitalism ("Satisfaction") to meditations on history and memory ("Deja Vu"). Taken as a whole, rock created an inclusiveness that was both troubled and smart. And within the vast field of '60s rock 'n' roll, it was above all Dylan and the Beatles who were most able to put the comic and historical vision into music.

But what can sustain the comic vision itself? To dwell in the comic attitude without lapsing into cynicism is strenuous. To distinguish reconciliation from resignation requires vigilance and fortitude—the kind Joni Mitchell, Carlos Santana, and Van Morrison have shown as they go on producing albums that carry forward and complicate what they first saw in the '60s. To live and work as an agent in history even while one knows that history might be meaningless or worse is heroic. (*Who is willing to save a world that's destined to die?*) While adolescents are endowed with such heroism, even if it's only a demand for high drama, as adults we grow out of it and must create it for ourselves. Few of us have done so. And that is why, for the past thirty years, we have been living in an age of cynicism, looking for something else but not yet finding it. Yet not quite giving up either. I think this, too, is what Merwin means by "our incompleteness and our choices."

What does it mean to me, then, as I look back from the near shore of the twenty-first century, that these songs of the '60s anticipated the difficulty I have now as I try to recover a richer memory of that decade, one that gives it a place in my present instead of consigning it to the oblivion of a reckless youth? It is as if these songs' own consciousness of the brevity of their vision and the futility of adolescence created a genie who could fly forward through time and greet me when I arrived here. And it is as if these songs managed to supersede their ephemerality and outmaneuver their futility by allowing me to experience thirty years ago what I experience today. They challenge me to sustain a vision that remembers more of what the '60s were about than public memory has allowed. Hearing four bars of an old song on the radio, I try to remember the loneliness, the breakthroughs, the vertigo of radicalization, and the awareness of a fundamental instability that looked like ecstasy at one moment, like evil the next. Catching a sudden slant of light, I try to hold it all in one gaze, as *Sgt. Pepper's* managed to do. It is as if I can begin to see these songs and the '60s as a whole, not as a moment that occurred once and was gone forever, but as a part of our present as real as anything I see and touch in this instant, this *now* that has just taken its place alongside these other fragments we call *the past*. After all, tomorrow never knows.

It remembers.

Music, Form, and Meaning

This book is predicated on three beliefs: First, that music is an intentional activity and that its intentions include the production of meanings; certainly, musicians and audiences assume that their musical activity will produce not just sounds but meaningful sounds. Second, that while a piece of music may not mean precisely the same things to each and every person, it will mean some shared things to listeners who collectively regard themselves as an audience for that music; if this sharing, or overlap, did not occur, music would be a merely private activity, like meditation, not a public activity that both requires and helps make a social group. Third, that some of the meanings produced through music can be used as a way to know ourselves and the world around us.

Because none of these assumptions is subject to indisputable verification (not even in the most rigorous ethnographic studies), they constitute a terrain of intense debate among philosophers and musicologists. As I prepared to write this book, I immersed myself in that debate for several months, hoping to find a consensus among experts about such basic questions as how music "means" things and what the relation might be between musical and linguistic meaning. Unfortunately, no such consensus exists.

However, although many would regard her work as rather dated by now, I found Susanne K. Langer's speculative hypotheses about musical meaning to be exceptionally helpful. In *Philosophy in a New Key,* Langer argues that music evokes feelings by giving us "presentational symbols" of them. By "presentational" she aims to distinguish music from language, which is, in her terms, a "discursive symbol" system. Whereas discursive symbols work by manifestly resembling or by standing for a thing (as the picture of a dog might resemble, or as the collar of a dog might stand for, a dog), presentational symbols work mysteriously, in ways that cannot be described precisely in the discursive symbology of language. The point of contact between a presentational symbol and the thing symbolized is *form,* which Langer defines as the relation between the parts, or elements, of a thing. Somehow, the form of the presentational symbol resembles (Langer's term is "iconic with") the form of the thing symbolized. Somehow, for example, the relationship among the elements of a piece of music will resemble the relationship among the elements of an emotion. If the music makes us feel sad, it is because the formal structure of sadness is somehow akin to the formal structure of this music.

Whatever its drawbacks, Langer's theory at least has the merit of accounting for the fact that when I listen to music I like and understand, I feel that I am both receiving and creating meaning. That is, I feel that my response to the music is to some extent determined by it and to some extent created by my subjective state at that moment. Langer's emphasis on form allows for this mix of determination and freedom that seems to characterize my listening to music. At the same time, Langer's distinction between presentational and discursive symbology helps describe, if it does not quite explain, why I feel that music has coherent meanings even though I am seldom able to put these into words.

Readers who balk at the suggestion that our emotional life might take certain "forms" might find it helpful to bear in mind that in other contexts we feel quite comfortable with this metaphor. When historians, for example, write about "moments," "eras," "epochs," or "ages" in history, they express our intuition (or simply reproduce our narrative) that in particular times and places people can share a tenor or tone of life, a set of historical conditions, however infinitely varied their individual lives must be. No two persons have precisely the same experience of anything. What they share, rather, is something like a ground or condition that *informs*—but does not entirely determine—their experiences. The metaphor of "form" seems applicable because it allows for a coexistence of similarity and difference. And to those who insist that to be real a form must be visible, I would point out that we can never actually see the form of a triangle (we see only particular triangles) yet we find it useful to think of "three-sidedness" as the form all triangles share.

Some readers might balk also at the notion, taken for granted throughout this book, that music is a way of knowing the world. To understand music as a way of knowing, it is helpful to rethink what we might mean by that word. The western tradition of philosophy has encouraged us to regard "knowing" as the attainment of a privileged position from which we look out, or back, at experience and see it as it "really" is. This tradition encourages us to esteem most highly those kinds of knowing—for example, mathematics and logic—that appear to be least contaminated by the messy stuff of everyday life. This way of thinking about knowing has, as a corollary, the view that the mind is essentially different from the body. Just as knowing occurs outside of experience, so too the mind is most itself when it disentangles itself from the limiting and distorting confines of embodiment. Not surprisingly, this tradition has difficulty imagining that an *aesthetic* experience of the senses has value in terms of cognition or knowledge in the mind. But a number of countertraditions have developed other understandings of knowledge and its relation to experience and embodiment. I have been influenced especially by pragmatism and phenomenology, both of which have managed to describe "knowing" as an activity of the human organism as a whole, not just that part we metaphorically designate "the mind."

The Form and Work of the Blues

I f popular music conveys certain meanings to its audience, however different these might be from the meanings of words, then the historian's job is to come up with words that convey the shape, if not the substance, of that music's meaning. One of the sharpest disappointments of my own research into the history of the blues and rock has been to find so few accounts that deal with music not just lyrics, sounds not just words, rhythms not just verses.

Fortunately, the blues have specific formal features that give them their distinctive aural qualities and that offer us a path into the ways the blues deliver meanings. The first of these we might call intonation. A blues song is not put together with notes that are utterly unfamiliar to a person schooled exclusively in the European musical tradition. In fact, the blues make constant use of the notes and sounds of music as Europeans know these. But at the same time, of course, the blues rigorously inflect and alter those notes—*blues* them—so that they fade into the background somewhat, serving more as a foil to be referenced than as the material out of which the music is made. In the words of musicologist Christopher Small, the blues performer feels European procedures "not as a fixed frame in which he has to work, but rather as a support around which the creative act can take place."

The blues in this way seem continually to mediate between two traditions and two worlds, and to meditate on the relationship between an abstracted whiteness and an intonated coloring, between a system of sounds approved by a society and a systematic interpretation of those sounds by those whom that society oppresses. In the European classical tradition, when an operatic voice or a virtuoso violinist "hits" a note, the miracle we are called to listen to is that of a mere mortal achieving an absolute. There it is—a high "C"—like the human realization of a Platonic form! In the blues, however, the musician reaches for something else. If the blues trumpet seeks and finds that high note, it does so not only to assert the miracle of human mastery but to project an intense and inward emotion into open space. Often the blues musician chooses this moment to most emphatically "bend" the note, teasing it up or down toward other notes in order to wring from it a breadth of feeling not conveyed by a single note sustained in its own exact form. The blues musician's altering of notes is not, of course, a misunderstanding, a cultural inability to hear the note as it is defined in European music; indeed, the blueing of the note would make little sense unless the performer and his audience already had that note in its European form in their aural vocabulary. Precisely that tension between traditions, between different musical universes and different social worlds, is a crucial part of what the inflected note is concerned to express. The note in its Euro-American form is not an ideality to be reached for and achieved but a notion to comment on, to infuse with the priorities of African musical traditions and the presence of the black performing self. The blues *sound* is for this reason continuously dialogical—a musical spanning of two social spaces. It's an example of what critics today would call "hybridity."

We can think of this feature of the blues as closely related to, perhaps even an expression of, a second formal feature: the call-and-response structure that, we have good reason to believe, captured Africans brought with them when they were transported as slaves to America. In the blues we almost always hear a conversation—between two people, two attitudes, two moods, and between an individual and a community. The *content* of that conversation is infinitely variable; so is its tone, which may be angry, good-humored, competitive, ironic, and so on. But if the voice of the soloist has nothing to say to the voice of the chorus, and if the voice of the instrument makes no comment on the voice of the singer, the song is unlikely to be a blues. If the band is not engaged in a relationship with its audience, and if that audience is not encouraging the band to push on or ease up, to aspire for more or settle back, it is unlikely to be a blues performance.

A similar conversational or dialogical dynamic can be heard and felt in the relation between improvisation and regularity in the blues. The blues are repetitive, and deliberately so. To an ear that can't get into the blues, the songs are all "the same" and therefore boring. Yet to performers and audiences who love the blues, their essential sameness is both a comfort and a challenge. The simple and familiar structure of a blues song allows us to perceive its outline as a whole, and thus to feel it as a whole, and thus in turn to notice each and every detail of the song's inscape that the blues performer is transforming and taking possession of. One can think of this dialogue as a conversation between individual and group or as an interplay of spontaneity and structure. As Albert Murray has written: "no matter how deeply moved a musician may be, whether by personal, social, or even aesthetic circumstances, he must always play notes that fulfill the requirements of the context, a feat which presupposes far more skill and taste than raw emotion." The blues is thus a structure that belongs to the community, but each blues performer makes his or her own house. Bessie Smith is not Sarah Vaughn, Robert Johnson is not Elmore James, Howlin' Wolf is not Muddy Waters. Each performer has to find a way to render the familiar new, thereby creating a self out of the materials given by others.

"I know why you're sitting up front," I once heard Clarence "Gatemouth" Brown say to the first rows of his audience. "You all just want to steal my licks." The "lick," a third formal feature of the blues, consists of relatively few notes, all taken from a single scale, yet combined and inflected in a new way. Made one's own. The lick is always a combination, or a combination lock, which other performers, friends and rivals, try to figure out and reproduce. Of course, the best blues performers not only master the licks of their predecessors but add to the repertoire others will inherit, thereby reproducing and extending the past. In other words, the blues lick is cultural memory at work and in the making. When a blues performer launches into improvising flight, the very wings on which he or she is borne aloft are a complex intermingling of tradition and invention, past and future, others and self. Thus, the blues lick replicates on a smaller scale the series of tensions—between European and African, between individual and community, between comfort and challenge, between the old and the new—that we hear making the blues *sound* what it is.

Finally, a tension of this sort can be felt also in the paradigmatic (1–4–1–4–5–4–1) chord progression of the blues. This progression begins by establishing a tense dialogue between the tonic (1) and subdominant (4) chords. The nature, or content, of that dialogue varies from song to song. The 4 chord might be a weary echo of the 1 chord; it might be a wry comment, or put-down, of the feeling the first has enunciated. But whatever specific emotional content they generate, the movement back and forth from the 1 to the 4, from the 4 to the 1, and from the 1 back to the 4 again builds suspense. We feel pressure and desire building within the song and within our gut: the blues want to burst through to a third place, to a third possibility beyond the tightly dualistic confines that have been established by the first two chords. Take, for example, Robert Johnson's "Love in Vain":

> *When the train, it left the station (1)*
> *with two lights on behind (4)*
> *When the train, it left the station (1)*
> *with two lights on behind (4)*

Here the chord movement works right alongside the lyrics to create in sound the tension created by the words: we want to know what the emotional outcome or resolution of this moment will be. This release, or resolution, will be the work of the dominant (5) chord. It tears open the woven fabric. It disrupts the dialogue. It creates movement out of stasis. Johnson sings:

> *Well, the blue light was my blues (5)*
> *and the red light was my mind (4)*

And whether the 5 chord is uplifting or dispiriting, mocking or joyous, it always points to a freedom won by the sudden and radical intensification of feeling it brings into the song:

> *Rock me baby, (1) rock me all night long. (4)*
> *Rock me baby, honey, (1) rock me all night long. (4)*
> *I want you to rock me baby, (5) like my back ain't got no bone. (4)*

For better or worse, though (depending on the song), the duration of the 5 chord is brief. Hard on its heels comes the familiar 4 chord, and then we descend back down the ladder of the 4 chord and then further down the "turn around" to the 1 chord and the condition established at the song's beginning. We are weary at heart, or maybe grateful, back where we started, ready to begin again. Booker T. ("Bukka") White once remarked that "the blues come from behind a mule." Behind the mule, the plowman reaches the end of the row and finds a momentary respite, even satisfaction; then he wheels the mule around and regards—with what emotion?—both the furrows dug and the unplowed field that calls to him, imperiously.

This series of interlocking and mutually reinforcing tensions— the pull between two musical traditions we hear in the intonation or bending of the blues note, the pull between community and individual we hear in the relation between instruments and voice, the pull between tradition and innovation we hear in the blues lick and in the dialogue between regularity and improvisation, the pull between stasis and change, or between the worldly and the transcendent we hear in the basic blues progression—is what constitutes the formal structure of the blues. It is what creates the blues *sound*. Taken as a whole, this sound makes perfect sense, sounds "right," because it so powerfully expresses what the early blues audience was *feeling*: an "explosive combination of promise and disappointment that constituted freedom for African Americans" in the post-Reconstruction decades. It was a condition of being both inside and outside, of being free yet unfree, of being released into new possibilities of individuality yet more deeply tied to community identity than ever before, of feeling happy and feeling unspeakably low, of transcendence and immobility, of connection and isolation. It was a condition, to use Du Bois's famous metaphor, of living behind a "veil": "It is a peculiar sensation, this double-consciousness, this sense of always looking at one's self through the eyes of others, of measuring one's soul by the tape of a world that looks on in amused contempt and pity." This doubleness is expressed in musical tensions at every moment in the blues, regardless of whether a particular song is happy or sad, exuberant or moody. This doubleness is what Ralph Ellison has called a combination of "the tragic and the comic":

> The blues speak to us simultaneously of the tragic and the comic aspects of the human condition and they express a profound sense of life shared by many Negro Americans precisely because their lives combined these modes. This has been the heritage of a people who for hundreds of years could not celebrate birth or dignify death and whose need to live despite the dehumanizing pressures of slavery developed an endless capacity for laughing at their painful experiences.

Could this heritage, embodied and expressed in the very *sound* of the blues, have been totally unavailable to the white teenagers who absorbed so much of that sound in their own music? When they first heard rhythm and blues and liked it, can their appreciation have failed utterly to take in these meanings of the blues? Is it possible for anyone to hear a musical form and not hear what that form was designed to deal with? Could white kids have simply liked the blues sound and not respected it? My answer to all these questions is No. While there is no evidence to suggest that white kids *consciously* heard the heritage within the blues, there is no evidence that black audiences did either. For that is not how music works. It is not discursive, indicative, definitive. It works beyond or beneath words and affects our cognitions in ways that we are seldom conscious of.

To take just one of literally hundreds of examples: in his rollicking twelve-bar blues, "Rainy Day Woman #12 & 35," Bob Dylan uses the pivotal emphasis of the 5 chord to identify comically with his listeners' loneliness and the familiar 4 chord to assure them that the emerging community of psychedelics will provide the companionship they need:

> Well they'll stone you when you're trying to be so good, (1)
> They'll stone you just like they said they would. (4)
> They'll stone you when you're trying to go home. (1)
> And they'll stone you when you're there all alone. (4)
> But I would not feel so all alone (5)
> Everybody must get stoned! (4)

Of course, each and every blues song uses the blues form in its own way. Ruby Smith's "Fruit Cakin' Mama" is an instance of what is now known as the "classic blues"—blues sung primarily in cities and towns, most often by women, between roughly 1910 and 1930. Structurally, this song is a standard blues (twelve bars with an *aab* stanza form draped across a 1–4–5 chord progression). Like so much of the classic blues, "Fruit Cakin' Mama" is a playful song about a woman's determination to be herself and to assert her power within social relationships. Ruby's voice is silky, sensual, strong, moving between a lilting tease and a mocking growl as she sings:

> I'm a fruit cakin' mama, (1) monkey men let me be. (4)
> I'm a fruit cakin' mama, (1) monkey men let me be. (4)
> 'Cause you can't get my peaches, (5) so don't go shakin' my
>   tree. (4)
>
> You can take me out men, but you sure can't make me fall.
> You can take me out men, but you sure can't make me fall.
> You can take me to my door, kiss me goodnight and that's all.
>
> Well I may be dumb, but I ain't deaf and blind.
> I may be dumb, but I ain't deaf and blind.
> I've seen enough of men to know just what is on their mind.
>
> Now I ain't no yes mama, I'll go riding in your car.
> I ain't no yes mama, but I'll go riding in your car.
> But I won't leave town 'cause I may have to walk too far.
>
> I've just never loved nobody, don't take me seriously.
> I ain't never loved nobody, don't take me seriously.
> I'm just a fruit cakin' mama, and 'taint nothin' else to me.

If the sound of the blues expresses a condition of double con-sciousness, the words Ruby Smith sings give that doubleness a par-ticular shape. Her song is about identity: who she really is in strug-gle with whom other people take her to be. Each stanza turns on the pivot of a "but" that drops like a veil between the expectations others have of her and the knowledge she has of herself. She is a pleasure-loving "fruit cakin' mama," *but* she is not loose or easy. She will go for a ride in a man's car, *but* if he gets fresh she is prepared to get out and walk home. She enjoys the company of men and will let them escort her to her door, *but* they should not count on being asked inside. Ruby walks, in short, a very fine line that she has drawn herself. She respects her own desires enough to disdain conventional expectations of "proper" female behavior. But that very respect also means that she is a capable guardian of her own integrity and will get what she wants on terms acceptable to herself. Ruby is asserting the existence of, and her right to, a middle space between Victorian prudery on the one hand and sub-mission to male desire on the other. She is asserting that she does *not* have to give up something essential to herself in order to live with dignity. While society might declare that for women especially no such space or possibility exists, her song helps bring it into being.

What's at stake in Ruby's song becomes even clearer when we look at the specifics of her situation as a black woman in the early decades of the century. As a number of historians have shown, black female identity at this time tended to be viewed by whites in terms of a sharp binary: a black woman meant a responsible and nurturing solicitude (the black mammy) or she signified unbridled sexual appetite (the black whore). Many middle-class women's clubs *within* the African American community responded to this binary by rigidly upholding Victorian standards of female probity and aggressively policing the behavior of African American women. They asserted, in other words, the truth of one side of the binary and the falsehood of the other. In their eyes, blues music and blues singers like Ruby Smith, Ma Rainey, and Bessie Smith represented the false side, and they worked hard to distance the black middle-class community from them. They would have been scandalized by the brazenly pleasure-loving, sensuous, and independent fruit cakin' mama of this song, seeing her as the very embodiment of everything white society accused black women of being.

Ruby's song, then, is a reply to three kinds of audience and a kind of compact with a fourth. To white folks (if any listened), it contested the binary prism through which they sorted and judged black women. To middle-class blacks who accepted that binary, it asserted an alternative, a way to be yourself without submitting to the classifying gaze of whites. To men, the explicitly referenced audience of the song, it said something powerful about sexual politics: don't imagine that your desire has priority over mine. And to the black women in her audience whose minds were not already made up, and who were dealing, in the particular way they had to deal, with the condition of the veil and double consciousness as black *women* experienced these, Ruby was confirming Du Bois's claim that it's possible to embrace both sides of a bifurcated identity—in this case one's desire *and* one's dignity. Her song is a working through of the general condition of the veil experienced by so many African American persons of both genders, expressing for both the conflict between surging expectations and repressive social structures, at once resisting those structures and asserting the possibility of a new relationship to them. It is about the pain of being labeled and about the necessity, even joy, of acknowledging a real identity behind that label. At the same time, Ruby Smith's blues is also working through the more specific, but still *formally* similar, conditions of many African American women in particular. These conditions, too, were the product of a complex tension between promise and disappointment, empowerment and oppression, freedom and restriction. When Ruby Smith walks a tightrope between social disapproval and male greed, defiantly proclaiming her identity as a "fruit cakin' mama" who cannot be subsumed or subordinated by social conventions, she is enacting a situation that was shared by many African American women (and no doubt by many white women as well). In these complex and layered ways then, the lyrics of her song develop and articulate with great specificity what the sound of the blues was always saying.

Like "Fruit Cakin' Mama," Muddy Waters's "Hoochie Coochie Man," a Chicago blues from the 1950s, is explicitly an assertion of personal identity—what one might call an "I am" song:

The gypsy woman told my mother before I was born,
You got a boy child's comin', gonna be a son of a gun.
He gonna make pretty women jump and shout,
Then the world wanna know what this all about,
But you know I'm here, everybody knows I'm here.
I'm the hoochie coochie man, everybody knows I'm here.

I got a black cat bone, I got a mojo too,
I got a John-the-Conqueror root, I'm gonna mess with you.
I'm gonna make you girls lead me by my hand,
Then the world'll know I'm the hoochie koochie man.
But you know I'm here, everybody knows I'm here.
I'm the hoochie coochie man, everybody knows I'm here.

On the seventh hour, of the seventh day,
On the seventh month, the seventh doctor say,
"You were born for good luck and that you'll see."
I got seven hundred dollars, don't you mess with me,
But you know I'm here, everybody knows I'm here.
I'm the hoochie coochie man, everybody knows I'm here.

If these lyrics seem to lack the dynamic complexities of "Fruit Cakin' Mama"—to be a song of simple assertion rather than of negotiation and struggle—that is because we are not hearing the sound of Muddy Waters's delivery. His voice, "bottomless" as someone has described it, sings these words with menace, exultation, and mystery. Its timbre requires us to take seriously the song's references to magic and voodoo—to the "black cat bone," the "mojo" hand, and the "John-the-Conqueror root." If we dismiss these too quickly as mere anachronisms, we'll fail to see that they point not just to particular beliefs and practices but to larger and vaguer mysteries. They point to a knowledge—to the fact that the song is clearly about *knowing*. The gypsy woman *knows* something the singer's mother doesn't know, and so does the seventh doctor. But most crucially, the song insists on something that *"everybody* knows" (you have to hear the way Muddy Waters draws out *"every*body"). Why, if everybody knows he's here, does the hoochie coochie man have to tell them that he is? The answer, I think, is that most people have repressed this knowledge, so that the work of the song is to bring this knowledge into consciousness, to remind us all of what we already know: that the hoochie coochie man is *here*.

Who, then, is the hoochie coochie man? Most directly, he is the musician as shaman. He deals in magic and mystery, and he represents those ways of seeing the world that get denied by commonsense values and conventional vision. He is a bluesman, and his music, like all music, is there to remind us that the surface of everyday life is undergirded by mystery. That beneath the world mapped by words is another world we can reach and describe only through the language of music. The mystery itself can't be named, only felt. We can point to it with phrases and metaphors—being requires nothingness, life is in league with death, rationality requires madness, the visible turns into the invisible, alternative modes of consciousness are all around us, the air is filled with voices—but these are not much better than the terms the song itself provides: a black cat bone, a mojo hand. The song reminds us that we're not supposed to explicate these mysteries (an absurd and impossible task by definition) but to acknowledge their *presence,* to remember that they are always *here,* like the hoochie coochie man himself. The song thus sets a standard for us. Like the hoochie coochie man, we should be able to live in this world and another, in this "here" and another. We should inhabit, in other words, a double consciousness because only a double consciousness can do justice to existence as humans encounter it. This is why, as Du Bois had claimed, double consciousness is not just a burden but a mystical gift of "second sight," a complexity of perception that is truer to the world as we find it than monocular vision, than the narrow-minded convention of empiricism.

At the same time, though, Du Bois's words should remind us that the gift of second sight can come out of intensely painful historical experience. And this is what the *sound* of Muddy Waters's voice tells us too. The threatening urgency within his voice is a response to something. To denial. To repeated denial that he is *here.* If "everybody knows I'm here" really means "everybody knows I'm here but they're pretending that I'm not," the question "Don't you know I'm here?" becomes more pointed. It means: "What's the matter with *you* that *you* don't know, that you refuse to acknowledge my presence?" Muddy's menacing tone and the violence carried by

"I'm gonna mess with you" and "don't you mess with me" underscore the fury of the hoochie coochie man. He is angry because he has been rendered invisible, and he brings all his musical resources to bear against the "you" who is so invested in denying knowledge of him.

If something like this is at work in the song, shouldn't we also hear it as an expression of a black man's rage against a culture—white culture—that refuses to acknowledge his humanity, power, and presence? Isn't there an affinity between the emotions of this song and the emotions that drive the main character of Ralph Ellison's *Invisible Man* (written at almost exactly the same time)? Isn't the song living in the contradiction that for African Americans second sight is both a burden and a blessing, a product of painful history that grants one special insight into that history? If so, not just the sound but the words of "Hoochie Coochie Man" are dealing with the same formal tensions, or dynamics, that are at work also in "Fruit Cakin' Mama" and countless other blues. The exact *content* of these emotions is different. Ruby Smith and Muddy Waters experienced in different ways the condition of living behind a veil, of coping with the "explosive combination of promise and disappointment that constituted freedom for African Americans," of reconciling "the tragic and the comic aspects of the human condition." But the underlying form of their experiences—a tug of war between empowerment and oppression, between feeling good and feeling bad, between comedy and tragedy—remains constant.

That form of experience is "iconic with," to use Susanne Langer's term, the form of the blues. And this helps explain in turn why white kids of the 1960s—and now millions more worldwide—find the blues form so expressive, so powerful, so right. They, too, live behind a veil, and they too experience an explosive combination of promise and disappointment that characterizes the modernity of the late twentieth century.

Introduction. "Living to Music"

"I wake up in the morning": John Cunnick, *Helix* (Seattle) vol. 2, no. 8, December 11, 1967, unpaginated. Cunnick's distinction between studying music and being involved in it has been interestingly discussed by Jeanne Bamberger as the distinction between "knowing" and "knowing about" music. See "Coming to Hear in a New Way" in *Musical Perceptions,* ed. Rita Aiello (New York: Oxford University Press, 1994), pp. 131–151. I believe Jon Blacking is making an analogous distinction when he writes that "music is not a language that describes the way society seems to be, but a metaphorical expression of feelings associated with the way society really is." Blacking, *How Musical Is Man?* (Seattle: University of Washington Press, 1973), p. 104.

the '60s fusion of rock music and psychedelics: In appendix 1, I deal briefly with the vexed issue of whether music has "meaning" and if so of what kind—emotional, cognitive, expressive, referential, and so on. My own discussion of popular music is essentially phenomenological, as the fundamental assumptions and values underlying the book as a whole are pragmatist. A useful overview of phenomenological approaches to music can be found in Edward Lippman, *A History of Western Musical Aesthetics* (Lincoln: University of Nebraska Press, 1992), pp. 437–469. The tendency among scholars of popular music today is to emphasize the ways music's "knowing" or noetic qualities are limited and mediated by social structures, what Teresa de Lauretis calls "technologies of gender." By contrast, one of the most forthright advocates of music's usefulness and reliability is Lawrence Grossberg. Simon Frith and Susan McClary also reject the notion that popular music is merely false consciousness, but they are more cautious and guarded. While I'm aware that all of '60s rock was mediated by certain institutions—record companies, reviewers, rock concert organizers, and promoters—I'm more interested here in the creativity exercised by individuals (especially those in the audience) within those constraints, playing with the cards they were dealt and trying to improvise games that seemed worthwhile. See Teresa de Lauretis, *Technologies of Gender* (Bloomington: University of Indiana Press, 1987); Lawrence Grossberg, "The Political Status of Youth and Youth Culture," in *Adolescents and Their Music: If It's Too Loud, You're Too Old,* ed. Jonathon S. Epstein (New York: Garland Publishers, 1994), pp. 25–46, and Grossberg, *We Gotta Get Out of This Place: Popular Conservatism and Postmodern Culture* (New York: Routledge, 1972); Simon Frith, *Sound Effects: Youth, Leisure, and the Politics of Rock 'n' Roll* (New York: Pantheon Books, 1981); Richard Leppert and Susan McClary, eds., *Music and Society: The Politics of Composition, Performance, and Reception* (Cambridge: Cambridge University Press, 1987); Susan McClary, *Feminine Endings: Music, Gender, and Sexuality* (Minneapolis: University of Minnesota Press, 1991). An exceptionally informed account of the business side of rock is Fred Goodman's *The Mansion on the Hill: Dylan, Young, Geffen, Springsteen, and the Head-on Collision of Rock and Commerce* (New York: Times Books, 1997). An interesting account of music and meaning produced from *within* the '60s can be found in George Steiner, "A Conversation with Claude Levi-Strauss," *Encounter,* April 1966; passage reprinted in *The Movement toward a New America,* ed. Mitchell Goodman (New York: Pilgrim Press/Alfred A. Knopf, 1970), p. 372.

"I become real to myself for the first time": Norman Mailer, quoted in *Conversations with Norman Mailer,* ed. Jay Michael Lennon (Jackson: University Press of Mississippi, 1988), p. 47.

roughly 20 million young people: I know of no reliable estimates of the audience for rock generally and for what was called the "college market" in particular. According to Robert C. Light, about half of the 75 million baby boomers went to college. If half of these, in turn, identified with the "we" Jon Landau and Dave Marsh refer to, then the audience would number approximately 19 million. Another way to estimate is to start with the fact that *The White Album* sold more than 2 million copies in the United States in the first ten days after its release in 1968 and remained the number one album for seven more weeks. Estimating the total sales figure to be 4 million, and calculating that at least three persons (siblings and friends) listened to each unit sold, then we would have a total "core" Beatles audience of about 12 million. If half of these took the Beatles as seriously as Cunnick and his friends took their music, then we're talking about 6 million persons. Light, *Baby Boomers* (New York: W. W. Norton, 1988), pp. 221–222.

Most historians of the political '60s: Todd Gitlin, *The Sixties: Years of Hope, Days of Rage* (New York: Bantam Books, 1987), is the notable exception to this general rule. More typical is Meta Mendel-Reyes's otherwise excellent *Reclaiming Democracy: The Sixties in Politics and Memory* (New York: Routledge, 1995), which tries to analyze '60s youth politics without dealing with "sixties culture (e.g. 'sex, drugs, and rock and roll,' Elvis, Jimi, Janis, the Beatles, the Stones, surfboards, beehives, split-levels, pillbox hats, marijuana, LSD, strobe lights, lava lamps, bellbottoms, headbands, beads, Haight-Ashbury, Andy Warhol, *The Graduate, Easy Rider, The Man from U.N.C.L.E.*)." Maurice Isserman's balanced and important *If I Had a Hammer: The Death of the Old Left and the Birth of the New Left* (New York: Basic Books, 1989) refers only in passing to music, mentioning Peter, Paul, and Mary and Bob Dylan. Indeed, Isserman writes that "the upheavals of the 1960s were produced by a complex interaction of demographics, economics, and politics" (p. xvii), implying that the counterculture was a product of, not a player in, those upheavals. Allen J. Matusow makes a game effort to write about "The Rise and Fall of a Counterculture," but his analysis consists merely of Nietzsche's Apollonian/Dionysian distinction, and his account is perforce superficial, consisting of phrases like "the Beatles induced mystic ecstasies with LSD" (p. 296) and the "Dionysian impulse in the hippie counterculture was made up in equal measures of drugs, sex, and music" (p. 293). Matusow, *The Unraveling of America: A History of Liberalism in the 1960s* (New York: Harper and Row, 1984). In his fine early account of the politics of the '60s, Godfrey Hodgson thought it sufficient to say that the years 1965 to 1968 "saw the illusion that chemistry could free the human mind spin through the full cycle from frenzied hope and bombastic prophecy to panic, paranoia and catastrophe" (p. 328). He repeatedly describes the counterculture's enthusiasm for LSD as a "craze" (pp. 328–329) and leaves it at that. Hodgson, *America in Our Time: From World War II to Nixon—What Happened and Why* (New York: Vintage Books, 1978).

"the gravest omission in my text may well be cultural": Jim Miller, *Democracy Is in the Streets: From Port Huron to the Siege of Chicago* (Cambridge: Harvard University Press, 1994), p. 5. Yet Miller quotes Richard Flack's remark that "to understand The Port Huron Statement, you have to understand Bob Dylan." I suspect that Miller himself would agree, and agree also with what rock critic Simon Frith said of John Lennon's work: it "confirmed what I believed then and believe still—that it is not possible to separate the hippy aspects of the 1960s youth culture . . . from the

political process which fed the student movement, the anti-war movement, May 1968, the women's movement, gay liberation." See Frith, *Music for Pleasure: Essays in the Sociology of Pop* (New York: Routledge, 1988), p. 75. But if conventional historiography cannot manage to discuss the deep connections between rock and politics, then new forms of history must be invented. This book is one such attempt.

"To make drug consciousness": David Farber, *Chicago '68* (Chicago: University of Chicago Press, 1988), pp. 221–222.

second class of books: Daniel Bell's chapter "The Sensibility of the Sixties" in *The Cultural Contradictions of Capitalism* (New York: Basic Books, 1976), pp. 120–145, set the tone for much of what followed. The locus classicus of '60s-bashing remains *Destructive Generation: Second Thoughts about the Sixties* (New York: Summit Books, 1989), by Peter Collier and David Horowitz. See also Peter Marin, "An American Yearning: Seeking Cures for Freedom's Terrors," *Harper's,* December 1996.

"The problem was that you didn't always know": Michael Herr, *Dispatches* (New York: Vintage International, 1991), p. 20.

"amnesias" and "oblivions": Benedict Anderson, *Imagined Communities: Reflections on the Origin and Spread of Nationalism* (London: Verso Press, 1983), p. 204. Interestingly, the specific example Anderson gives is of the oblivion that falls between infancy and adulthood: "Out of this estrangement comes a conception of personhood, *identity* (yes, you and that naked baby are identical) which, because it cannot be 'remembered,' must be narrated."

"There are profound things that went wrong": Newt Gingrich, quoted in the *New York Times,* November 10, 1994, p. A1.

"hip capitalism": Thomas Frank, *The Conquest of Cool: Business Culture, Counterculture, and the Rise of Hip Consumerism* (Chicago: University of Chicago Press, 1997), p. 26. Frank neatly summarizes the ironies that abound in cultural memory of the '60s on pp. 1–7.

"the permanent revolution": R. W. Davenport and the Editors of *Fortune, USA, the Permanent Revolution,* quoted in Godfrey Hodgson, *America in Our Time,* p. 77.

"the sound of mountains crashing": Norman Mailer, *Miami and the Siege of Chicago* (New York: Signet Books, 1968), p. 142.

the most authoritative study of national drug use: The Monitoring the Future Study (MTF), Institute for Social Research, University of Michigan (for the National Institute on Drug Abuse).

"We know that age to be utterly beyond reach": W. S. Merwin, *The Second Book of Four Poems* (Port Townsend, Wash.: Copper Canyon Press, 1993), p. 2.

Chapter 1. "Something That Never Happened Before"

"A few days after the first performance": Greil Marcus, "The Beatles," in *The Rolling Stone Illustrated History of Rock & Roll*, ed. Jim Miller (New York: Random House/Rolling Stone: 1980), p. 181. Marcus is quoting Bob Dylan, who remembered: "We were driving through Colorado [and] we had the radio on and eight of the Top Ten songs were Beatles songs. In Colorado! . . . Everybody else thought they were for teenyboppers, that they were gonna pass right away. But it was obvious to me that they had staying power. I knew they were pointing in the direction where music had to go. . . . It seemed to me a definite line was being drawn. This was something that never happened before" (p. 179).

the recent and shocking rumor that Paul was dead: Deday LaRene's authoritative account (*Creem,* vol. 2, no. 6 [undated], pp. 5–8) of the "Paul Is Dead" rumor ("number nine" said backwards is "turn me on, dead man") traced it to Fred LaBour's article for *The Michigan Daily.* LaBour himself had heard it on the street. See also Barbara Suczek, "The Curious Case of the 'Death' of Paul McCartney," in *The Beatles Reader,* ed. Charles P. Neises (Ann Arbor: Pierian Press, 1984), pp. 27–39.

the Beatles had bought an island: In fact, Lennon had bought an island off the coast of Ireland and offered it as a place for hippies and others in the rock culture to camp out.

"the decade now drawing to a close": Richard Rovere, *New York Times Magazine,* December 14, 1969.

smart, liberal, college-educated white men: This view was widely held in liberal circles. Benjamin DeMott, in the issue of the *New York Times Magazine* just cited, wrote that "a powerful lesson taught by the Vietnam War . . . was that bureaucrats, diplomats, generals, and presidents who allow themselves to be locked into orthodox, culturally sanctioned patterns of thought and assumption make fearful mistakes" (p. 124). DeMott is right about the "lesson," but he should have included the profit motive among the "culturally sanctioned patterns of thought" the power elite was (is) "locked into." Cf. Bob Dylan's "Masters of War."

tripling the number of American dead (from 16,000 to 57,000): This figure is from James Carroll's beautiful memoir, *An American Requiem: God, My Father, and the War That Came between Us* (Boston: Houghton Mifflin Co., 1997), p. 192. The exact numbers are 16,459 and 56,835.

"The fact that we were buying the records": Jon Landau, "John Wesley Harding," in *The Age of Rock: Sounds of the American Cultural Revolution,* ed. Jonathan Eisen (New York: Vintage Books, 1969), p. 219.

"Another clue from the Beatles": Review of *Abbey Road* by Deday LaRene, *Creem,* vol. 2, no. 5 (undated), p. 5.

"The Beatles' music had just become popular": Stan Kaplan, quoted in Annie Gottlieb, *Do You Believe in Magic? The Second Coming of the Sixties Generation* (New York: Times Books, 1987), p. 39.

"Everything before them is sort of blurry": Dave Marsh, in *Creem,* vol. 2, no. 5 (undated), p. 22.

"Man, what done got into them ofays?": Eldridge Cleaver, *Soul on Ice* (New York: McGraw-Hill, 1968), p. 198.

"Suddenly you could breathe freely": Vaclav Havel, quoted in Jim Miller, *Democracy Is in the Streets: From Port Huron to the Siege of Chicago* (Cambridge: Harvard University Press), p. 5.

"In the beginning": Miller, *The Rolling Stone Illustrated History of Rock & Roll,* p. 1.

"We all dressed up": John Lennon, interviewed by Jann Wenner in *Rolling Stone Interviews, 1967–1980* (New York: St. Martin's, 1981), p. 130.

"Feeling the press of complexity upon the emptiness of life": The Port Huron Statement, in Miller, *Democracy Is in the Streets,* p. 330.

"One, two, three, fuck!": Greil Marcus in Miller, *The Rolling Stone Illustrated History of Rock & Roll,* p. 180.

Beatles expert Mark Lewisohn: Quoted by Mark Hertsgaard in *A Day in the Life: The Music and Artistry of the Beatles* (New York: Delacorte Press, 1995), p. 26. Hertsgaard's is the best single book on the music of the Beatles.

federal penitentiary on McNeal Island: From Vincent Bugliosi, *Helter Skelter: The True Story of the Manson Murders* (New York: Bantam Books, 1975), p. 197.

"something fundamental had changed": Cleaver, *Soul on Ice,* p. 198.

"stared straight ahead, didn't twitch once": Nik Cohn, *Rock from the Beginning* (New York: Stein and Day, 1969), pp. 165–166.

"The Beatles changed American consciousness": Allen Ginsberg, quoted in Geoffrey and Brenda Giuliano, *The Lost Beatles Interviews* (New York: Dutton Books, 1994), p. 371.

"Somehow Sgt. Pepper's *did not stop the Vietnam War"*: *Rolling Stone Interviews, 1967–1980,* p. 163.

"it becomes necessary to stabilize precisely because stability is not natural": Jacques Derrida, "Remarks on Deconstruction and Pragmatism," in *Deconstruction and Pragmatism,* ed. Chantal Mouffe (London: Routledge, 1996),

pp. 83–84. The reference to the "founding and irreducible" primacy of change is also to Derrida, id.

"What I can say about the Beatles": Warren Zevon, quoted in Giuliano, *The Lost Beatles Interviews,* p. 373.

"Where did you get the idea for the haircuts?": Quoted in Giuliano, *The Lost Beatles Interviews,* p. 13.

"What did you expect to find here in Australia?": Quoted in Giuliano, *The Lost Beatles Interviews,* p. 21.

"Do you plan to record any anti-war songs?": Quoted in Giuliano, *The Lost Beatles Interviews,* p. 38.

"How has your image changed since 1963?": Quoted in Giuliano, *The Lost Beatles Interviews,* p. 88.

"Why do you think you're so popular?": Quoted in Giuliano, *The Lost Beatles Interviews,* p. 13.

"In 1965, the average person": Ellen Willis, "Records, Rock, Etc.," *The New Yorker,* July 6, 1968, reprinted in *Rock She Wrote: Women Write about Rock, Pop, and Rap,* ed. Evelyn McDonnell and Ann Powers (New York: Delta, 1995), p. 420.

"Thank You Girl" (1963) "shows Lennon and McCartney cultivating their audience": Ian MacDonald, *Revolution Is in the Head: The Beatles' Records and the Sixties* (New York: Henry Holt, 1994), p. 44.

"Through the centuries, artists and visionaries": Gene Youngblood, reprinted in *Kaleidoscope* (Milwaukee), vol. 1, no. 5, December 22–January 4, 1968, p. 2.

"our gods are created by a conscious or unconscious fear of aloneness": Bani Shorter, *Susceptible to the Sacred: The Psychological Experience of Ritual* (New York: Routledge, 1996), p. 21.

"We write songs": Paul McCartney, quoted in William J. Dowlding, *Beatlesongs* (New York: Fireside, 1989), p. 161.

"If we have any influence on youth at all": John Lennon, quoted in Giuliano, *The Lost Beatles Interviews,* p. 120.

"infinitely precious and possessed of unfulfilled capacities": The Port Huron Statement, in Miller, *Democracy Is in the Streets,* p. 332.

"the Beatles affected not only the feel": Greil Marcus, "The Beatles," in Miller, *The Rolling Stone Illustrated History of Rock & Roll,* p. 182.

1996 was the highest-grossing year in Beatles history: Report on National Public Radio, "All Things Considered," October 22, 1996.

"a sense of limitless, unbounded futurity": Geoffrey Stokes, Ken Tucker, and Ed Ward, *Rock of Ages: The Rolling Stone History of Rock & Roll* (New York: Summit Books, 1986), p. 279.

"You get to the bit where you think, if we're going to do philosophy": Quoted in Dowlding, *Beatlesongs*, pp. 33–34.

Chapter 2. "Heartbreak Hotel"

"The inner events of an adolescent": Peter Marin, "The Open Truth and Fiery Violence of Youth: A Sort of Soliloquy," *The Center Magazine*, no. 2 (January 1969), pp. 61–74, reprinted in *The Radical Vision: Essays for the Seventies,* ed. Leo Hamalian and Frederick R. Karl (New York: Thomas Y. Crowell, 1970), p. 330.

"lonely? Ah yes": Bob Dylan, "Outlined Epitaphs," *Lyrics, 1962–1985* (New York: Alfred A. Knopf), p. 116.

"I experienced my oppression": Neumann also writes: "In everyday life, the forces of repression are omnipresent but veiled. Civil disobedience is the reagent that precipitates these repressive forces out of the formless fluidity of our humdrum existence." Neumann, "Motherfuckers Then and Now: My Sixties Problem," in *Cultural Politics and Social Movements,* ed. Marcy Darnovsky, Barbara Epstein, and Robert Flacks (Philadelphia: Temple University Press, 1995), pp. 27, 71.

"(You Ain't Nothin' but a) Hound Dog": The song has a quirky history best told by Greil Marcus in *Mystery Train: Images of America in Rock 'n' Roll Music* (New York: Obelisk/Dutton, 1975), p. 155:

> Jerry Lieber and Mike Stoller were Jewish boys from the East Coast who fell in love with black music. Hustling in Los Angeles in the early fifties, they wrote "Hound Dog" and promoted the song to Johnny Otis, a ruling R & B bandleader who was actually a dark-skinned white man from Berkeley who many thought was black. Otis gave the song to [black blues singer Willie Mae] Thornton, who made it a number one R & B hit in 1953. Otis also took part of the composer's credit, which Lieber and Stoller had to fight to get back. Elvis heard the record, changed the song completely, from the tempo to the words, and cut Thornton's version to shreds.
>
> Whites wrote it, a white made it a hit, yet there is no denying that "Hound Dog" is a "black" song, unthinkable outside the impulses of black music, and probably a rewrite of an old piece of juke joint fury that dated back beyond the birth of any of these people. Can you pull justice out of *that* mess?

"But that was just a lie!": Big Mama Thornton sings "but I could see through that."

"Second sight": W. E. B. Du Bois, *The Souls of Black Folk* (New York: Penguin Books, 1989), p. 5.

Elvis's "voice became a growl": Stanley Booth, "A Hound Dog, to the Manor Born," in *The Age of Rock: Sounds of the American Cultural Revolution,* ed. Jonathan Eisen (New York: Vintage Books, 1969), p. 52.

"to musick": See Christopher Small, *Music of the Common Tongue: Survival and Celebration in Afro-American Music* (London: John Calder, 1987). Small is correct, I think, in arguing that "music is not primarily a thing or a collection of things, but an activity in which we engage. One might say that it is not properly a noun at all, but a verb." He goes on to explain: "In order to narrow that gap that is assumed to exist between performers and listeners in European musicking, I define the word to include not only performing and composing . . . but also listening and even dancing to music" (p. 50). I use the term in the same way.

The ecstasy might derive from Elvis's personal discovery: Following the lead of Greil Marcus, most of those who have written about Elvis privilege the authenticity of his early work with Sun, thereby reproducing the older (Romantic) preference for the "folk" over the "modern" and the "mass." But my view is exactly the opposite. What interests me is the effort to name the particular kind of excellence a mass audience recognizes and responds to.

One dwells in one's place in history: Many artists, historians, psychologists, and philosophers have tried to put into words what this new condition— which I am simply calling "modernity"—feels like and means. Martin Heidegger called it "the peculiar dictatorship of the public realm," a condition in which "so-called 'private existence'" is merely a futile negation or denial of the public, "an offshoot that depends upon the public and nourishes itself by a mere withdrawal from it." One fateful consequence of this erosion of a meaningfully "private" self is that "language . . . falls into the service of expediting communication along routes where objectification— the uniform accessibility of everything to everyone—breaks out and disregards all limits." In other words, the construction of one's "self" out of others' views of oneself, and the attendant feeling that one's innermost being is always open and available to the gaze of others, promotes a worldview in which we have no respect for, or even belief in, the radical otherness of the people around us. We are all essentially "the same," which is to say that we are each essentially nothing. We deny what Heidegger elsewhere calls the "concealedness" of each other and of Being, and in so doing we lose sight of the mysteries that give existence meaning. For only out of concealedness can come revelation, and only in revelation is meaning vouchsafed to us. Heidegger, "Letter on Humanism," in *Basic Writings,* ed. David Farrell Krell (New York: HarperCollins, 1977), p. 221.

This new self they dubbed a "social self": A very clear and helpful overview of what he calls the American "discourse about self," with its "optimistic" and "pessimistic" poles, is provided by John P. Hewitt, *Dilemmas of the American Self* (Philadelphia: Temple University Press, 1989), pp. 4–10. The most influential account of the social self was offered by George Herbert Mead in *Mind, Self, and Society: From the Standpoint of a Social Behaviorist*, ed. Charles W. Morris (Chicago: University of Chicago Press, 1934), pp. 140, 194. See also James Livingston, *Pragmatism and the Political Economy of Cultural Revolution, 1850–1940* (Chapel Hill: University of North Carolina Press, 1994).

the "changing American character": David Riesman (with Nathan Glazer and Renel Denney), *The Lonely Crowd: A Study of the Changing American Character* (New Haven: Yale University Press, 1961), pp. 22–23, 157, 158. Riesman's analysis of the social conditions of postwar America is just one of many attempts to understand what it was (and is) like to live in the conditions that have been variously described as "modernity," "postmodernity," "post-scarcity" or "abundance," and "late capitalist." Some of these (those of Jacques Ellul, for example, and of Theodore Roczak) stress the importance of technology as a force that has dehumanized and separated men and women from the world. Others (those of Erik Erikson, D. W. Winnicott, and Heinz Kohut) are more narrowly psychologistic, emphasizing stages of personal development and relations between parents and children and changing patterns of child-rearing. Most popular among '60s political radicals were the analyses of the Frankfurt school generally and of Herbert Marcuse in particular; these ascribe to modern capitalism a tendency to seek ever greater control of man's erotic and imaginative life, leaving man feeling lost and alienated from the world he has made and dreaming of a "revolution" that would be a "liberation of consciousness," not just seizure of the means of production. Daniel Bell has suggested that late capitalism is inherently self-contradictory insofar as its encouragement of hedonism undermines the work ethic and capital accumulation. Scholars today are probably most familiar with Christopher Lasch's critique of the narcissistic drift of American individualism, and with Michel Foucault's pessimistic account of the ways social power insinuates itself into the everyday life of individuals, controlling them less by physical force than by intellectual, emotional, and psychological manipulation. Different as they are, what all these accounts have in common is an intense anxiety about the relation between society and personhood. All of them are useful, and most will appear in these pages, but I have preferred to emphasize the work of Riesman and his colleagues because they were writing in a tradition and in a vocabulary closer than the others to the history and vocabulary of rock 'n' roll. They provide an explanatory theory that is also a primary source.

"Postmodern," "alienation," and "surplus repression" do not appear in any rock songs I know of. But as we shall see, the loneliness evoked in countless rock 'n' roll songs has everything to do with the "loneliness" of the "other-directed" or "social" self. While teenagers of the '50s and '60s were responding and adjusting all the time to an increasingly technologized and bureaucratized world, and while they observed an inverse correlation between conformity and meaning in their parents' lives, they were somewhat more preoccupied with the difficulties of establishing their identity in relation to their peers, parents, neighbors, and community. Riesman's vocabulary helps us see how and why the twin poles of "love" and "loneliness" that structure rock 'n' roll speak to the problems of a broader social condition, one in which we are asked again and again to be ourselves while also being told that we should never assert our selfhood at the expense of the social fabric. In *Constructing the Self, Constructing America* (Reading, Mass.: Addison-Wesley, 1995), Philip Cushman makes the case that the profession of psychotherapy (especially through the work of D. W. Winnicott and Heinz Kohut) reflected and contributed to modernity's "construction of the empty self" (p. 268). See also Christopher Lasch, *The Culture of Narcissism: American Life in an Age of Diminishing Expectations* (New York: W. W. Norton, 1978); Daniel Bell, *The Cultural Contradictions of Capitalism* (New York: Basic Books, 1976).

teenagers of the late '50s and '60s suddenly had money: The figures are from Grace Palladino, *Teenagers: An American History* (New York: Basic Books, 1996), p. 195, and David Farber, *Chicago '68* (Chicago: University of Chicago Press, 1988), p. 219; he derives them from Landon Jones, *Great Expectations* (New York: Coward, McGann, and Geoghegan, 1980).

"The mission of the adult world is to help teenagers become adults": Grace and Fred M. Hechinger, *Teen-age Tyranny* (New York: Morrow, 1963), quoted by Palladino, *Teenagers,* p. 198.

"the revelatory mystery of the happening": Norman Mailer, *The Armies of the Night* (1968; New York: Penguin Books, 1994), p. 68.

"If I could find a white man who had the Negro sound": The story was told by Marion Keisker, Phillip's secretary, and is passed along by (among many others) Peter Guralnick in *Feel Like Going Home: Portraits in Blues and Rock 'n' Roll* (New York: Harper and Row, 1989), p. 172.

"Rock 'n' roll faith is faith in the music's black elements": Simon Frith, *Sound Effects: Youth, Leisure, and the Politics of Rock 'n' Roll* (New York: Pantheon Books, 1981), p. 20.

"there are lots of reasons why blues should attract a white audience": Guralnick, *Feel Like Going Home,* pp. 22–23.

Without denying that the white assimilation: Thirty years of varied scholarship have established beyond the shadow of a doubt that white audiences, musicians, producers, and record companies have appropriated and exploited African American music forms and performers. More recent scholarship, most notably Eric Lott's *Love and Theft: Blackface Minstrelsy and the American Working Class* (New York: Oxford University Press, 1993), has elaborately theorized the relation between white audiences and African American cultural production, often in psychologistic terms of "lack," "projection," and "alterity." While I have found much of this work immensely valuable, I am troubled somewhat by its presumption that an unverifiable analytical model knows the truth about musical experience that the duped participants themselves are unaware of. And whether intended or not, the effect of much of this criticism is to accuse the pleasure and ignore the knowing that rock music can offer its various white audiences. For example, in *Instruments of Desire: The Electric Guitar and the Shaping of Musical Experience* (Cambridge: Harvard University Press, 1999), Steve Waxman follows Lott in regarding rock as a "putting on of blackness" in "an attempt to compensate for a perceived lack in the composition of whiteness . . . by drawing on the sexual excess that African-American men were thought to embody" (p. 4). Unfortunately, this conception of rock as in essence a form of false consciousness makes it difficult, if not impossible, to discuss other dimensions of the experiences rock music provides. In any case, I hope that it's possible to acknowledge rock's pleasures and to try to articulate its noetic qualities without it being assumed that such aims in themselves constitute a denial of the complex history of race and American music.

"refused it peremptorily, with a glance": Du Bois, *The Souls of Black Folk*, p. 4.

"this is the dwarfing, warping, distorting influence": James Weldon Johnson, *The Autobiography of an Ex-Colored Man*, in *Three Negro Classics*, ed. John Hope Franklin (New York: Avon Books, 1965), p. 403.

"explosive combination of promise and disappointment": Ellen Carol DuBois, review of *To Keep the Waters Troubled*, in the *New York Times Book Review*, February 14, 1999, p. 31.

That form was the blues: The bibliography of the blues is immense. I have learned most from Amiri Baraka, *Blues People: The Negro Experience in White America and the Music That Developed from It* (New York: William Morrow, 1963), p. 55; James Baldwin, "Many Thousand Gone," in *Notes of a Native Son* (Boston: Beacon Press, 1955); James H. Cone, *The Spirituals and the Blues: An Interpretation* (New York: The Seabury Press, 1972); Ralph Ellison, *Shadow and Act* (New York: Vintage Books, 1972); Guralnick, *Feel Like Going Home;* Richard Middleton, *Pop Music and the Blues: A Study of the Relationship and Its Significance* (London: Victor Gollancz, 1972); Albert Murray, *Stomping the Blues* (New York: Da Capo, 1976). See also Houston A. Baker, Jr., *Blues, Ideology, and Afro-American Literature:*

A *Vernacular Theory* (Chicago: University of Chicago Press, 1984); Stephen Calt and Gayle Deane Wardlaw, *King of the Delta Blues: The Life and Music of Charlie Patton* (Newton, N.J.: Rock Chapel Press, 1988); William Ferris, *Blues from the Delta* (New York: Da Capo, 1978); Alan Lomax, *The Land Where Blues Began* (New York: Pantheon Books, 1993); Jon Michael Spencer, *Blues and Evil* (Knoxville: University of Tennessee Press, 1993).

The idea that the blues form deals with specific historical conditions is developed in Middleton's generally overlooked *Pop Music and the Blues*. I discovered Middleton's book late in my research. It offers a similar but richer and more detailed account than mine of the cultural work of the blues and of its usefulness to other audiences. He argues that what I am calling the "condition of the veil" is "nothing more than an extreme prophecy of general developments in the West" and that the blues are "perhaps capable of showing us the kind of response to alienation that we need" (p. 26).

Obviously, my life as a white kid in the '50s: Writing about the blues, I'm haunted by a moment in novelist John Wideman's memoir in which he tells how he felt when a white college classmate arrogantly laid claim to blues expertise, "trespassing on the private turf of my music, the black sounds from home." *Brothers and Keepers* (New York: Penguin Books, 1984), pp. 28–30. Standing outside the blues, I have had to rely on what I have read and even more on what I have heard, knowing that my response to the blues is shaped by my own history. Yet even as I write "my history," I feel the solidity of such a construct disintegrating in my awareness that African American life, history, and culture started flowing into mine from the day I was born, and then more steadily from the day I heard a blues structure deep within the songs of Elvis Presley. My desire to understand rock music more fully requires me to stand at a place where cultural differences are less important than cultural entanglings, where history is a collage of astounding complexity, and where language is too blunt an instrument to do justice to the nuances of interconnection.

if we think of "loneliness" as: Loneliness is the vernacular word not just for the condition of heartbroken solitude but for "alienation" and "anomie" and their ramifying implications. Loneliness points toward uprootedness, exile, social isolation, and meaninglessness—in short, toward those emotional states that seem so prevalent as to characterize the late twentieth century. The history of the word "lonely" further uncovers some of its latent meanings. For centuries, lonely meant "single" or "solitary," and a "lonely" tree was not one that had feelings but one that stood alone, apart from other trees. A lonely man, similarly, was one who was solitary. Not until the early nineteenth century, at the height of Romanticism, did "lonely" come to mean "dejected because of want of company or society;

sad at the thought of being alone." This use may have had early anteced-ents, but with a twist, in the word's Old Norse roots, "laun" and "lain," which meant "to conceal, hide; to be silent about, disguise." The state of being lonely has about it something secretive, concealing, and self-protective. We speak of being "wrapped" in loneliness, as if it were a cloak that comforted even as it oppressed. The lonely man is to some extent hidden from the eyes of society in a double sense: he may be solitary and therefore out of sight, or he may be "sad at the thought of being alone" and, even if surrounded by a crowd, nevertheless concealed by the screen of his emotion.

"ever feels his two-ness": Du Bois, *The Souls of Black Folk,* p. 5.

"Blues Power!" shouts Albert King: In the song of this title, on *Live Wire* (Stax/Volt, 1968).

"The Dead's music . . . is primarily an imitation of Negro blues": Burton H. Wolfe, "The New Music and the New Scene," in Eisen, *The Age of Rock,* p. 33.

to make our own self out of nothing: In 1968 psychologist Kenneth Keniston, the most astute observer of '60s middle-class youth, coined the term "post-modern youth" to describe "an emergent stage of life [that] intervenes between adolescence and adulthood, a stage of life made possible by the affluence of the post-modern world, and made necessary by the ambiva-lence that world inspires" in the young. Postmodern youth adopted a style characterized chiefly by instability, mobility, flux, he argued, because they saw the world changing so fast that the concept of a fixed identity had become meaningless to them. "The term 'identity' as ordinarily used sug-gests a greater fixity, stability, and 'closure' than most . . . post-modern youth possess." Postmodern youth try on identities and attitudes as they might try on clothes. They live indefinitely in a state of "limbo" between adolescence and adulthood, and they remain intensely loyal to this condi-tion. To be a postmodern youth is, then, to inhabit a seam between two realities, to inhabit a "self" so fluid that it barely counts as a self, and yet, as Keniston writes, to maintain a deep faith in "a self that transcends, but is often hidden by, . . . social roles." For these young people, the most important thing in "a man's life is the quality of his personal relationships; the greatest sin is to be unable to 'relate' to others in a direct, open, trust-ing, and one-to-one way." Keniston's analysis employs somewhat different terms than Mead's and Riesman's, but like theirs it describes a condition in which youth are caught between two mutually contradictory paradigms of selfhood and citizenship. Just as the "other-directed" self oscillates be-tween a need for the expectant, self-defining gaze of others and a desire to escape from that gaze into lonely solitude, so postmodern youth oscillate between a clear perception that the world is ruled by flux and uncertainty and a desire to transcend that chaos through relationships that are "real," through intimacy that is "open," and through compelling intersubjective encounters in which each person affirms and celebrates the reality of the other. Keniston, *Young Radicals: Notes on Committed Youth* (New York: Harcourt, Brace, and World, 1968), pp. 264–290.

Keniston's analysis remains indispensable, and I have drawn on it heavily.

Chapter 3. "Something's Happening Here"

"In my earlier poems": Quoted in "Adrienne Rich: The Poetics of Change," by Albert Gelpi, in *American Poetry since 1960,* ed. Robert P. Shaw (Cheadle, Cheshire: Carcanet Press Ltd., 1973), p. 133.

"really thinking for the first time": A full account of this meeting can be found in Peter Brown and Steven Gaines, *The Love You Make* (New York: McGraw-Hill, 1983), pp. 157–158. The authors put the date of the meeting as August 28, but by my calculation—based on the Beatles' performing schedule—it is more likely to have occurred on Sunday, August 30. Certainly it took place some time that weekend. It's worth noting that the whole story of the meeting might be apocryphal—Brown and Gaines cite no sources—but it does receive some corroboration elsewhere. See The Editors of Rolling Stone, *The Ballad of John and Yoko* (Garden City, N.Y.: Rolling Stone Press, 1982), p. 52.

"By 1969, according to a Gallup Survey": Cited in Godfrey Hodgson, *America in Our Time: From World War II to Nixon—What Happened and Why* (New York: Vintage Books, 1978), p. 330.

In the Sunday New York Times that was delivered: The photo of Philadelphia rioters is on page A76, Barnett's vow is on page A51, the report on Princeton on page A78, the report on pesticides on page A49, the report on blue whales on page A11, Erwin Strassman's small breasts and large brains are on page A42, the coverage of Beatlemania on page A95, the review of the Beatles concert on page A9, the best-seller list on page 8 of the *Book Review,* the ruminations on Vietnam on page E5, and Lyndon Baines Johnson's lie about what had happened in the Gulf of Tonkin is on page A1. Like so many other newspapers, the *Times* unquestioningly accepted Johnson's version of events and reported as fact that the "retaliatory action was taken after North Vietnamese patrol boats had fired on United States destroyers." Those were the days.

"Your hump . . . GIVE ME YOUR HUMP!": Terry Southern and Mason Hoffenberg, *Candy* (New York: G. P. Putnam's Sons, 1964), p. 148.

"the slippery thing, all covered with jelly": Mary McCarthy, *The Group* (New York: Harcourt, Brace, and World, 1963), p. 67.

"it is increasingly assumed that": Vance Packard, *The Naked Society* (New York: D. McKay Co., 1964), p. 12.

McCartney, who "seems to have had an out-of-body experience": Quoted in Brown and Gaines, *The Love You Make,* p. 158.

"There's no question that the shift from alcohol to grass": Annie Gottlieb, *Do You Believe in Magic? The Second Coming of the Sixties Generation* (New York: Times Books, 1987), p. 166.

"One conclusion . . . forced upon my mind": William James, *The Varieties of Religious Experience* (1902; New York: Modern Library, 1929), pp. 378–379.

"God is in everything": Paul McCartney interview in *International Times,* in Geoffrey and Brenda Giuliano, *The Lost Beatles Interviews* (New York: Dutton Books), p. 101.

"really affected the way I feel about human communication": Bonnie Wolf, quoted in Gottlieb, *Do You Believe in Magic?* p. 176.

"LSD and mescaline suppress the mind's ability": Charles Perry, *The Haight-Ashbury: A History* (New York: Random House/Rolling Stone Press, 1984), p. 253.

"Up until LSD": George Harrison interview in *International Times,* in Giuliano, *The Lost Beatles Interviews,* p. 104.

"musical universe": Paul Valéry, *The Art of Poetry,* trans. Denise Folliot (1939; New York: Vintage Books, 1961), pp. 71–72.

"the mirror of the world": See the discussion of Suzanne Langer in appendix 1.

"change the nature of work": Bruce Jackson, *Wake Up Dead Man! Afro-American Worksongs from Texas Prisons* (Cambridge: Harvard University Press, 1972), p. 30.

the blues as an "area" created by blacks: Amiri Baraka, *Blues People: The Negro Experience in White America and the Music That Developed from It* (New York: William Morrow, 1963), p. 55.

Music is experienced as immediate: "Sounds come from outside the body, but sound itself is near, immediate." John Dewey, *Art and Experience* (1934; New York: Perigree Books, 1980), p. 237.

"in groups . . . we would sit around, listening": Todd Gitlin, *The Sixties: Years of Hope, Days of Rage* (New York: Bantam Books, 1987), p. 202. A superb account of the qualities of psychedelicized rock can be found in John Hicks's *Sixties Rock: Garage, Psychedelics, and Other Satisfactions* (Urbana: University of Illinois Press, 1999), pp. 58–74.

"*Week after week we go inside the music*": Sandy Darlington, *San Francisco Express Times,* vol. I, no. 8, March 14, 1968, p. 11.

"*nothing less than . . . the self itself*": Benjamin DeMott, "Rock Saves?" in *Supergrow: Essays and Reports on Imagination in America* (New York: E. P. Dutton, 1969), pp. 55–60.

I and my friends desperately ransacked the world: For the first and fullest treatment of this theme, see Albert Goldman's wonderful essay, "The Emergence of Rock," first published in April 1968 and reprinted in *The Sixties: Art, Politics and Media of Our Most Explosive Decade,* ed. Gerald Howard (New York: Paragon House, 1991), pp. 343–364. In "Why Do Whites Sing Black?" (*New York Times,* December 14, 1969), he wrote that white kids "are trying to save their souls. Adopting as a tentative identity the firmly set, powerfully expressive mask of the black man, the confused, conflicted, and frequently self-doubting and self-loathing offspring of Mr. And Mrs. America are released into an emotional and spiritual freedom denied them by their own culture" (p. 25). Where Goldman comes up short, though, is in understanding the rock culture's use of black idioms and music as "adoption," which is at bottom synonymous with "appropriation" or even "theft." White kids did not sing like black performers because they wanted to be black nor did white kids listen to Janis Joplin, say, or Otis Redding merely because they wanted to put on a black mask. They were drawn to black expressive forms because they *already* felt "black," because those forms *already* made sense to them by speaking so powerfully to their conditions.

As Buffy St. Marie scolded us: Quotes can be found in *Our Time: An Anthology of Interviews from EVO,* ed. Allen Katzman (New York: Dial Press, 1972), p. 213.

"*American river*": Allen Ginsberg, *Howl* (1956; San Francisco: City Light Books, 1982), p. 18.

"*I went into the bedroom with my girlfriend*": Jeff Maron, quoted in Gottlieb, *Do You Believe in Magic?* p. 177.

The famous "death of the ego": Most commentators on the '60s psychedelic scene would agree with Jay Stevens that "there was a point, during every LSD user's career, when the trips to the Other World became negative." Stevens, *Storming Heaven: LSD and the American Dream* (New York: Harper and Row, 1987), p. 342.

Chapter 4. "I Was Alone, I Took a Ride"

"*O to break loose*": Robert Lowell, "Walking Early Sunday Morning," in *Near the Ocean* (New York: Noonday Press, 1971), p. 13.

"Between every human consciousness and the rest of the world": Aldous Huxley, "Culture and the Individual" (1963), in *Moksha: Writings on Psychedelics and the Visionary Experience,* ed. Michael Horowitz and Cynthia Palmer (Los Angeles: J. P. Tarcher, 1977), p. 248.

"the fountain has not played itself out": R. D. Laing, "The Transcendental Experience," reprinted in *The Sixties: Art, Politics and Media of Our Most Explosive Decade,* ed. Gerald Howard (New York: Paragon House, 1991), p. 205.

"in a world of pettiness constructed by adults": Jacques Attali, *Noise: The Political Economy of Music* (Minneapolis: University of Minnesota Press, 1985), p. 110.

"between us and It, there is a veil": Laing, "The Transcendental Experience," p. 205.

"DRUGS BREAK PATTERNS": Tuli Kupferberg, "The Hip and the Square: The Hippie Generation," in *Notes from the New Underground,* ed. Jesse Kornbluth (New York: Viking Press, 1968), p. 208.

"People coming down from LSD": Charles Perry, *The Haight-Ashbury: A History* (New York: Random House/Rolling Stone Press, 1984), p. 249.

McCartney's earliest experiences with LSD: Mark Lewisohn calls it "Tamla Motown inspired." Lewisohn, *The Beatles Recording Sessions* (New York: Harmony Books, 1988), p. 72.

"a quantum jump not only into tomorrow": Lewisohn, *The Beatles Recording Sessions,* p. 70.

"introduced LSD and Leary's psychedelic revolution": Ian MacDonald, *Revolution in the Head: The Beatles' Records and the Sixties* (New York: Henry Holt, 1994), p. 150.

"consummation": Willfred Mellers, *Twilight of the Gods: The Music of the Beatles* (New York: Schirmer Books, 1973), p. 81.

"touching down from a different galaxy": Tim Riley, *Tell Me Why: A Beatles Commentary* (New York: Alfred A. Knopf, 1988), p. 199.

"No John Lennon vocal had ever sounded like that before": Lewisohn, *The Beatles Recording Sessions,* p. 72.

"There were five in all": MacDonald, *Revolution in the Head,* p. 152.

"I want to sound as though I'm the Dalai Lama": Lennon, quoted in Lewisohn, *The Beatles Recording Sessions,* p. 72.

"The sound is the sound of the electronic age": Ralph Gleason, quoted by Nat Hentoff in *The Age of Rock: Sounds of the American Cultural Revolution,* ed. Jonathan Eisen (New York: Vintage Books, 1969), p. 3.

Heidegger was struggling to invent a richer vocabulary: Martin Heidegger, "The Question Concerning Technology" (1954), in *Basic Writings,* ed. David Farrell Krell (New York: HarperCollins, 1977), pp. 308–341.

"I'm trying to take people with me": This and subsequent quotations are from the Paul McCartney interview in *International Times,* no. 6, January 16–29, 1967, p. 9.

"There is an essential dichotomy of moralities in America": Aldo Giunta, in Kornbluth, *Notes from the New Underground,* pp. 211–212.

"not just dropping out into Limbo or Nirvana": Ralph Gleason, "The Power of Non-Politics or the Death of the Square Left" (1967), in Kornbluth, *Notes from the New Underground,* p. 216.

"the most striking feature [of the mescaline experience] is its profound impersonality": Aldous Huxley, "Mescaline and the 'Other World'" (1955), in Horowitz and Palmer, *Moksha,* pp. 61–62.

Chapter 5. "Never Do See Any Other Way"

"Politics has the function of bringing people out of isolation": The Port Huron Statement, quoted in Jim Miller, *Democracy Is in the Streets: From Port Huron to the Siege of Chicago* (Cambridge: Harvard University Press, 1994), p. 333.

"We're as much influenced by everybody else": George Harrison interview, "The Way Out Is In," *International Times,* no. 13, May 18–June 2, 1967, p. 9.

"The key to the meaning of the song": Quoted on liner notes to CD release of *Are You Experienced?* (MCA Records, 1993), p. 9.

"'Hey Joe' is a blues arrangement": *Are you Experienced?* liner notes, p. 6.

"blues and rock and whatever else happens": *Are You Experienced?* liner notes, p. 8.

"a 12-bar blues flipped upside-down": *Are You Experienced?* liner notes, p. 14.

Hendrix takes "you further and further into your mind": Marshal Rubinoff, "RockЯɔoЯ," *The Sun* (1968), p. 11.

"I'm sitting here listening to 'Foxy Lady'": Terri Sutton, "Women, Sex, and Rock 'n' Roll," *Puncture* (summer 1989), reprinted in *Rock She Wrote: Women Write about Rock, Pop, and Rap,* ed. Evelyn McDonnell and Ann Powers (New York: Delta, 1995), p. 380.

"You'll always have cats to stand up there": *Are You Experienced?* liner notes, p. 15.

"Heavy rock is rebellion and disgust": Old Mole, in *The Movement toward a New America,* ed. Mitchell Goodman (New York: Pilgrim Press/Alfred A. Knopf, 1970), p. 383.

This was, in essence, a tragic attitude: I'm drawing here on the work of Northrup Frye in *Anatomy of Criticism: Four Essays* (Princeton: Princeton University Press, 1957), pp. 35–67, and of Hayden White, *Metahistory: The Historical Imagination in Nineteenth Century Europe* (Baltimore: Johns Hopkins University Press, 1973).

Balloons rose into the sky: As Allen Ginsberg said: "After the apocalypse of Hitler and the apocalypse of the Bomb, there was here [in *Sgt. Pepper's*] an exclamation of joy, the rediscovery of joy and what it is to be alive." Quoted in Geoffrey and Brenda Giuliano, *The Lost Beatles Interviews* (New York: Dutton Books, 1994), p. 95.

"'Love' remains the great unfulfilled need": Richard Poirier, "Learning from the Beatles," in *The Age of Rock: Sounds of the American Cultural Revolution* (New York: Vintage Books, 1969), pp. 171–172.

"There's something happening": George Harrison interview, *International Times,* May 18–June 2, 1967, p. 9.

"Who is the Underground?": M. Preston Burns, "What Is the Underground?" *Avatar,* June 9, 1967, in *Notes from the New Underground,* ed. Jesse Kornbluth (New York: Viking Press, 1968), p. 210.

"The exhilaration, the sense of change and purpose": Simon Frith, "Rock and the Politics of Memory," in *The 60s, Without Apology,* ed. Sohnya Sayres, Anders Stephanson, Stanley Aronowitz, and Frederic Jameson (Minneapolis: University of Minnesota Press, 1984), pp. 61–62. Not just the songs of these great artists but many others—"Itchycoo Park," "Dance to the Music," "Do You Believe in Magic?"—expressed the hope that music was a magical kingdom in which one had no need for loneliness. Psychedelics gave substance to this hope by taking people there—there to a world in which *everything connects,* in which even one's lonely consciousness has a place, its place, where one belongs. And in the act of dwelling there, one feels an emotion that can only be called "love," though it is also so full of awe that "love" seems trivial and inappropriate. Yet that was exactly the paradox, or surprise, that the Beatles and the Grateful Dead and Van Morrison and others played upon: "love," this word debased by countless pop songs, turns out suddenly to be luminous and alive, casting a radiance back over pop music and revealing its prophetic nature. The pure joy of *She loves you, yeah yeah yeah* could now be seen as a cosmic affirmation disguised, even to its creators, as just another piece of bubblegum. In the beginning they misunderstood, but now they got it: the word is good.

"Hope. Our new music reflects the hope": Warren Steel, *Avatar*, no. 7, September 1, 1967.

"I don't believe that it ends with our Western logical thought": Paul McCartney interview, *International Times*, January 16, 1967, p. 8.

"I know I'm going to need a new set of rules": Paul McCartney interview, *International Times*, January 16, 1967, pp. 8–9.

"The whole commune was relieved": Dotson Rader, "Up against the Wall" (1968), in *The Radical Vision: Essays for the Seventies*, ed. Leo Hamalian and Frederick R. Karl (New York: Thomas Y. Crowell, 1970), p. 192.

"There can be no revolution when Life turns its cameras on": John Wolfe, *The Distant Drummer* (Philadelphia), vol. I, no. 1, November 1967, p. 9.

"the danger in work like much of the Beatles'": Alan Beckett, "Stones," *New Left Review*, no. 47 (January–February 1968), pp. 24–29.

Chapter 6. "Evil" Is "Live" Spelled Backwards

"Evil is 'live' spelled backwards": Deday LaRene, *Creem*, vol. II, no. 7 (undated), p. 17.

"Oh God, no, please don't!": Tim Ireland's testimony about the early morning of August 9 is from Vincent Bugliosi's *Helter Skelter: The True Story of the Manson Murders* (New York: Bantam Books, 1975), p. 4.

Manson's own version: See Bugliosi, *Helter Skelter*, pp. 321–331.

"If you started the wrong way": Aldous Huxley, quoted in Jay Stevens, *Storming Heaven: LSD and the American Dream* (New York: Harper and Row, 1987), p. 46.

It was the Rolling Stones: Alan Beckett, "Stones," *New Left Review*, no. 47 (January–February 1968).

"If it takes a bloodbath": Ronald Reagan, quoted in Hans Koning, *Nineteen Sixty-Eight: A Personal Report* (New York: W. W. Norton, 1987), p. 59.

"It must be a wonderful feeling to kill a pig": Mark Rudd, quoted in Todd Gitlin, *The Sixties: Years of Hope, Days of Rage* (New York: Bantam Books, 1987), p. 400.

"liberal" is someone who thinks that cruelty: Judith Shklar, quoted in Richard Rorty, *Contingency, Irony, Solidarity* (Cambridge: Cambridge University Press, 1989), p. 74. This rejection of liberalism can be understood as a backlash by what political theorist Michael Sandel has called the tradition

of "civic republicanism" against the increasingly dominant ideology of "neutral liberalism."

This metamorphosis was misunderstood at the time: An early exception was Frank Bardacke's "Blow Their Minds," from *Steps* 1 (December 1966), reprinted in *The Movement toward a New America,* ed. Mitchell Goodman (New York: Pilgrim Press/Alfred A. Knopf, 1970), pp. 378–380.

Dylan's discovery of LSD: See Bob Spitz, *Dylan: A Biography* (New York: W. W. Norton, 1989), pp. 273–274.

"a psychodrama of self-validation": Morris Dickstein, *Gates of Eden: American Culture in the Sixties* (New York: Basic Books, 1977), p. 268.

"Liberal consciousness": Greg Calvert, quoted in Gitlin, *The Sixties,* p. 383.

"I hate this weird liberal mass of nothingness": Mark Rudd, quoted in Gitlin, *The Sixties,* p. 393.

"had little meaning for kids who dropped out": David Lewis Stein, *Living the Revolution: The Yippies in Chicago* (Indianapolis: Bobbs-Merrill, 1969), p. 5.

some absolute poverty: I think there are affinities between this desire of '60s youth and what Richard Poirier has described as an American hankering for "bareness" (the word is Emerson's) "telling us . . . that any access to superfluity, to the power for new creation, depends on the admission that our own subjectivity, which we like to associate with depth, is itself bare and barren." *Poetry and Pragmatism* (Cambridge: Harvard University Press, 1992), p. 71.

"the delicate spores of the new fierceness that will change America": The first Yippie manifesto (1968), quoted in Stein, *Living the Revolution,* p. 6.

"their only choice": Shin'ya Ono, quoted in Gitlin, *The Sixties,* p. 391.

"We are against everything": Gitlin, *The Sixties,* p. 400.

brilliant articles for Ramparts: David Horowitz, "Sinews of Empire," in *Divided We Stand,* ed. Editors of *Ramparts* (San Francisco: Canfield Press, 1970), p. 83. Harvard's Center for International Affairs, wrote Horowitz,

> is probably unmatched in its tight interlacing of the knots of power. Among the key individuals who were involved in the creation of the Center were: Robert R. Bowie, its first director and head of the State Department Policy Planning Staff under John Foster Dulles (the dean of Harvard's Graduate School of Public Administration which gave Bowie his legitimizing "university appointment"); Henry A. Kissinger, who became associate director; Dean Rusk of the Rockefeller Foundation, who followed J. F. Dulles first at the Foundation and then in the State Depart-

ment; James A. Perkins of the Carnegie Corporation, who went on to become president of Cornell and a director of the Chase Manhattan Bank; Don K. Price, vice president of the Ford Foundation, formerly of the staff of Harvard's School of Public Administration, who later returned to become dean after his stint at Ford. McGeorge Bundy, who originally organized the Center, went on to become the overseer of JFK's national security policy. Bundy later left the White House to become head of the Ford Foundation, his key White House post being filled by the MIT Center's [Walt] Rostow. When Nixon took over, there at the head of foreign policy planning was Henry A. Kissinger, fresh out of Harvard's Center for International Affairs.

"forced revolution": Gitlin, *The Sixties,* pp. 381–382.

"The real division is not between": Jane Alpert, quoted in Gitlin, *The Sixties,* p. 402.

"there is still a missing link": Gitlin, *The Sixties,* p. 402.

"By their refusal, their mischief, their infiltration": Jacob Brockman, "My Generation" (October 1968), in *Smiling through the Apocalypse:* Esquire's *History of the Sixties,* ed. Harold Hayes (New York: McCall, 1969), pp. 635–640.

"I lost interest in the White Album*"*: Geoff Emerick, quoted in Mark Lewisohn, *The Beatles Recording Sessions* (New York: Harmony Books, 1988), p. 143.

"the rot had set in": George Harrison, quoted in Lewisohn, *The Beatles Recording Sessions,* p. 163.

But it is comedy nonetheless: Because so many accounts of the '60s oversimplify the culture or cohort I am writing about, I want to emphasize again that it was both critical and self-critical, engaged and disengaged. Only by seeing and holding both of these visions together at the same time can we recover the more complex and comedic understanding I am trying to describe. For example, in 1970 Yale political scientist Robert Dahl wrote an early critique of this '60s, claiming that "the greatest obstacle to democratization . . . is not that bugbear with which the Left, old and new, is invariably so obsessed, an elite of wealthy men or even the military-industrial complex . . . , but rather the military-industrial-financial-labor-farming-educational-professional-consumer-complex . . . that might be called the American people." *After the Revolution? Authority in a Good Society* (New Haven: Yale University Press, 1970), p. 110.

But Dahl was not telling young people anything they didn't already know simply by looking around them or by listening to Dylan records.

Their feeling that the "political" had become coextensive with "the American people," with all of American life, required them either to become apolitical or to become more radically and self-destructively political. Eben Given wrote in the *Avatar,* for example, that "In this world there is a roaring and a grinding of gears. We are walking in a cyclone of sounds and smells and colors. We cannot escape it, no Himalayan hut is high enough. Be it without—or within us. We can't escape it any more than we can escape our own mind and finally our own feelings. We can't escape it because we've created it. We're not here by any accident of fate. We're here only inheriting what is ours" (quoted in *Notes from the New Underground,* ed. Jesse Kornbluth [New York: Viking Press, 1968], p. 26). This sense of being unable to "escape" created the "pressure" George Harrison referred to and led to the desperate search for "some way out of here." But the prevailing vision of the rock audience was that, as Given argues, there is no escape, there is no way out.

Afterword. "Our Incompleteness and Our Choices"

"Oedipa wondered": Thomas Pynchon, *The Crying of Lot 49* (New York: Harper and Row, 1965), p. 95.

"the very ontological foundations are shaken": R. D. Laing, "The Transcendental Experience," in *The Sixties: Art, Politics and Media of Our Most Explosive Decade* (New York: Paragon House, 1991), p. 198.

Hendrix would "pop his head around the corner": Eddie Kramer, quoted in CD liner notes for *Electric Ladyland* (MCA Records, 1993), p. 20.

"It is a sign of our times": Ralph Waldo Emerson, *Collected Works,* vol. 1 (Cambridge: Harvard University Press, 1971), p. 213.

"Beginning with the 'new sound' of the Beatles": Daniel Bell, *The Cultural Contradictions of Capitalism* (New York: Basic Books, 1976), p. 122. The single most useful summary of historical interpretations of the period focuses on the events of May 1968 in France. It is Philippe Beneton and Jean Touchard's "The Interpretations of the Crisis of May/June 1968," originally published in the *Revue françaises des sciences politiques* (summer 1970) and translated by Keith A. Reader in *The May 1968 Events in France: Reproductions and Interpretations* (New York: St. Martin's Press, 1993). See also Maurice Isserman, "The Not So Dark and Bloody Ground: New Works on the 1960s," *American Historical Review* 94 (October 1989), pp. 990–1010, and Paul Lyon's fine historiographical essay, "The Sixties Legacy," in *New Left, New Right, and the Legacy of the Sixties* (Philadelphia: Temple University Press, 1996), pp. 192–222.

'60s *"counterculture worked . . . harm"*: Francis Fukuyama, "Dust Off the Ramparts," review of *Opposing the System* by Charles Reich in *The New York Times Book Review,* November 26, 1995, p. 7.

"a surge in a long immobile glacier": Lester Thurow, "Why Their World Might Crumble," *Real Times,* November 1995, p. 78.

"What appeared to them to be constraints": Regis Debray, *Modeste contribution aux disscours et ceremonies officielles du dixieme anniversaire* (Paris: François Maspero, 1978), p. 14 (my translation). This view is also held by Ian MacDonald, who writes: "The irony of modern right-wing antipathy to the Sixties is that this much-misunderstood decade was, in all but the most superficial senses, the creation of the very people who voted for Thatcher and Reagan in the Eighties. . . . What mass society unconsciously began in the Sixties, Thatcher and Reagan raised to the level of ideology in the Eighties: the complete materialistic individualisation—and the total fragmentation—of Western society." *Revolution in the Head: The Beatles' Records and the Sixties* (New York: Henry Holt and Co., 1994), pp. 29–30.

"the therapeutic sensibility": Christopher Lasch, *The Culture of Narcissism* (New York: W. W. Norton, 1978), p. 7.

"Rape is as common as bullshit": "Haight/Hate," Communication Company leaflet, August 1967, reprinted in *Notes from the New Underground,* ed. Jesse Kornbluth (New York: Viking Press, 1968), p. 247.

"Is love a fond hallucination?": Lionel Mitchell, "Look as Down Here," *East Village Other,* January 10, 1967, reprinted in Kornbluth, *Notes,* p. 228.

"If nature was a veil": Norman Mailer, *The Armies of the Night* (1968; New York: Penguin Books, 1994), pp. 92–93.

"Those who remember the past are condemned to repeat it": Michael Herr, *Dispatches* (New York: Viking International, 1991), p. 254.

"the man who comes back through the Door in the Wall": Aldous Huxley, quoted in Jay Stevens, *Storming Heaven: LSD and the American Dream* (New York: Harper and Row, 1987), pp. 67–68.

"We know that age to be utterly beyond reach": W. S. Merwin, *The Second Book of Four Poems* (Port Townsend, Wash.: Copper Canyon Press, 1993), p. 2.

Americans can't forget or expunge the '60s: Even those who are too young to remember the '60s live in the shadow the '60s cast in cultural memory. See, for example, two witty essays in *Next: Young American Writers on the New Generation,* ed. Eric Liu (New York: W. W. Norton, 1994): David Greenberg, "In the Shadow of the Sixties" (pp. 69–80), and Ian Williams, "Trash That Baby Boom" (pp. 174–186).

"a historical phenomenon, completely understood": Friedrich Nietzsche, *The Use and Abuse of History*, trans. Adrian Collins (Indianapolis: Bobbs-Merrill Co., 1957), p. 11.

Appendix 1. Music, Form, and Meaning

"presentational symbols": This term and those that follow are more fully defined in Susanne K. Langer, *Philosophy in a New Key: A Study in the Symbolism of Reason, Rite, and Art* (Cambridge: Harvard University Press, 1942), chap. 8: "On Significance in Music," pp. 204–245. I agree with Langer that "there are certain aspects of the so-called 'inner life'—physical or mental—which have formal properties similar to those of music— patterns of motion and rest, of tension and release, of agreement and disagreement, preparation, fulfillment, excitation, sudden change, etc." (p. 228). I would assume that what constitutes such similarities varies from culture to culture. I concur also with Langer's reply to positivists who equate meaning with verbal articulation—what they criticize "as a weakness, is really the strength of musical expressiveness: that *music articulates forms which language cannot set forth*" (p. 233).

As noted above, not all musicologists agree. For example, Stephen Davies argues that the "central ideas of Langer's theory—indescribable forms, undemonstrable iconicity, and unstatable laws of projection—are unintelligible." *Musical Meaning and Expression* (Ithaca: Cornell University Press, 1994), p. 132. Indeed they are if the theory is asked to explain entirely, to render transparent, the way that music is meaningful. No theory can meet that criterion if the symbology of music and other art forms is simply beyond, or to one side of, language. The earliest and still influential argument that music is self-referential and cannot express emotions (or ideas) is Eduard Hanslick, *The Beautiful in Music* (1884), while the most important recent argument for the self-referentiality of music is probably Peter Kivy's *Sound Sentiment: An Essay on the Musical Emotions* (Philadelphia: Temple University Press, 1989).

Readers will have to decide the matter for themselves. In addition to Langer, they can find sophisticated arguments on behalf of musical meaning and referentiality in Wilson Coker, *Music and Meaning: A Theoretical Introduction to Musical Aesthetics* (New York: Free Press, 1972), and in Leonard B. Meyer's magisterial *Emotion and Meaning in Music* (Chicago: University of Chicago Press, 1956).

influenced by pragmatism and phenomenology: See, for example, John Dewey, *Art and Experience* (1934; New York: Perigree Books, 1980). On music and phenomenology, see note to page 1. An unusually lucid account of the way phenomenology helps describe the ways we experience music can be found in Harris M. Berger, *Metal, Rock, and Jazz: Perception and the Phenomenology of Musical Experience* (Hanover, N.H.: University Press of New England, 1999), pp. 19–28.

Appendix 2. The Form and Work of the Blues

"not as a fixed frame": Christopher Small, *Music of the Common Tongue: Survival and Celebration in Afro-American Music* (London: Jonathan Calder, 1987), p. 200.

"no matter how deeply moved a musician may be": Albert Murray, *Stomping the Blues* (New York: Da Capo, 1976), p. 98.

"the blues come from behind a mule": Quoted in Houston A. Baker, Jr., *Blues, Ideology, and Afro-American Literature: A Vernacular Theory* (Chicago: University of Chicago Press, 1984), p. 188.

"explosive combination of promise and disappointment": Ellen Carol DuBois, review of *To Keep the Waters Troubled*, in *The New York Times Book Review*, February 14, 1999, p. 31.

"It is a peculiar sensation, this double-consciousness": W. E. B. Du Bois, *The Souls of Black Folk* (New York: Penguin Books, 1989), p. 5.

"The blues speak to us simultaneously of the tragic and the comic": Ralph Ellison, *Shadow and Act* (New York: Vintage Books, 1972), p. 235.

her situation as a black woman: see Hazel Carby, "It Just Be's Dat Way Sometimes: The Politics of Women's Blues," *Radical America* 20, no. 4 (June–July 1986), pp. 9–22, in which she argues that classic blues are "a discourse that articulates a cultural and political struggle over sexual relations" (p. 12). See also Paula Gidding, *When and Where I Enter: The Impact of Black Women on Race and Sex in America* (New York: Morrow, 1984), and Angela Y. Davis, *Blues Legacies and Black Feminism: Gertrude "Ma" Rainey, Bessie Smith, and Billie Holiday* (New York: Pantheon Books, 1998).